Playa Girón/Bay of Pigs

Bay of Pigs

1961: Washington's first military defeat in the Americas

Playa Girón

Fidel Castro

José Ramón Fernández

foreword by Jack Barnes

Pathfinder

NEW YORK   LONDON   MONTREAL   SYDNEY

Edited by Steve Clark and Mary-Alice Waters

Copyright © 2001 by Pathfinder Press
Copyright © 1999 by José Ramón Fernández: *Testimonio, mapas y tablas, presentados por José Ramón Fernández en el juicio de la Demanda del pueblo de Cuba al gobierno de los Estados Unidos por daños humanos*

ISBN 978-0-87348-925-6
Library of Congress Control Number: 2001131111
Manufactured in Canada

First edition, 2001
Fifth printing, 2011

Cover design: Eric Simpson

Cover photo: Cuban revolutionary troops reach the sea at Bay of Pigs on April 19, 1961, near the end of the three-day battle. On the horizon, still burning, is the *Houston*, one of two ships of the invasion fleet destroyed by Cuba's Revolutionary Air Force in the opening hours of combat. *(Granma)*

Back cover photo: José Ramón Fernández (left) and Fidel Castro at the Bay of Pigs, April 1961. (Courtesy José Ramón Fernández)

Maps taken from *The Bay of Pigs: The Leaders' Story of Brigade 2506* are used by permission of W.W. Norton & Company Inc. Copyright © 1964 by Haynes Johnson.

Pathfinder
www.pathfinderpress.com
E-mail: pathfinder@pathfinderpress.com

Titles in this series

Continued on next page

The Bolivian Diary of Ernesto Che Guevara (1994)

To Speak the Truth
BY FIDEL CASTRO AND ERNESTO CHE GUEVARA (1992)

How Far We Slaves Have Come!
BY NELSON MANDELA AND FIDEL CASTRO (1991)

U.S. Hands Off the Mideast!
BY FIDEL CASTRO AND RICARDO ALARCÓN (1990)

In Defense of Socialism
BY FIDEL CASTRO (1989)

*Che Guevara: Economics and Politics
in the Transition to Socialism*
BY CARLOS TABLADA (1989)

Contents

Fidel Castro

Fidel Castro has been first secretary of the Communist Party of Cuba since its founding in 1965. He served as president of the Council of State and Council of Ministers from 1976 to 2008. As commander in chief of Cuba's armed forces, he directed operations from the battlefront in April 1961 during the defense of the revolution against the U.S.-organized invasion at the Bay of Pigs.

Born in 1926, Fidel Castro was raised in Oriente province in eastern Cuba. In 1945 he entered the University of Havana where he became a leader of student protests against U.S. imperialist domination and for social justice in Cuba. When the Orthodox Party was organized in 1947 in opposition to government corruption, Castro became a founding member and central organizer of its revolutionary-minded youth. He was one of the party's candidates for Cuba's House of Representatives in the 1952 elections, which were canceled following a U.S.-backed coup by Fulgencio Batista in March of that year.

Following the coup, Castro organized a new revolutionary movement to overthrow the dictatorship. On July 26, 1953, he led that movement to attack the army garrisons in Santiago de Cuba and in nearby Bayamo, aiming to spark a popular insurrection. The attack failed and over fifty captured revolutionaries were murdered. Castro was sentenced to fifteen years in prison on the Isle of Pines. His courtroom defense speech, "History Will Absolve Me," was smuggled out of prison and later distributed in tens of thousands of copies across Cuba, becoming the program of the revolutionary movement.

Released in May 1955 after a mass amnesty campaign, he organized the founding of the July 26 Movement a few weeks later. In July he went to Mexico and from there organized preparations for landing in Cuba to lead an armed popular insurrection against the Batista regime. On December 2, 1956, he returned to Cuba on the yacht *Granma*, at the head of an expeditionary detachment of eighty-two men that initiated the revolutionary war from the Sierra Maestra mountains. He commanded the Rebel Army during the 1956–58 revolutionary war. In May 1958 he was elected general secretary of the July 26 Movement.

After the revolutionary triumph on January 1, 1959, Castro was appointed Cuba's prime minister by the Council of Ministers in February of that year. He was elected president in 1976. He was commander in chief of Cuba's Revolutionary Armed Forces from 1959 to 2008.

José Ramón Fernández

José Ramón Fernández commanded the main column of the revolutionary Cuban forces that repelled the CIA-organized invasion at the Bay of Pigs in April 1961 and defeated the mercenaries at Playa Girón.

Fernández is currently vice president of the executive committee of the Cuban government's Council of Ministers, a deputy to the National Assembly, and a member of the Central Committee of the Communist Party of Cuba. He is president of the Cuban Olympic Committee.

Born in Cuba in 1923, Fernández was a young officer in Cuba's armed forces at the time of the March 1952 coup by Fulgencio Batista. Together with other similarly inclined officers and soldiers, Fernández worked in secrecy to depose the brutal U.S.-backed Batista dictatorship. He was part of an unsuccessful revolt on April 4, 1956, by army officers who became popularly known as *los puros* (the pure ones). For his participation in that failed attempt, Fernández was arrested, court-martialed, and incarcerated in the infamous penitentiary on the Isle of Pines. He remained in prison for almost three years.

On the Isle of Pines Fernández came to know a number of revolutionary-minded fellow prisoners, among them members and leaders of the July 26 Movement. Won to the political perspective of that movement, he acted for more than a year as military instructor to these political prisoners, who organized their own battalion within the prison.

On January 1, 1959, news reached the prison of Batista's

flight from Cuba in face of the advancing Rebel Army backed by a general strike and growing revolutionary upsurge throughout the country. As the dictatorship's command structure disintegrated, Fernández and other imprisoned July 26 Movement leaders took over the prison, forced their release, and quickly assumed political and military command over the entire Isle of Pines.

Summoned to Havana the next day, he was asked by Fidel Castro to head up a school for cadets to train Cuba's new revolutionary armed forces. Fernández agreed.

Fernández continued on active duty in the Revolutionary Armed Forces through the 1960s. He was deputy minister of the FAR until 1970; deputy minister of education in 1970–71; and minister of education from 1972 to 1991. Since 1978 he has been vice president of the Council of Ministers.

Fidel Castro and José Ramón Fernández (at center, facing camera) at Playa Girón, April 1961.

Jack Barnes, the author of the foreword, has been national secretary of the Socialist Workers Party since 1972. An organizer of the Fair Play for Cuba Committee, actions in defense of Black rights, and the anti–Vietnam War movement, Barnes was a leader of the Young Socialist Alliance (YSA) in the early 1960s, serving as its national chairperson in 1965. He has been a member of the Socialist Workers Party National Committee since 1963, a national officer of the party since 1969, and has carried central responsibility for the party's work internationally.

As a contributing editor of the Marxist magazine *New International,* Barnes is the author of numerous articles, including, "U.S. Imperialism Has Lost the Cold War," "The Fight for a Workers and Farmers Government in the United States," and "The Politics of Economics: Che Guevara and Marxist Continuity." Among his recent books and pamphlets are *Malcolm X, Black Liberation, and the Road to Workers Power, The Working Class and the Transformation of Learning* and *Capitalism's World Disorder.* He was one of the reporters who conducted the interviews published as *Making History: Interviews with Four Generals of Cuba's Revolutionary Armed Forces.*

Foreword

"The October Crisis was a continuation of the U.S. fiasco at Girón. The defeat they suffered there led them to risk an atomic war. Girón was like a bone sticking in their throats, something they don't accept to this day. In war one either wins or loses. But they can't admit having lost in their efforts to dominate such a small country."

DIVISION GENERAL ENRIQUE CARRERAS
REVOLUTIONARY ARMED FORCES OF CUBA
OCTOBER 1997

On the morning of April 18, 1961, readers of daily newspapers across the United States woke up to front-page headlines proclaiming, "Rebels Near Havana, Invade Four Provinces." An Associated Press news dispatch reported that "Cuban rebel forces" had landed within thirty-eight miles of Havana and at numerous other points on the island. Citing a press release from the "Cuban Revolutionary Council," the dispatch said that much of the Cuban militia had already defected to the invading forces and "in the next few hours" the deciding battle for the country would be fought. "Rebel" forces were "in control of the Isle of Pines and had freed some 10,000 political prisoners held there."

Most Americans took the story as good coin, expecting to soon hear that the "pro-Communist dictator" Fidel Castro had been ousted.

Around the country, however, in dozens of cities and on a number of college campuses, there were pockets of individuals who knew from the beginning that every word of the AP story was a lie. We had been carrying out an intensive educational campaign for weeks. We had been getting ready for the invasion we knew was coming, preparing to act here in the Yankee heartland side by side with the Cuban people the moment it happened. Between April 17 and April 19, as the battle was being fought in Cuba, we confidently took to the streets, organized speak-outs, posted marked-up newspaper clippings, and went on the radio asserting that, all press reports to the contrary, the U.S. government-organized and -financed invasion was being defeated, not winning.

As we had been doing for months, we pointed to the immense popularity of the revolution among the Cuban people in response to the measures the new government was organizing them to take. The Mafia-run gambling dens and brothels, a national shame, had been shut down. Land had been distributed to more than 100,000 tenant farmers, sharecroppers, and squatters. House and apartment rents, as well as electricity and telephone rates, had been slashed. Racial discrimination was outlawed and equal access not only made law but enforced. Public beaches, previously off limits to Blacks, had been opened to all. A nationwide campaign to eliminate illiteracy had been launched—part of a broader extension of public education to the countryside, among the poor, and for women. Popular militias had formed in factories, other workplaces, schools, neighborhoods, and towns across the island, as Cubans demanded arms and military training to defend their new conquests. The huge money-gouging U.S. monopolies had been nationalized, as well as the major landed, commercial, and industrial property holdings of the wealthy Cuban families who had been the social and political base of the Batista dictatorship.

Through more than two years of popular mobilization, the

workers and farmers of Cuba had begun transforming not only their country but themselves, we explained. It was precisely for this reason that Cubans could, and would, fight to the death to defend their revolution—and do so successfully.

Only thirty-six hours after the initial AP stories made headlines across the United States, the counterrevolutionary "rebel forces"—who had landed not thirty-eight miles from Havana or on the Isle of Pines, but near the Bay of Pigs on the southern coast of the island—had been ignominiously routed at Playa Girón by Cuba's popular militias, Revolutionary National Police, and Rebel Army. Not only the decisiveness, but also the speed of the April 19 defeat was crucial. The strategic plan authorized by President John F. Kennedy called for the 1,500-man mercenary force to establish and hold a beachhead on an isolated slice of Cuban territory long enough to declare a provisional government and appeal for direct military intervention by Washington and its closest allies in Latin America.

The shock of this very first military defeat of U.S. imperialism in the Americas began to register in Washington, and among its defenders in pressrooms, factories, and schools across the country. In the weeks that followed, as bitter and self-serving recriminations among organizers of the invasion spilled out, more and more information about the U.S.-run military operation and the background of the individual Cuban "freedom fighters" began to make its way into the mainstream press in the United States.

As these facts became known, supporters of the Cuban Revolution took full advantage to spread the truth, point to the accuracy of what we had been arguing for months, and underline the sober exactitude of the speeches and statements of leaders of the Cuban Revolution over the previous two years.

The first issue of *Time* magazine to appear after the Cuban victory, for example, revealed that the purported authors of the Cuban Revolutionary Council press release cited so authoritatively by AP, including "prestigious" figures such as José Miró Cardona, not only knew nothing of the timing of the invasion but had actually been held as quasi-prisoners by the U.S. government while the operation was under way. The press release issued in their name had in fact been written by the CIA officers in charge of the invasion, while the members of the CIA-created Cuban government-in-exile were held incommunicado under military guard in a barracks at the deserted Opa-Locka airfield near Miami.

Both the AP wire story and *Time* magazine article, and the use we made of them, were part of the intense argument that raged on a number of campuses, as well as in factories, rail yards, and other workplaces throughout the United States during the opening years of the Cuban Revolution. It was a propaganda battle that, from one end of the country to the other, became a confrontation in the streets both during the days surrounding the U.S.-organized invasion at the Bay of Pigs and a year and a half later during the October "missile" crisis.

This political battle that began more than forty years ago was one that changed the lives of a not-insignificant number of young people in the United States. It transformed the communist movement here in a way that paralleled the profound changes taking place in Cuba and elsewhere around the world. Nothing since the October 1917 Bolshevik Revolution in Russia has had such an impact.

There are moments in history when everything ceases to be "normal." Suddenly the speed of events and stakes involved intensify every word and action. Neutral ground seems to disappear. Alignments shift and new forces come together. The polite conventions of civil discourse that normally reign in bourgeois circles evaporate, including within the "academic community."

April 1961, when the bombing and invasion of Cuba by

mercenaries organized, financed, and deployed by Washington met the fearless resistance and lightning victory of the Cuban people, was such a moment.

*

At the time I was one of the organizers of the campus Fair Play for Cuba Committee (FPCC) at Carleton College, a small, very respectable liberal arts school in Northfield, Minnesota, a few miles south of the twin cities of Minneapolis-St. Paul. The billboard at the Northfield city limits welcomed visitors to "Cows, Colleges, and Contentment." The contentment was sorely tried by the rise of the Cuban Revolution and by the historic and irreconcilable conflict of class forces reflected at the Bay of Pigs. The cows continued to fare well.

The experiences we went through at Carleton were not unique. To one degree or another they were repeated at several dozen colleges and universities across the United States.

The January 1959 victory of the Cuban Revolution, combined with Washington's intense hostility to the economic and social transformation being wrought so close to U.S. shores, led three Carleton students to decide to visit Cuba in 1960, each at different times, to see for themselves. I was one of those students, spending the summer in Cuba to study the economic changes taking place there. I was deeply affected by these ten weeks of daily participation together with other young people and with the workers and farmers of Cuba in actions that constituted one of the most important turning points of the revolution. Returning for my senior year, I was determined to find those in the United States whose response to what was happening in Cuba was similar to mine. I had two intertwined goals: to work together with whomever possible to oppose Washington's attempts to crush the Cuban Revolution, and to find among them those who wanted to organize their lives to emulate here the example set by the Rebel Army and Cuba's working people.

From the spring of 1960 on, every political person in the
world knew an invasion of Cuba was imminent. Reports on
the CIA recruitment and training facilities in Florida, Louisiana, and Guatemala circulated for months. Despite heavy
government pressure on mostly pliant journalists and pub-
lishers alike, bits and pieces of news found their way into
print. Cuba's foreign minister, Raúl Roa, speaking before
United Nations bodies at least three times publicly detailed
the scope of the preparations under way. He made it clear
beyond challenge that the only question was exactly when
and where the invasion would occur, not whether.

Under the impact of experiences in Cuba, we organized a
socialist study group on campus to read and discuss Marxist
theory—from *The German Ideology* and other early works
by Karl Marx that had recently been published in English
translation for the first time, to the *Communist Manifesto*,
to works by communist leaders in the United States. We
organized other students to subscribe to the *Militant* newsweekly—which we had begun reading in Cuba and was our
most thorough, regular, and reliable source of information
about the revolution.

Early in 1961, convinced the invasion could not be more
than weeks away, we organized a campus chapter of the Fair
Play for Cuba Committee, and began to carry out virtually
nonstop political education activities to lay the groundwork for
deepening and broadening opposition to Washington's plans.

The bulletin board in the student union soon became a
battleground. Every day we posted clippings with the lat-
est news reports from the big-business dailies and weeklies,
from the Minneapolis *Tribune* to *Newsweek*—marked up
and annotated to underscore Washington's acts of aggression against Cuba and to expose the fabrications and self-
contradictory information emanating from U.S. government
sources. We also tacked up speeches by Cuban leaders that
we clipped out of the *Militant*, and we made the unqualified

assertion that their assessment of the U.S. rulers' response to the advance of the revolution would soon be proven correct. Opponents of the revolution, from liberals to ultra-right-wingers, would reply by posting articles they thought bolstered their views; we would answer the next day, often using the very same sources to expose their arguments. We were learning a valuable lesson about the existence, and effectiveness, of imperialist disinformation campaigns.

No one tried to tear down clippings or halt the debate, however, which we counted as our first victory. We had done what communists in plants and mills across the country were simultaneously doing: we had taken the moral high ground, proving that defenders of Cuba, not our opponents, were the ones pressing for debate, for openness, for reading the press critically and discussing the facts.

In February 1961 we had initiated a series of public meetings on Cuba. These programs were sponsored by Challenge, a lecture series we had established earlier in the school year after winning support from the student government for the initiative. The campus newspaper, the *Carletonian*, described the program as designed to "challenge the underlying beliefs and assumptions of the student body by bringing to the campus 'numerous intelligent and committed individuals who hold dissenting views which are not heard by the Carleton student body.'"

Challenge had already had a broad impact on campus. It organized debates on U.S. covert operations in Laos. Marxist literary critic Annette Rubinstein, an editor of *Science and Society* magazine, had lectured on Shakespeare. Challenge sponsored a debate on the May 1960 San Francisco "riots" against the so-called House Un-American Activities Committee (HUAC). We held a showing and discussion of *Salt of the Earth*, the blacklisted movie about the unionization battle of largely Mexican zinc miners in the Southwest in face of posse violence and ferocious red-baiting. A member of the International Union of Mine, Mill, and Smelters Workers spoke after the film about their 1950 strike and ongoing battle against the mine operators. Another program on the unions—an "unknown institution" at Carleton in those years—featured Mark Starr, the longtime education director of the International Ladies' Garment Workers' Union.

All these events were controversial on campus. But nothing compared to what broke out around programs on Cuba.

A letter to the editor in the *Carletonian* in March 1961 complained of the "rude treatment" a visiting professor allegedly received from several students who had challenged him on the facts in response to statements he made about Cuba. He acknowledged at the Challenge meeting that he wasn't an authority on the subject and later had to admit to the student paper he had never even been to Cuba.

The following week two members of the National Fair Play for Cuba Committee spoke on campus about the Cuban Revolution and the deepening struggle for Black rights throughout the United States. One was Robert F. Williams, a founding member of Fair Play who two years earlier had been removed by top NAACP officials as president of the Monroe, North Carolina, chapter for organizing fellow Black war veterans into armed self-defense of their community against racist thugs and nightriders. The other speaker was Ed Shaw, Midwest organizer of Fair Play, who was a typesetter and member of the International Typographical Union from Detroit, as well as a leader of the Socialist Workers Party. That meeting had a powerful impact on campus. What impressed us above all was that Williams and Shaw each talked about both the struggle for Black rights and the Cuban Revolution with similar ease and insight.

The next week, four Carleton students who had visited or lived in Cuba—three of them organizers of the campus Fair Play for Cuba Committee—presented a slide show and debated the issues.

We organized to make sure that every issue of *The Carletonian* carried articles, letters, cartoons, and other commentary that was part of the deepening discussion about the Cuban Revolution among students and faculty. Jim Gilbert, a supporter of Fair Play who had visited Cuba during the Christmas break at the end of 1960, wrote an extensive article describing his experiences and observations about the social and political gains of the Cuban people. By chance Gilbert had visited Playa Girón, where the revolutionary government was focusing development efforts that had already begun transforming conditions of life and work for the impoverished residents of the Zapata Swamp, previously one of the most isolated and backward regions of the country. Little did we know at the time the special significance Playa Girón would have in a matter of weeks, not only for the Cuban people but for the work of supporters of the Cuban Revolution.

The unfolding debate at Carleton, as elsewhere, was deeply affected by hearing accounts in early 1961 of the murder of young literacy campaign workers in Cuba by CIA-financed and -armed counterrevolutionary bands in remote areas. Homilies from liberal opponents of the revolution about the need to see both sides of the story seemed brutally hypocritical beside photos of Cuban teenagers lynched for the crime of teaching peasant families to read and write. Or for the crime of having on a militia uniform as they walked home at night, unarmed.

Supporters of the revolution also put a spotlight on the unjust and brutal treatment of prorevolutionary Cubans in the United States. Only days before the Bay of Pigs invasion, Francisco Molina, an unemployed Cuban worker who supported the revolution, was convicted in New York City on second-degree murder charges. *The Carletonian* carried the story. Molina had been framed and found guilty of murder for the accidental death of a young Venezuelan

girl during a fight, provoked by an assault by Cuban counterrevolutionaries, that broke out in a New York restaurant
during Prime Minister Fidel Castro's September 1960 visit
to speak before the United Nations General Assembly. On
grounds of "national security," the judge prevented Molina's
defense attorneys from pursuing the identity and other rel-
evant information about the counterrevolutionary Cubans
involved in the incident. As the respectable press howled
about the lack of justice in Cuba, the class character of "justice" in the United States could not have been more clearly
demonstrated for us.

During these same weeks, a major fight involving much
greater forces than those at Carleton alone broke out over
campus recognition of the student Fair Play for Cuba Committee. In early February the student government association, by a two-thirds majority, approved an application for
recognition from the campus chapter of the FPCC. A very
vocal minority objected, arguing that a group avowedly dedicated to "dissemination of material both of fact and opinion on contemporary U.S.-Cuba affairs" and establishing
"broader understanding of U.S.-Cuba relations" could not be
a legitimate campus organization since, they charged, the
FPCC was "vulnerable to communist influence." A cartoon
in the following issue of the campus paper depicted Nikita
Khrushchev, Mao Zedong, and Fidel Castro standing behind
Carletonian editor John Miller, who had run an editorial
supporting recognition of Fair Play, and chortling, "Well,
boys, what'll we put in next week's *Carletonian?*"

The large majority vote by the student government association didn't settle the matter, however. A faculty meeting
also had to approve the charters of all student organizations
before they could be recognized, normally a formality following a favorable student government recommendation.
After stalling for a month on technicalities, in mid-March
the faculty assembly took up the FPCC application, along

with a letter from three students objecting to recognition of the campus chapter. Appended to the letter were excerpts from the records of the Senate Internal Security Subcommittee, chaired by Democratic Party senators James Eastland of Mississippi and Thomas Dodd of Connecticut, which was at that time conducting a congressional witch-hunt hearing on "communist influence" in the Fair Play for Cuba Committee.

Dean of the College Richard Gilman told a closed faculty meeting he "had information saying that the Socialist Workers Party have a special and partisan interest in the Fair Play for Cuba Committee—that they are using it for their own purposes." According to *The Carletonian*, "Gilman admitted that this information presented was not documented evidence but rather was the 'opinion' of two sources," whose identity he refused to reveal because of the "nature of the information and the sources."

The campus paper reported that a request from the campus Fair Play organizers that they be given even "one documented incident to indicate use of the FPCC by another political group for purposes other than those enumerated in its charter" was denied. Also refused was a request that they be provided with the identities of even one of the purported "sources" so they could "confront Fair Play's accusers" and either refute or corroborate their "opinions."

A few days before the faculty vote on recognition, Gilman asked me to drop by his office. He handed me copies of expurgated pages from an FBI file on the Fair Play for Cuba Committee containing informers' reports on meetings of the committee in Minneapolis-St. Paul, including garbled comments attributed to individuals identified as members of the Socialist Workers Party. When the dean asked me if I recognized any of the names, I assured him I did, and considered a number of them my comrades. They were members of the party I was soon to join. I also protested that I knew them well enough to assure him they could not have made the kinds of remarks attributed to them by the FBI's apolitical stooges.

"That really makes no difference, does it Jack?" was Gilman's only reply. It was a very short meeting.

It wasn't the facts or content that mattered, it was the accusation, or rather the threat behind the accusation. That was the message. This was the tried-and-true witch-hunting method machined during the war administration of Franklin Roosevelt, broadened in use by Harry Truman, then honed over more than half a decade in the late 1940s and early 1950s by Richard Nixon, Joseph McCarthy, and their ilk. It was a method still very much in use in 1961. "X" and "Y" were known members of the Socialist Workers Party, a communist organization, and the Socialist Workers Party was on the Attorney General's List of Communist or Subversive Organizations—in those days that was often sufficient to end further discussion.

Even with all this, Gilman wasn't sure enough of a majority to allow a faculty vote on recognition of the Fair Play for Cuba Committee. On March 11 the faculty accepted the dean's recommendation not to act on the student government proposal, pending clarification of some matters about which he was awaiting "further information." Everyone got the point. The school year would soon be over, and the central leaders of the committee were seniors. The dean and others hoped their "problem" would be eliminated before the next academic year began.

But wars register sharpening not diminishing class struggle. Far from disappearing, their "problem" was about to get worse.

✳

With the bombing of the Cuban airports on April 15; the April 16 mass mobilization that registered the socialist character of the revolution, politically preparing the Cuban people for the impending invasion; and the April 17 landing of the mercenary forces at the Bay of Pigs followed by their crushing defeat fewer than three days later—all documented by Fidel Castro and José Ramón Fernández in the pages that follow—everything ceased being normal.

One of the routines of campus life at Carleton was the lunchtime reading of the day's news dispatches. In each dormitory dining room, as a sit-down lunch was being served by student waiters working for their scholarship funds, the head waiter would read a handful of the morning's press dispatches from United Press International. UPI's teletype service was provided free of charge by Lucky Strike cigarettes to the campus radio station on condition that Lucky Strike be acknowledged as the sponsor of all news programs. Which it was. Except when "The Sleepy Fox," who hosted the morning wake-up music and news program, sometimes announced the sponsor was a popular brand of Havana cigar. He also prepared students for the day by opening with the "July 26 Hymn," an antidote to "The Star-Spangled Banner" with which radio and TV stations in the United States signed on and off each broadcast session.

On Monday, April 17, the dry, slightly cynical style of the lunchtime news readings changed. Initial reports of the assault on Cuba were suddenly greeted by slightly flushed right-wingers leading rhythmic chants of "War! War! War!" The rapidity of the transformation, and the incipient violence that lay so close to the surface beneath the "political debate," was something none of us had seen before.

Three days later, for those who had led the chants, the unimaginable had happened. You could almost see the ranks of supporters of Fair Play for Cuba expanding as the news readers flatly intoned UPI dispatches announcing the utter rout of the mercenary forces at "Cochinos Bay." We were surprised as some campus workers, instructors, and students

Top: Cadres of right-wing Young Americans for Freedom tried to bust up April 18, 1961, speak-out called by campus Fair Play for Cuba Committee at University of Minnesota. A small core of the largely hostile crowd pelted speakers with snowballs and milk cartons. Confrontation sparked extensive debate on campus. **Bottom**: April 19, 1961, picket line in Detroit, Michigan. Photo was "Exhibit 39" in publication issued by Senate Internal Security Subcommittee in June 1961. Booklet contains the witch-hunting committee's unsuccessful effort to grill Ed Shaw, Midwest organizer of Fair Play for Cuba Committee (at center left in photo). "I will not be intimidated into cooperating with . . . your efforts to suppress the free expression of public indignation over the illegal and immoral invasion of Cuba by the U.S. Government and its Central Intelligence Agency," Shaw told the subcommittee.

we barely knew—who had remained poker-faced during the previous three days—came up with a handshake or smile to say something friendly, even if not openly mentioning Cuba.

The year 1961 in Cuba was "The Year of Education," when more than 100,000 young people, the big majority of them teenagers, left their homes and spread out across the country to eradicate illiteracy from Cuba before the year was up. In unexpected ways, 1961 was the year of education for us as well.

One of our biggest lessons was what happens in an imperialist country when war begins.

In a matter of hours on April 17, the broad undecided center had shrunk to a voiceless kernel. Months of concentrated political action preparing for the war fell into place in a few decisive days. Committed builders of the Fair Play for Cuba Committee at Carleton in early 1961 had been fewer than half a dozen. But now came the payoff for the weeks of education, propaganda work, writing, talking, pushing for and organizing open political debate, and taking up the challenges of every opponent on every issue. As the workers and peasants of Cuba inflicted a crushing defeat on U.S. imperialism, support for the political positions we had been defending exploded overnight. But only because we were there, we were prepared, and we were ready to respond.

The sharp and violent polarization that erupted as the first shots were fired taught us another big lesson. As opponents of the U.S.-sponsored invasion, we were in the streets within hours. But so too were the ultra-right-wing cadres of the Young Americans for Freedom (YAF) who mobilized to try to physically prevent Fair Play for Cuba Committee actions from taking place.

On the steps of the University of Minnesota student union on April 18, where the campus FPCC had called a protest speak-out, a largely hostile crowd of several hundred swelled to well over a thousand as right-wingers pelted the speakers with snowballs and milk cartons, while the cops smiled. With the predominantly liberal and pacifist rally organizers unprepared to defend the meeting, John Greenagle, state chairman of the YAF, forced his way onto the platform to deplore the defeat of Batista, while a few other students appealed for tolerance and dialogue. Even one of those who had been lined up to speak as an opponent of the invasion rushed to take his distance from the Cuban Revolution, bleating out, "We don't support Castro. Once again the Cuban people are under the heel of a dictator, but is an American-supported invasion the way to help them? Is this armed force any better than Batista or Castro?"

An effigy of the "commie" Fair Play for Cuba Committee was hung in front of the chemistry building the next morning.

Similar confrontations took place at other schools across the United States, from Madison, Wisconsin, to Providence, Rhode Island.

We learned in practice what Batista and the Cuban Revolution had already taught us from afar: that in the United States, too, we would have to defeat the reactionary thugs in the streets even to have the right to make our positions known.

We got an education in liberalism, too, as our faculty friends went silent or absented themselves, rather than take on a dean (a supposedly reserved and tolerant one, of course) waving the Attorney General's list and FBI informer reports in their faces. We saw student allies who had previously been staunch defenders of the Cuban Revolution, or at least of Fair Play's right to function like other campus organizations, suddenly develop cold feet; they were discovering that future career plans were incompatible with continued association with friends who were becoming communists.

Others made the opposite life decisions in a matter of days.

Our understanding of these class questions was accelerated immeasurably by the fact we were sharing our day-by-day experiences, talking about them into the wee hours of the night with communist workers in the Twin Cities. They were people like V.R. Dunne, who had been a member of the Communist International at its founding, a leader of the Teamsters strikes and organizing drives in the Upper Midwest during the 1930s, and one of the first victims railroaded to prison by the federal government under the infamous Smith "Gag" Act for opposition to U.S. imperialism leading up to and during World War II.

These workers pointed us to the history of the class struggle in the United States, to the lessons we needed to learn from the workers and farmers whose fighting legacy we inherited. They drew on this rich history to help us understand what we had to be prepared for as we went up against the most violent and brutal ruling class in the world.

Above all, they taught those of us who, like themselves, were so strongly and passionately attracted to the example being set by the fighting workers and peasants of Cuba that the challenge—*for us*—was not there. Cuba's workers and farmers had proven they could take care of themselves. They helped us see that *our* fight was in the United States. That Washington, to paraphrase Cuban Division General Enrique Carreras, would never be able to get that bone out of its throat.

Those workers like Dunne and others helped us see that the contest would end only with the defeat of the revolution in Cuba or a victorious socialist revolution in the United States.

"There is one thing we can most certainly tell Mr. Kennedy," Fidel Castro told a cheering crowd in Cuba on March 13 of that year. "A victorious revolution will be seen in the United States before a victorious counterrevolution in Cuba."

That had become our conviction too. As beyond belief as

this appeared to the average American, it seemed the only *realistic* perspective to us, and we set out to speed the day.

The continual interchange between new, young activists, mostly on the campuses, and communist workers whose experiences on the job and in the unions paralleled ours as we all went through the same rapid political shifts and changes, helped deepen our understanding of what we were living through. Our rail worker comrades reported receiving a friendly nod from fellow workers for telling the truth about Cuba in the same way that we were being encouraged in many indirect ways by those on campus we had not previously realized were following so closely what we were saying and doing.

We came to appreciate that everything depended on the political work done beforehand. We learned firsthand how dangerously wrong and class-biased were the fears and semihysterical reactions of many of our campus-based colleagues. The source of reaction was not "backward American workers" but the U.S. ruling class. And the danger came also from those who, whether they owned up to it or not, had set out on a life course to camouflage, help divert attention from, and politically rationalize the rapacious and brutal actions of that ruling class. The battle before us was first of all a political battle inside the working class, as part of the working class.

*

As Cuban workers and farmers pressed forward their socialist revolution and U.S. aggression mounted in reaction to their gains, the lessons transformed the way we looked at the battle for Black rights in the United States as well. The mass proletarian struggle to bring down the Jim Crow system of legal segregation throughout the South, with its various forms of discrimination extending throughout the country, was marching toward bloody victories at the same time that the Cuban Revolution was advancing. We could see in practice that there were powerful social forces within the United States capable of carrying out a revolutionary social transformation like the working people of Cuba were bringing into being.

The core of the activists defending the Cuban Revolution were young people who had cut their political eyeteeth as part of the civil rights battles, supporting the Woolworth lunch counter sit-ins and joining or supporting marches and other protests in Alabama, Georgia, Mississippi, and elsewhere in the South.

The many faces of reaction, some in Ku Klux Klan hoods, others with sheriff's uniforms and FBI jackets protecting them; the lynchings and murders on isolated country roads; the dogs and water cannons unleashed on protesters—all were burned in our consciousness as part of the lessons we were learning about the violence and brutality of the U.S. ruling class and the lengths to which it will go to defend its property and prerogatives.

And we were learning lessons, too, from the armed self-defense organized by Black veterans in Monroe, North Carolina, and elsewhere in the South. Immediately following the U.S. defeat at the Bay of Pigs, during a debate in the Political Committee of the United Nations General Assembly, Cuban Foreign Minister Raúl Roa read a message that former Monroe NAACP president Robert F. Williams had asked him to convey to the U.S. government.

"Now that the United States has proclaimed military support for people willing to rebel against oppression," Williams wrote, "oppressed Negroes in the South urgently request tanks, artillery, bombs, money, use of American air fields and white mercenaries to crush racist tyrants who have betrayed the American Revolution and Civil War."

We rapidly came to see that the legal and extralegal violence directed against those fighting for their rights and dignity as human beings here in the United States was one and the same as the mounting overt and covert aggression against the people of Cuba. We placed the struggle for Black rights in the world. It became totally intertwined for us with the stakes in defending the Cuban Revolution.

This was exemplified above all by the convergence of the Cuban Revolution and Malcolm X, whose voice of uncompromising revolutionary struggle—by any means necessary—was then increasingly making itself heard. Fidel Castro met with Malcolm at the Hotel Theresa in Harlem during the Cuban delegation's trip to the United Nations in 1960. Malcolm invited Che Guevara to address a meeting of the Organization of Afro-American Unity during Che's trip to New York in 1964.

For us, these and other expressions of the growing mutual respect and solidarity that marked relations between Malcolm X and the Cuban leadership were further confirmation of our own developing world view.

*

The April 1961 actions condemning the U.S.-organized invasion of Cuba—held in a score of cities across the United States, as well as a number of small college towns—registered an important moment in U.S. politics in another regard.

In many cities, for the first time in decades, these were united front actions, called under the banner of the Fair Play for Cuba Committee and organized both by those identified with the *Militant* newspaper and by those who looked for leadership to the *Daily Worker*, newspaper of the Communist Party. Representatives of each of these historic currents in the broad working-class movement joined July 26 Movement speakers and prominent individuals not affiliated with any current on speakers' platforms from New York to Detroit, from Minneapolis to San Francisco. The actions were testimony to the impact of the Cuban Revolution as well as the leadership of the July 26 Movement.

The potential for unified actions had received a boost during the summer of 1960 when scores of young people from the United States, affiliated and unaffiliated, traveled to Cuba, many of us participating in the July 26 celebration in the Sierra Maestra mountains and attending the First Latin American Youth Congress in Havana. We took part in the wide-ranging political debate among young people from all over the Americas and the world, trying to understand the onrushing struggle we were part of and thinking through the questions addressed by Che Guevara in his opening speech to the youth congress, where he asked: "Is this revolution communist?"

The answer Guevara gave posed the issues we were all discussing. "After the usual explanation as to what communism is (I leave aside the hackneyed accusations by imperialism and the colonial powers, who confuse everything)," Guevara responded, "I would answer that if this revolution is Marxist—and listen well that I say 'Marxist'—it is because it discovered, by its own methods, the road pointed out by Marx."

Guevara's explanation coincided well with the conclusions I was groping toward during that decisive summer, when all the major imperialist-owned industries in Cuba were nationalized by massive mobilizations of working people from one end of the island to the other. Guevara's view was far from a unanimous one, however, and we spent many long hours debating among ourselves the political and theoretical issues that were posed.

Despite sharp political differences over the dynamic of the revolution in Cuba and class politics in the United States, the fact that different currents were able to come together in action against the U.S. government, even if briefly, registered the weight of the Cuban Revolution in the Americas, and the degree to which it opened up a historical potential to shatter old molds and alter the relationship of class forces that had for years dominated what was broadly considered the "left."

*

The campus Fair Play for Cuba Committees and the actions in response to the U.S.-sponsored invasion at the Bay of Pigs also dealt one of the first blows to anticommunist witch-hunting and red-baiting. As the Carleton example illustrated, the hearings of the Senate Internal Security Subcommittee aimed at dividing and destroying the effectiveness of Fair Play simply failed to have the same effect on students they would have had several years earlier.

Throughout these same months of intense political action in defense of Cuba, Committees to Abolish HUAC, the House Un-American Activities Committee, had been mushrooming on campuses across the country. On April 21, one day after a Union Square demonstration of 5,000 in New York City condemning the U.S. invasion, nearly the same number turned out for an anti-HUAC rally in the city to protest the imminent jailing of several prominent civil liberties and civil rights activists for refusing to cooperate with the House committee.

Among students, especially, conviction that the U.S. rulers were lying about Washington's total control of the invasion and other actions against Cuba went hand in hand with rejection of the government's witch-hunt methods. Openness to searching for the truth about Cuba was incompatible with a belief that the opinions of some should not be heard because they were communists or were labeled communists.

In a prelude to what happened during the opening years of the anti–Vietnam War movement in the mid- and late 1960s, the witch-hunting moves of right-wing students and faculty, far from paralyzing organizing efforts, became targets of derision and scorn. The majority of students awakening to political life simply refused to support attempts to exclude members and supporters of the Socialist Workers Party and Communist Party, or any other group, from the Fair Play for Cuba Committee.

✻

The victory at Playa Girón punctured the myth of U.S. imperialism's invincibility. It left us with the conviction that the Cuban Revolution would be at the center of the class struggle inside the United States as long as the working class was in power in Cuba, and we had become convinced that such would be the case for the rest of our political lives. The U.S. rulers could never accept revolutionary Cuba and would never stop trying to get rid of it and the example it set. Their most vital class interests were at stake. That was the truth we had to bring to working people in the United States and prepare to act on.

Within a matter of days of the Bay of Pigs defeat, President Kennedy stepped up covert operations against Cuba and began organizing directly from the White House even more extensive military preparations for a U.S. invasion. We didn't know the scope of those operations at the time, nor that the administration only a year and a half later would push them to the brink of unleashing a nuclear war. But we did know that Fidel Castro was speaking the truth to the people of Cuba and the world in his April 23 report on the victory at Playa Girón when he emphasized that the victory "does not mean that the danger is past. Quite the contrary. We believe that the danger is now great, above all, the danger of direct aggression by the United States."

The victory of Cuban working people at Playa Girón, together with the concentrated class-struggle experience we had gained over a few months of intense action, had in a matter of a few days transformed a group of young people for the rest of our lives. Before the Bay of Pigs there had been only one member of the Young Socialist Alliance at Carleton College, myself, and one at the University of Minnesota, John Chelstrom, an eighteen-year-old freshman who, when everyone else froze in front of the rabidly hostile crowd, stepped forward and led off the April 18 speak-out on the steps of the student union, not only opposing the invasion but openly identifying himself with the Cuban Revolution.

Between those days of concentrated politics, and similar experiences lived through during the October 1962 "missile" crisis, we recruited scores of young people who were won to the communist movement not for months or years, but for life. At Carleton College alone during that brief span, these recruits included over a dozen who later became leaders of the communist movement—national officers of the Young Socialist Alliance, national officers and National Committee members of the Socialist Workers Party, editors of the *Young Socialist*, the *Militant*, the *New International*, leaders of the movement's industrial trade union work, and of countless defense committees and coalitions, editors of Pathfinder Press—individuals who to this day remain committed to the political current and active along the political course they became convinced of in those decisive days. In fact, forty years later, a large majority of them were involved in bringing this book into print!

Through those experiences four decades ago, we were won not just to an ideological position or a moral stance, but to a course of political conduct and, most importantly, to the habits consistent with it. With a sense of history, we signed on for the duration, recognizing that the revolutionary fight for power is a struggle that can only be waged country by country, and possibly the most satisfying victory of all will be in the United States. For us, what Cuban workers and peasants had accomplished was the example in our own political lifetime of the necessity and the possibility of revolution, of how to fight to win, of the capacity of ordinary human beings to transform themselves as they confront challenges and take on responsibilities they would have previously deemed impossible. We and millions like us were the only ones who could "remove the bone"—by following the example the revolutionary militias, police, and army had set in smashing the invasion at the Bay of Pigs.

*

The pages that follow are not solely a celebration of the victory at Playa Girón on the occasion of its fortieth anniversary. Rather, in clear and unambiguous words, these pages register accurately the historical accomplishments achieved there.

The July 1999 testimony offered by José Ramón Fernández draws its unusual power not only from being the firsthand account of the field commander of the main column that fought and defeated the U.S.-organized invasion, but also from his use of the major accounts published by those who recruited, trained, and commanded the enemy forces. He points not only to what the revolutionary leadership of Cuba knew and did at the time, guaranteeing the decisive victory at Playa Girón. Fernández also cites the judgments and opinions rendered in the maps and charts the mercenary forces later drew for themselves, as well as the balance sheets of top CIA officials during the months and years that followed their totally unexpected defeat.

The three speeches by Cuban commander in chief Fidel Castro excerpted here capture the intensity of the moment, the stakes for the people of Cuba, and their confidence in ultimate victory. The same is true of the April 15 calls to battle by Raúl Castro and Che Guevara, as well as the war communiqués issued by the revolutionary government between April 17 and the victory on April 19. The confidence marking each of them is born not of some unfounded belief in military invincibility, but of the recognition that history and justice are on their side, and that the price the empire will have to pay to conquer them is one no capitalist politician will be capable of doing or willing to try.

The U.S. rulers, and those who follow their lead, still to this day cannot grasp what Fidel Castro stressed in his April 23 report to the Cuban people on the victory at Playa Girón, and what José Ramón Fernández underlines in his testimony: that the military strategy and tactics of those who planned the invasion at the Bay of Pigs were sound; the defeat was rooted in their class blindness to what the men and women of Cuba had wrought, to the *objective* power of a just cause and of an armed and revolutionary people committed to defend it and acting with the decisiveness and speed necessary to shape the course of history.

The invading forces lost their will to fight before they ran out of bullets. During three days of battle, they could never even get off the beaches, and additional U.S. air or naval support would have made no difference to the ultimate outcome.

Most importantly, for those of us living and working in the United States, this is a book about the future of the class struggle here. It is about the workers and farmers in the imperialist heartland, and the youth who are attracted to the line of march of these toilers—workers and farmers whose revolutionary capacities are today as utterly discounted by the ruling powers as were those of the peasant and proletarian masses of Cuba. And just as wrongly.

Cuba's victory at Playa Girón registered the first great defeat of U.S. imperialism in the Americas. It will not be the last.

That will occur right here.

Jack Barnes
MARCH 2001
NEW YORK CITY

Publisher's note

The transcript of the testimony by José Ramón Fernández before the Provincial People's Court of the City of Havana in July 1999 is published here in full, together with reproductions of the maps and charts he presented. As with all material in this book, the titles, subheadings, and footnotes are the responsibility of the editors.

To aid the reader with historical events, names, places, and other information that may be unfamiliar, we have included biographies of the authors and several maps, as well as a chronology, a glossary, and a list of further reading.

This book is being published by Pathfinder simultaneously in English and Spanish. The 1961 speeches and documents included here have either been out of print or not easily accessible in either language for several decades. In English some are appearing for the first time, and all are published in new and more accurate translations. The April 16 speech by Fidel Castro has been translated into English for the first time; the April 23 report to the Cuban people on the battle of Playa Girón has been newly translated; and the May 1 speech was previously published only in an unreliable English text prepared by the U.S. government's Federal Broadcast Information Service. The April 15 calls to arms by Raúl Castro and by Ernesto Che Guevara are translated and published here in English for the first time.

The translation into English of the Fernández testimony was the work of volunteers Paul Coltrin and Matilde Zimmermann. Final editing of this and other translations into

English was done by Michael Taber. Paul Coltrin helped with translation into Spanish of introductory material and annotation. Final editing of the text in Spanish was the responsibility of Luis Madrid.

This book would not have been possible without the assistance of José Ramón Fernández and members of his staff in Havana, Cuba. A special thanks is due Iraida Aguirrechu, also of Havana, for her help in researching information for the footnotes, chronology, glossary, and further reading. Delfín Xiqués of *Granma* and Manuel Martínez of *Bohemia* provided invaluable assistance in searching the archives of those publications to find many of the photographs displayed in these pages.

Through their contributions on many fronts, volunteers for the Pathfinder Reprint Project across North America and around the world made it possible to produce this book with speed and quality. They formatted and proofread the text, scanned speeches for editorial preparation, and worked miracles with some of the illustrations and photographs to make them usable and print-ready. Volunteers on Pathfinder's editorial staff and in its printshop did essential work in preparing the cover, text, and photo insert—and did so in face of tight deadlines—making this book as attractive and readable as possible for all those who will put it to use.

Rebel Army commander Camilo Cienfuegos (third from right) leads caravan of peasants into Havana, July 26, 1959. Half a million peasants came to the capital to celebrate implementation of the first agrarian reform law, which distributed land to over 100,000 rural toilers and their families. The measure had been enacted in May.

SAN ANTONIO DE LOS BAÑOS   CIUDAD LIBERTAD

FAKE LANDING, APRIL 18   HAVANA

BAHÍA HONDA   MANAGUA   MATANZAS

GUANIGUANICO   DEL RÍO   HAVANA   JOVELLANOS   COLÓN

PINAR DEL RÍO   PINAR   MATANZAS   SANTA CLARA

ZAPATA PENINSULA   CIENFUEGOS   LAS VILLAS   ESCAMBRAY

PLAYA GIRÓN

ISLE OF PINES   BAY OF PIGS

INVASION, APRIL 17

Cuba and the Caribbean, 1961

ATLANTIC OCEAN

GULF OF MEXICO   Bahamas

Cuba   Puerto Rico

Jamaica   Haiti

Mexico   Br. Honduras (Belize)   Dominican Republic

Guatemala   Honduras

El Salvador   CARIBBEAN SEA

Nicaragua

Costa Rica

PACIFIC OCEAN   Venezuela

Panama   Colombia

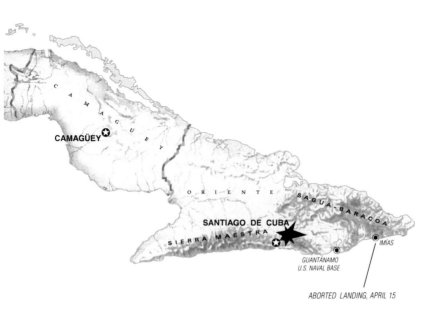

CAMAGÜEY⊙

O R I E N T E

S A G U A - B A R A C O A

SANTIAGO DE CUBA

S I E R R A   M A E S T R A

⊙ IMÍAS

GUANTÁNAMO
U.S. NAVAL BASE

ABORTED LANDING, APRIL 15

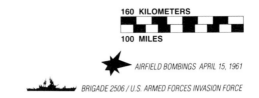

160 KILOMETERS

100 MILES

★ AIRFIELD BOMBINGS APRIL 15, 1961

BRIGADE 2506 / U.S. ARMED FORCES INVASION FORCE

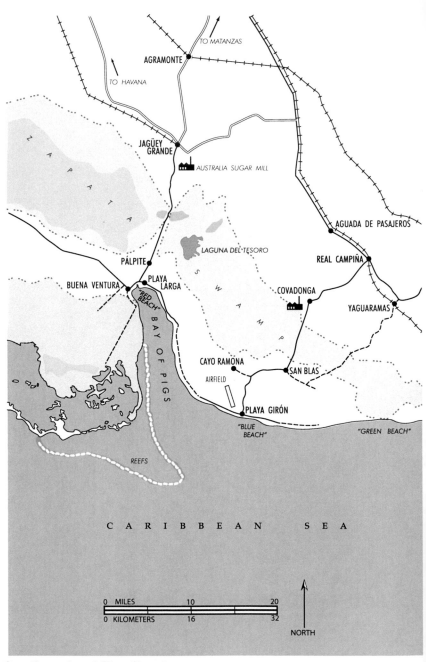

Southern Las Villas Province

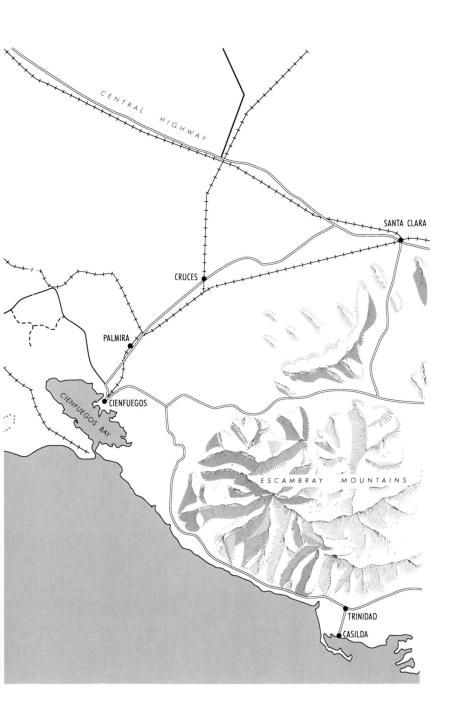

CENTRAL HIGHWAY

SANTA CLARA

CRUCES

PALMIRA

CIENFUEGOS

CIENFUEGOS BAY

ESCAMBRAY MOUNTAINS

TRINIDAD

CASILDA

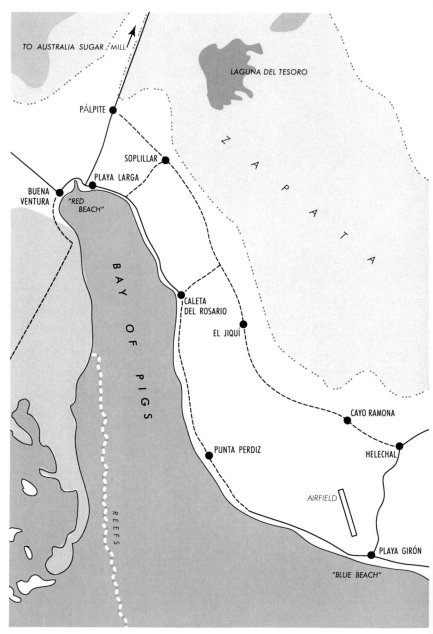

Zapata Swamp and the Bay of Pigs

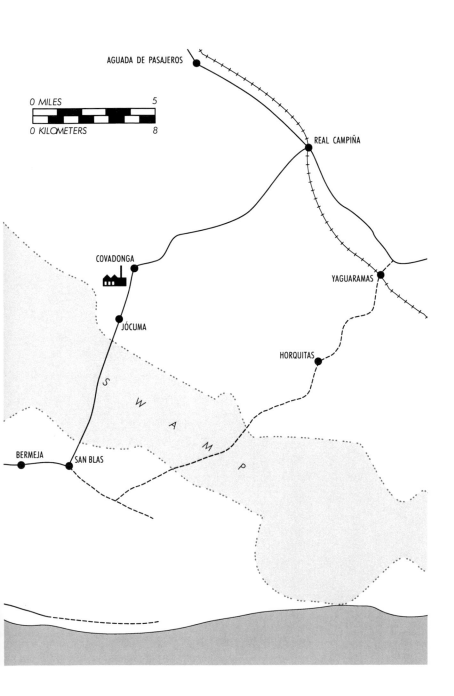

AGUADA DE PASAJEROS

0 MILES 5

0 KILOMETERS 8

REAL CAMPIÑA

COVADONGA

YAGUARAMAS

JÓCUMA

HORQUITAS

S

W

A

M

P

BERMEJA

SAN BLAS

They cannot forgive us because
we made a socialist revolution
right under their very nose

Fidel Castro
April 15–16, 1961

On April 15, 1961, in what Fidel Castro described as "a monstrous, cowardly act," eight planes from the CIA-organized Brigade 2506 launched simultaneous bombing raids against the Havana-area San Antonio de los Baños and Ciudad Libertad airfields, as well as the Antonio Maceo airport in Santiago de Cuba. The raids were conducted on orders from U.S. president John F. Kennedy in preparation for an invasion at the Bay of Pigs two days later. This unsuccessful attempt to destroy the revolution's handful of combat aircraft on the ground was carried out by Pentagon-supplied B-26 bombers bearing counterfeit insignia of Cuba's Revolutionary Air Force. Seven Cubans were killed and fifty-three injured in the sneak attacks.

Immediately following the assault, Fidel Castro mobilized all revolutionary military units and placed them on a state of alert. His statement to the Cuban people following the issuance of those orders opens this section.

The next day a massive funeral procession in Havana honored those killed. Hundreds of thousands of Cuban working people marched in the procession to the Colón Cemetery. At the conclusion, Fidel Castro addressed the crowd—in whose front ranks were members of the Revolutionary National Militias carrying their rifles—and before the world pointed to the socialist character of the Cuban revolution.

Included here is the main portion of the concluding section of his remarks.

Statement to the people of Cuba

At 6:00 a.m. today, April 15, 1961, U.S.-made B-26 bombers simultaneously attacked points in Havana, San Antonio de los Baños, and Santiago de Cuba, according to reports received so far.

Our antiaircraft batteries opened fire on the attacking planes, hitting some and forcing one to retreat in flames.[1]

Planes of the Revolutionary Air Force took off immediately in pursuit of the enemy.

As this report is being written, numerous explosions continue to be heard, as a consequence of a fire at a munitions dump close to the FAR airfield. No deaths have yet been reported, although there are many wounded. The attack was carried out by surprise and in a cowardly manner.

Our country has been the victim of criminal imperialist aggression in violation of all norms of international law.

The Cuban delegation to the United Nations has received instructions to directly accuse the government of the United States of being behind this aggression against Cuba.

The order has been given to mobilize all combat units of the Rebel Army and Revolutionary National Militias. All commands have been put on a state of alert.

---

1. That plane, which had bombed the Ciudad Libertad airfield, exploded in a ball of fire over the Caribbean. Another B-26 hit by antiaircraft fire over Ciudad Libertad made an emergency landing in Key West, Florida, while a plane hit over San Antonio de los Baños airfield had to land in the Cayman Islands.

If this air attack is the prelude to an invasion, the country will be on a war footing. With an iron fist, it will resist and destroy any force that attempts to land on our soil.

The people will be kept fully informed.

Every Cuban must occupy their assigned post, whether in a military unit or a workplace, with no interruption in production, the literacy campaign, or a single revolutionary task.

Our country will resist any enemy attack firmly and calmly, sure of its victory.

Patria o muerte!

Venceremos!

Fidel Castro Ruz

Speech to ceremony honoring those killed in imperialist assault on Cuban airfields

Fidel Castro

Yesterday at 6:00 a.m., as everyone knows, three groups of bombers penetrated the national territory from abroad and attacked three points of the national territory. At each of these points, men defended themselves heroically. In each of these points, the courageous blood of the defenders was shed. In each of these points there were thousands, or at least hundreds, of witnesses to what happened.

It was something that was expected. It was something that had been expected every day. It was the logical culmination of the burning of canefields, of the hundreds of violations of our airspace, of the pirate air incursions, of the pirate attacks on our refineries by ships that penetrated at dawn.[2]

---

2. The U.S. government-organized bombing of Cuban sugar mills and canefields and other air incursions by planes taking off from the United States began in October 1959. Many of these attacks, together with other events leading up to and in the aftermath of the invasion at the Bay of Pigs, are indicated in the chronology at the back of this book.

On March 13, 1961, a speedboat carrying recoilless artillery clandes-

It was the consequence of what everyone knows. It was the consequence of the plans of aggression that have been brewed in the United States with the complicity of the lackey regimes in Central America. It was the consequence of the air bases that everyone knows about, because they have even written about it in the U.S. newspapers and news agencies themselves, and these news agencies and newspapers are tired of speaking of the mercenary armies that are being organized, of the airfields that have been prepared, of the planes that the U.S. government has supplied, of the Yankee instructors, of the air bases established in Guatemalan territory.[3]

All the people of Cuba knew this; all the world knew this. Yesterday's attack was carried out in the presence of thousands and thousands of men. What do you think the Yankee rulers have said about such an incredible thing? Because it's no longer a case of the explosion of *La Coubre*, which was carried out as a cunning undercover act of sabotage.[4] It's now a question of a simultaneous attack on three points of the national territory with machine-gun fire, bombs, missiles, and warplanes that everyone saw. We're talking about a public act, an anticipated act, an act that the world knew of even before it was conducted.

---

tinely entered the harbor at Santiago de Cuba, firing at the Hermanos Díaz oil refinery, leaving one dead and one wounded.

3. In May 1960 the CIA established the first of several bases and airfields in Guatemala for counterrevolutionary Cuban-born military forces. As early as October of that same year Cuban foreign minister Raúl Roa, speaking before the United Nations, publicly exposed the exact location and other details of these training camps, and in January 1961 the *New York Times* ran a front-page article headlined, "U.S. Helps Train an Anti-Castro Force at Secret Guatemalan Air-Ground Base."

4. See the March 4, 1960, entry in the Chronology at the end of this book.

In order for us to set the historical record straight, in order to establish the historical proof, in order for our people to learn once and for all, and in order to let the peoples of the Americas know—to whom only a single ray of truth may get through—I'm going to explain to the people. I'm going to show the people how the imperialists proceed. [*Applause*]

Did you think the world was going to find out about the attack on Cuba? Did you think the world was going to find out what happened? Did you think or could you conceive that it would be possible to try and silence the echo around the world of the criminal bombs and missiles they fired yesterday at our country? Would it have occurred to anyone that someone would try to deceive the entire world, to hide the truth from the entire world, to trick the entire world?

Yesterday they attacked our land in a cunning and criminal attack. The whole world knew about it. There were Yankee planes, Yankee bombs, and Yankee weapons, as well as mercenaries paid by the Yankee Central Intelligence Agency. They destroyed the nation's wealth. They ended the lives of young people, many of whom were still in their teens. [*Shouts*] But not only this. Yesterday the U.S. government also tried to trick the world. The U.S. government yesterday tried to trick the world in the most cynical and shameless manner anyone could ever imagine. [*Applause*]

I have here the proofs. I have here the proofs of how imperialism acts, of the whole workings of imperialism, of how imperialism not only commits crimes against the world, but how it tricks the world. It tricks the world not only through stealing its oil, its minerals, the fruit of the peoples' labor, but it tricks the world morally, palming off untruths and the most sensational lies anyone could imagine.

We are going to read to our people what imperialism is telling the world. We are going to show what the world learned yesterday, what they told the world, and what perhaps they made tens upon tens of millions of human beings believe.

This is what was published in thousands upon thousands of newspapers, and was read aloud yesterday over thousands upon thousands of radio and television stations about what happened in Cuba. This is what a considerable part of the world learned through the Yankee agencies.

[Castro reads several news dispatches from the U.S. press agency United Press International (UPI). He then reads several from the Associated Press.]

The following are the AP dispatches: [Shouts]

"MIAMI, April 15, AP—Three Cuban bomber pilots, fearing betrayal in their plans to escape Fidel Castro's government, fled today to the United States after strafing and bombing the airports in Santiago and Havana.

"One of the two twin-engine bombers from the Second World War landed at Miami International Airport, with a lieutenant at the plane's controls. He described the way in which he and three of the twelve pilots of B-26 aircraft who remain in the Cuban Air Force, had for months planned to flee Cuba.

"Another plane that took part in the raids landed at the U.S. naval air station at Key West. Two Cubans were aboard. The names of the pilots were withheld. The immigration authorities took the Cubans into custody and impounded their planes.

"Approximately 100 Cuban refugees gathered at the Miami airport and cheered and applauded as the pilot was hurried through customs and taken to an undisclosed destination."

Listen to this: "Edward Ahrens, district director of the U.S. Immigration Service read aloud the following statement prepared by the pilot of the Cuban Air Force . . ." In other words, not only do they state that he is Cuban, they have the gall to state that they're not giving his name, so that no one will know who he is. Not only do they seek to hide the name of this gentleman who has just committed a crime, but in addition the director of immigration reads his statement aloud. You see the degree of cynicism, you see how shameless imperialism's officials and leaders are. You see how they invent a horrendous cover story—down to the smallest detail. . . .

So this is what they have told the world. Not only did UPI and AP give the world the news that "Cuban pilots, who left with their planes and dropped bombs," but they also spread this tale throughout the world. And what do you think tens of millions of people in the world read yesterday, published and aired in thousands upon thousands of different newspapers, radio and television stations? What do you think they have said in Europe, in many parts of Latin America, in many parts of the world?

Not only have they stated such a thing, they have fabricated a complete story, with details and names, scheming up everything. Hollywood would never have come up with something like this, ladies and gentlemen![5]

OK, that is what UPI declares. That is what AP declares. That is what the mercenaries declare. That's the declaration given by the director of immigration, while he says he is not giving out the name so that the pilot is not revealed, after stating that he'd just taken the plane. . . .

But it doesn't stop there. Now we're going to unmask imperialism's charlatan in the UN, who passes for a man who's illustrious, liberal, left-wing, etc., etc.: Mr. Adlai Stevenson, who is another perfectly shameless individual. The trick continues, that is, the attempt to trick the world. Already UPI and AP have given out the tale, thousands of reactionary newspapers . . . and they themselves publish it,

---

5. According to a report on the Bay of Pigs by a committee headed by U.S. General Maxwell Taylor, the plan for the fake defections and strikes on Cuban airfields was approved by President John F. Kennedy at an April 5 White House meeting with top CIA and Pentagon officials.

with the main newspapers welcoming the news of the desertion of these pilots.

The delegate from "María Ramos's pussycat"[6] arrives at the UN. "The U.S. ambassador Adlai Stevenson rejected Roa's statements[7] and repeated the declaration of President John F. Kennedy that there would not under any condition . . ." I repeat: . . . there will not under any condition be any intervention in Cuba by United States armed forces. Stevenson showed the commission United Press International photographs that portray two planes landing today in Florida after having participated in the air raids against three Cuban cities."

Then Stevenson says: "It has the markings of Castro's Air Force on the tail," he says, pointing to one of them. "The Cuban star and the initials FAR—Fuerzas Armadas Revolucionarias—are clearly visible. I will gladly exhibit this photo." Stevenson added that the two planes in question were piloted by officers in the Cuban air force, and that the crew consisted of men who deserted from Castro's regime. "No personnel from the United States participated in today's incident, and the planes were not from the United States," he stated. "They were planes from Castro himself that took off from his own fields."

"The Cuban minister said that 'this morning's air raids are undoubtedly the prologue to a large-scale invasion attempt organized, supplied, and financed by the Government of the United States. The Cuban government,' Roa

---

6. An expression for someone who does something and then tries to pretend they didn't.

7. On April 15 Cuban foreign minister Raúl Roa rose before the UN General Assembly to "accuse . . . the imperialist government of the United States of being the main culprit for this brutal attack on Cuba's territorial integrity, independence, and sovereignty." Roa was able to complete the accusation before being gaveled out of order.

said, 'solemnly accuses the government of the United States before this commission and before world public opinion of trying to employ force to settle their differences with member states.'"

Here we have, as other peoples have seldom had, the opportunity of knowing what imperialism is—inside and out, on every coast, top to bottom. Here we have the opportunity of appreciating how its whole financial, propaganda, and political apparatus works, as well as its mercenaries, secret bodies, and officials, who, with such tranquility and in an almost unheard-of manner, are tricking the world. Try to imagine how we would have known what's happening in the world. How we would have been able to know what's happening in the world, if this were the only version and the only explanation that countless people around the world are getting!

In other words, they organized the attack, prepared the attack, trained the mercenaries, supplied the planes, supplied the bombs, prepared the airports—everyone knows it. The attack occurs and they calmly state before the world that it's not so. This is a world that they know would rise up in indignation in face of such a monstrous, cowardly act that violates the rights of the peoples and is a violation of peace! [*Applause*]

And these miserable gringo imperialists, after shrouding seven homes in mourning, after murdering a handful of young people who were not millionaire parasites—because those we've come here to bury were not millionaire parasites, they were not mercenaries who sold themselves for foreign gold, they were not thieves. They are true sons of our people! [*Prolonged applause*]

They were young workers, children from families of ordinary people who never stole anything from anyone, who never exploited anyone, and who had a right to live more than the millionaires. They had more right to live than the parasites and the *gusanos!*[8] [*Applause*] Because they did not live off the labor of others, like the Yankee millionaires. They did not live off foreign gold, like the mercenaries and gusanos who have sold out to imperialism. [*Shouts of "Down with them!"*] They did not live off vice or theft, and they had a right to have their lives respected. And no miserable imperialist millionaire has the right to send planes, bombs, and missiles to snuff out these young and cherished lives of the homeland! [*Applause*] . . .

What the imperialists cannot forgive is that we are here. What the imperialists cannot forgive is the dignity, the integrity, the courage, the firmness of ideas, the spirit of sacrifice, and the revolutionary spirit of the people of Cuba. [*Applause*]

That is what they cannot forgive, that we are here under their very nose. What they cannot forgive is that we have made a socialist revolution right under the very nose of the United States! [*Applause and shouts*] That we defend this socialist revolution with these guns! [*Applause*] That we defend this socialist revolution with the same courage shown yesterday when our antiaircraft artillery riddled the aggressor's planes with bullets! [*Applause and shouts of "Venceremos!" and other revolutionary slogans.*]

This revolution is not defended with mercenaries. This revolution is defended by men and women of the people.

Who has the weapons? Do the mercenaries perhaps have the weapons? [*Shouts of "No!"*] Because mercenaries and millionaires are the same thing. Do the little rich boys perhaps have the weapons? [*Shouts of "No!"*] Do the overseers perhaps have the weapons? [*Shouts of "No!"*] Who has the weapons? [*Shouts*] In whose hands are these weapons now be-

---

8. *Gusanos* (Spanish for "worms") was the term used by supporters of the revolution to refer to the counterrevolutionary groups in exile that were plotting against the revolution.

ing raised? [*Shouts*] Are they the hands of playboys? [*Shouts of "No!"*] Are they the hands of the rich? [*Shouts of "No!"*] Are they the hands of the exploiters? [*Shouts of "No!"*]

Whose hands are now raising these weapons? Aren't they the hands of workers? [*Shouts of "Yes!"*] Aren't they the hands of peasants? [*Shouts of "Yes!"*] Aren't they hands hardened by work? [*Shouts of "Yes!"*] Aren't they hands that create? [*Shouts of "Yes!"*] Aren't they the hands of the humble, of ordinary men and women? [*Shouts of "Yes!"*] And who are the majority of the people—the millionaires or the workers? The exploiters or the exploited? The privileged or the working people? [*Shouts*]

Do the privileged have the weapons? [*Shouts of "No!"*] Are the privileged a minority? [*Shouts of "Yes!"*] Are the working people a majority? [*Shouts of "Yes!"*] Is it democratic to have a revolution in which the working people have the weapons? [*Shouts of "Yes!" Applause and shouts of "Fidel, Fidel!" and various revolutionary slogans.*]

Compañero workers and peasants, this is the socialist and democratic revolution of the working people, with the working people, and for the working people. [*Applause*] And for this revolution of the working people, by the working people, and for the working people we are prepared to give our lives. [*Shouts*]

Workers and peasants, men and women of our homeland: Do you swear to defend to the last drop of blood this revolution of the working people, by the working people, and for the working people? [*Shouts of "Yes!"*]

Compañero workers and peasants of the homeland: yesterday's attack was the prelude to the mercenaries' aggression. Yesterday's attack, which cost seven heroic lives, aimed to destroy our planes on the ground. But the mercenaries failed; they did not destroy our planes, and the bulk of the enemy planes were damaged or shot down. [*Applause*]

Here, in front of the graves of our fallen comrades; beside the remains of the heroic youth, children of workers and children of ordinary working men and women, we reaffirm our determination. Just as they faced the bullets, just as they gave their lives, we state that no matter when the mercenaries come, no matter who we face, that we are all proud of our revolution, proud to defend this revolution of the working people, for the working people, and by the working people. And we will not hesitate to defend it to the last drop of blood. [*Applause*]

Long live the working class! [*Shouts of "Long live!"*]

Long live the peasants! [*Shouts of "Long live!"*]

Long live the humble! [*Shouts of "Long live!"*]

Long live the martyrs of the homeland! [*Shouts of "Long live!"*]

Forever long live the heroes of the homeland! [*Shouts of "Long live!"*]

Long live the socialist revolution! [*Shouts of "Long live!"*]

Long live free Cuba! [*Shouts of "Long live!"*]

Patria o muerte! Venceremos! [*Applause*]

Let us sing the National Anthem, compañeros. [*Those present sing the National Anthem.*]

Compañeros, all units need to head toward the site of their respective battalions, in view of the mobilization order to maintain the country in a state of alert in face of the imminent mercenary aggression that can be deduced by all the events of the last weeks and yesterday's cowardly attack.

Let us march to the Militia Houses.

Let us form up the battalions and prepare to go confront the enemies, with the national anthem on our lips, with the words of the patriotic anthem, with the cry of "To battle," with the conviction that "to die for the homeland is to live" and "to live in chains is to live plunged in ignominy and shame."

Compañeros, let us march to our respective battalions and wait there for orders. [*Applause*]

"Long live our socialist revolution!" April 17, 1961, issue of *Revolución*, daily newspaper of the July 26 Movement.

RAÚL CORRALES

Militia members in Pinar del Río during January 1961 mobilization against escalating danger of U.S.-backed invasion.

Imperialism has always been our great teacher

Ernesto Che Guevara and Raúl Castro
April 15, 1961

With a U.S.-organized attack imminent, central leaders of the revolution were sent to take command of the revolutionary military forces in different areas of the country: Raúl Castro to Oriente province in eastern Cuba, Ernesto Che Guevara to Pinar del Río in western Cuba, and Juan Almeida to Santa Clara to head the Central Army.

On April 15, the day of the bombing attack on the airfields, Guevara was due to give a speech in Pinar del Río celebrating the demobilization of militia units from that province that had participated in the campaign to eliminate bands of counterrevolutionaries in the Escambray mountains. He used the occasion, as he says, not to say "good-bye" following the victory in the Escambray but to say "see you soon—very soon" and to prepare the working people of Pinar del Río for the battle against the imminent invasion.

Simultaneously, at the other end of the country, Raúl Castro called on the people of Oriente to return to the posts they had occupied during the national mobilization in January, when the revolution faced an increased danger of U.S. aggression during the transition between the administrations of President Dwight D. Eisenhower and John F. Kennedy. The call to mobilize was broadcast throughout Oriente province.

Concluding words of speech by Ernesto Che Guevara in Pinar del Río, April 15, 1961

Imperialism has always been our great teacher, the one that has taught us the most. Whenever our spirits have flagged, whenever we have considered sitting down to rest, imperialism has shown us, as it is doing today, that in a revolution one cannot rest, and that to keep advancing our weapons must be readied anew. We must be prepared for the next battle and continue being prepared, eliminating step by step everything that is despicable, everything that represents the past, and creating, in the midst of the fight, a new world.

Most likely they will now attack our production centers. They will probably hit all the vital points and in this way try to break us. The role of the people is more and more important: to wield a rifle and work beside their machines, with a pick or machete, producing every day, becoming disciplined in order to produce more; becoming disciplined in order to fight better when the battle is joined; waging combat in a revolutionary way against all our weaknesses and against all attempts to divide us.

The task is not easy, because we face an imperialist encirclement, direct armed assaults, and there is much to do. But nothing is impossible.

In the coming days the people will probably have to forego some of the comforts they are accustomed to. There will be shortages, days when production will be curtailed because the men are going into the trenches, or because the raw materials needed for production are not arriving. We must prepare for those days. We must steel our spirit. We must once again become disciplined, organize ourselves into revolutionary committees, organize young people into the Rebel Youth, organize the women into their organizations, unite all the political parties under the single banner of progress for Cuba, and work and prepare for the struggle together.

We cannot say when it will end. Just as today we were originally planning to say "good-bye" but it became instead "see you soon"—very soon. Imperialism always interferes and disrupts our peaceful plans. That's why we must prepare for a long and harsh war, and not think about peace until imperialism has been destroyed completely.

Our actions contribute to their destruction—peacefully— simply by removing their sources of cheap supplies, forcing them to pay what they owe, to pay for what they used to take for free. We contribute to their destruction by showing the Americas our shining example.

And they in turn, as we've said before, try to strike a blow at the vanguard of the Latin American revolution, which is here in Cuba.

This is the broad framework of the struggle.

Should we be outraged? It is our right and our duty to be outraged at their aggression. But we should not let that stop us from thinking clearly, dispassionately, knowing that the struggle will continue and that no protests before any international body will block the empire's actions. Because the empire understands the language of force, and by ourselves we are not strong enough to make them understand that language in their own home. That's why the struggle will take place here.

That's why these militia members here, and those all over Cuba, will return again and again to their posts. That's why, just as with the airfield today, the arson attack against El Encanto yesterday, and the assault on the Santiago refinery before it, our workplaces, our centers of production and defense, will be attacked and in some cases destroyed.

Every time that happens, over the bodies of our fallen comrades, over the rubble of our demolished factories, we must take the oath we always take, with increasing confidence and determination.

Patria o muerte!
Venceremos!

Call to arms by Raúl Castro broadcast to the people of Oriente province, April 15, 1961

People of Oriente:

Today at dawn mercenary planes, paid for by criminal Yankee imperialism, bombed the Antonio Maceo Airport in Santiago de Cuba. We have not had to mourn great losses, even though the loss of Cuba's sons is the least important thing right now. In other cities on the island, mercenary aircraft have similarly trampled on the homeland's soil, dropping Yankee imperialism's bombs.

What does this mean? That the moment has come for all Cubans to take up arms to wipe out the hated ones who seek to trample on the sacred homeland.

People of Oriente, militia members, members of the Rebel Army: mobilize!

The head of each militia and army unit must, in a calm and orderly way, report to the site where weapons are stored. Everyone must take up their posts. Everyone must take up the rifle with which we will pay the price for our freedom. As a first step, in a calm and orderly way, everyone must take up the same post they held during the January mobilization. Production should be maintained at the highest level possible. The CTC [Confederation of Cuban Workers] should call an immediate mobilization, without stopping production. The women's federation too should heed the call to take up their posts. The Rebel Youth, despite their young age, should also take up their rifles to save the homeland.

Everyone to their posts. The enemy has attacked. We will annihilate the enemy and internal reaction. The homegrown traitors, wherever they seek to utilize the confusion that this cunning and treacherous attack may have caused, should be eliminated wherever they carry out counterrevolutionary acts. Annihilate the *gusanos*. Let us fulfill the oath we have made to our 20,000 dead, to our sons and daughters, to the Americas, and to the world.

Annihilate the invader!

Patria o muerte!

Venceremos!

Commander Raúl Castro

War communiqués
to the Cuban people
and the peoples of the world

April 17–19, 1961

Top: Worker and peasant militia members mobilize to confront invasion. **Bottom:** April 18, 1961, issue of *Revolución*: "Everyone to their posts in combat and work!"

Declaration of a state of alert

Havana, April 17, 1961

The Commander in Chief and Prime Minister of the government of the republic declares the country to be on a state of alert and

Orders:

The Rebel Army, the militias, and all security forces to increase vigilance and proceed without hesitation against those seen committing, or trying to commit, acts of sabotage, firing of weapons, or other attacks.

The Committees for the Defense of the Revolution to redouble their vigilance, unmasking and denouncing counterrevolutionaries and their actions.

Urges:

Workers, peasants, intellectuals, and all working people to remain at their posts and redouble their efforts in the fields of production and education.

The entire population to maintain the strictest order and discipline, and to cooperate in crushing the mercenaries, fifth-columnists, saboteurs, and counterrevolutionaries in general.

Everyone into action for a free and sovereign Cuba.

Everyone into action for the revolution of redemption of the working people—Cuba's patriotic, democratic, and socialist revolution—with the cry of: *Patria o muerte! Venceremos!*

Fidel Castro Ruz
COMMANDER IN CHIEF
AND PRIME MINISTER

To the peoples of the Americas and the world

HAVANA, APRIL 17, 1961

U.S. imperialism has launched its long-announced and cowardly aggression against Cuba. Its mercenaries and adventurers have landed in one part of the country.

The revolutionary people of Cuba are fighting them with courage and heroism, and are sure of crushing them.

We nevertheless ask the solidarity of the peoples of the Americas and the world.

We ask our Latin American brothers in particular to make the U.S. imperialists feel the indomitable force of their actions. Let the world know that the peoples, the workers, the students, the intellectuals, and the peasants of Latin America are on Cuba's side, with its revolution to redeem the poor, its patriotic and democratic revolution, and with its revolutionary government.

Redouble the struggle against the main enemy of humanity: Yankee imperialism.

All of Cuba is on its feet with the slogan of *Patria o muerte!*

Our battle is your battle.

Cuba will win!

Osvaldo Dorticós Torrado
PRESIDENT OF THE REPUBLIC

Fidel Castro Ruz
PRIME MINISTER

To the people of Cuba

THE ORDER TO BATTLE

Havana, April 17, 1961

By sea and by air, invading troops are attacking various points of the nation's territory in southern Las Villas province, backed by warplanes and warships.

The glorious soldiers of the Rebel Army and the Revolutionary National Militias are already locked in combat with the enemy at all landing points.

They are fighting to defend the sacred homeland and the revolution against the attack by mercenaries organized by the imperialist government of the United States.

Our troops are already advancing on the enemy, sure of victory.

The people are already mobilizing to carry out the slogans of defending the homeland and maintaining production.

Forward, Cubans! Let us answer with fire and sword the barbarians who scorn us and seek to return us to slavery. They come to take away the land that the revolution gave to the peasants and cooperativists; we fight to defend the land of the peasant and the cooperativist. They come to take away the people's factories, the people's sugar mills, the people's mines; we fight to defend our factories, our sugar mills, our mines. They come to take away from our children and from our peasant women the schools that the revolution has opened for them everywhere; we defend the schools of our children and of the peasantry. They come to take away from black men and women the dignity that the revolution has returned to them; we fight to maintain the supreme dignity of each and every human being. They come to take away from workers their new jobs; we fight for a free Cuba with jobs for every working man and woman. They come to destroy the homeland, while we defend the homeland.

Forward, Cubans! Everyone to their posts of combat and work!

Forward, Cubans! The revolution is invincible, and against it and the heroic people that defend it, all enemies will be shattered!

Let us cry out, with more ardor and firmness than ever, at a time when Cubans are already laying down their lives in battle:

Viva Cuba libre!
Patria o muerte!
Venceremos!

Fidel Castro Ruz
COMMANDER IN CHIEF
AND PRIME MINISTER OF THE
REVOLUTIONARY GOVERNMENT

To the people of Cuba

HAVANA, APRIL 17, 1961
The revolutionary government informs the people that the armed forces of the revolution continue to fight heroically against enemy forces in southwestern Las Villas province, where mercenaries have landed with imperialist support.

In the coming hours, the people will be given details of the successes obtained by the Rebel Army, the Revolutionary Air Force, and the Revolutionary National Militias in the sacred defense of our homeland's sovereignty, of the revolution's victory.

Fidel Castro Ruz
COMMANDER IN CHIEF
PRIME MINISTER OF THE
REVOLUTIONARY GOVERNMENT

To the people of Cuba

HAVANA, APRIL 19, 1961

U.S. participation in the aggression being carried out against Cuba was dramatically proved this morning, when our antiaircraft batteries downed a U.S. military plane, flown by a U.S. pilot, that was bombing the civilian population and our infantry in the area of the Australia Sugar Mill.

The name of the U.S. aggressor pilot, whose body is in the hands of the revolutionary forces, is Leo Francis Berliss. His documents include a pilot's license, number 08323-1M, expiration date December 24, 1962. His Social Security card number is 014-07-6921. His motor vehicle registration card lists his address as 100 Nassau Street, Boston 14, Mass. The registered address of the Yankee pilot is 48 Beacon Street, Boston. His height: 5 feet, 6 inches.

Documents concerning the aggressive flight mission over our country were also found in the clothing of the Yankee pilot.

This is one of four enemy military planes shot down this morning, making a total of nine planes downed since the mercenary attack began on the Zapata Peninsula, an attack that will be completely crushed within a matter of hours.

General Staff of the
Revolutionary Armed Forces

To the people of Cuba

HAVANA, APRIL 19, 1961, YEAR OF EDUCATION[1]
Forces of the Rebel Army and the Revolutionary National Militias took by assault the last positions held by the invading mercenary forces in the national territory. Playa Girón, which was the last point occupied by the mercenaries, fell at 5:30 p.m.

The revolution has emerged victorious, although it has paid a high price in valuable lives lost by revolutionary combatants who confronted the invaders and attacked them without letup, without a single minute of truce, thus destroying in less than seventy-two hours the army organized over many months by the imperialist government of the United States.

The enemy has suffered a staggering defeat. One part of the mercenaries tried to reembark at various points and was hounded by the Revolutionary Air Force. The rest of the mercenary forces, after suffering many dead and wounded, were completely scattered in swampland, with no escape possible.

A large quantity of U.S.-made weapons was seized, among them various Sherman tanks. A complete inventory of the war matériel seized has not yet been made.

In the coming hours, the Revolutionary Government will keep the people fully informed.

Fidel Castro Ruz
COMMANDER IN CHIEF OF THE
REVOLUTIONARY ARMED FORCES

---

1. In recognition of Cuba's campaign to wipe out illiteracy in one year, 1961 had been designated the "Year of Education."

Militia members across Cuba mobilize to defeat invasion.

Commander Efigenio Ameijeiras (left) head of Revolutionary National Police, with members of police battalion at Playa Girón. The battalion took some of the heaviest casualties in the fighting.

The Cuban people, rifles in hand, were convinced of their cause

José Ramón Fernández
Testimony before the Provincial
People's Court of the City of Havana
July 12, 1999

In 1999 eight Cuban organizations joined together to file suit before the Provincial People's Court of the City of Havana to demand that Washington be compelled to pay damages for the consequences of its forty-year ongoing effort to overthrow the Cuban Revolution. The organizations bringing suit—the Central Organization of Trade Unions of Cuba (CTC), the National Association of Small Farmers (ANAP), the Federation of Cuban Women (FMC), the Federation of University Students (FEU), the Federation of High School Students (FEEM), the José Martí Organization of Pioneers, the Committees for the Defense of the Revolution (CDR), and the Association of Combatants of the Cuban Revolution (ACRC)—together comprise the majority of the Cuban people.

The court hearings in *The People of Cuba v. the U.S. Government* included scores of witnesses giving firsthand testimony detailing the concrete results of U.S. crimes against the Cuban people— thousands of deaths and billions of dollars in physical damage. On November 2, 1999, the court handed down a damage ruling against Washington of $181 billion.

Among those called to testify before the court was José Ramón Fernández, commander of the main column that attacked the CIA-organized forces at Playa Larga and Playa Girón. The following is the court transcript of his testimony.

Footnotes and subheadings are the responsibility of the editors.

Testimony before the Provincial People's Court of the City of Havana

José Ramón Fernández

PRESIDENT: The Court hereby convenes the afternoon session. Will the clerk please have the witness come forward.

SECRETARY: The Court calls upon the witness José Ramón Fernández Álvarez to testify.

On July 12, 1999, in the City of Havana, before the Provincial People's Court of the City of Havana, with myself as secretary, an individual was called forth to testify and was informed of the consequences of failure to fulfill this obligation.

PRESIDENT: The witness's name is José Ramón Fernández Álvarez.

FERNÁNDEZ: Yes, sir.

Questioned about the general provisions of Article 329 of the Law of Civil, Administrative, and Labor Procedures, the witness answered that his name was as it appears above, that he is a native of the city and province of Santiago de Cuba, that he is a Cuban citizen, seventy-five years old, married, with the occupation of public servant, that he is not depen-

89

dent on any of the parties in this legal proceeding, and that he has never been convicted of perjury.

PRESIDENT: You are aware that in testifying before the Court you must tell the truth, and you shall be held responsible for any failure to do so. We are going to ask you the question that was duly submitted to the Court by the lawyers for the plaintiff. In giving your answer you should explain to the Court how you came to have knowledge of the events you will be discussing.

Please indicate whether it is true that you played a primary role in leading the actions to confront the mercenary invasion at Playa Girón, and describe the details of your participation.

FERNÁNDEZ: Compañero president, compañeros of the Court:

We cannot discuss Playa Girón and its meaning without going back to its roots and viewing it as the culmination of a stage of the U.S. effort to destroy the Cuban Revolution, a stage whose final outcome was the defeat of Brigade 2506 on the sands of Playa Girón.

Most striking and surprising is the magnitude of the CIA plan, with not a single detail overlooked, whether military, economic, or political. These include: efforts to prepare and trigger an insurgency in mountainous regions; efforts to destabilize and subvert the entire country including the use of terrorism; attempts to create a psychological climate conducive to the objective of destroying the Revolution; recruitment and training centers to ensure the optimal preparation of the mercenary brigade for conventional limited-range battles, including supplying it with technical resources, i.e., weapons and equipment of all types, including fighter planes and heavily armed ships; the assembling and structuring of these forces; the manipulative and deceptive—and, at the same time, domineering—role of U.S. military and political leaders in working with the members of these forces; and many other aspects.

The magnitude of these plans has been covered up by the enemies of the Revolution, who are more concerned with attributing the defeat to the mistakes and deficiencies of the U.S. administrations involved rather than finding the true causes of the debacle.

It is also necessary to mention here the measures taken by the Revolution, under Fidel's leadership, to foil the enemy's plans. To be noted are the actions against banditry and against infiltration by the CIA and by counterrevolutionary organizations operating both in Cuba and the United States; the fight against sabotage, which reduced to ashes some of the country's most important retail and industrial establishments; the crushing of all the truly record number of attempts to assassinate the Commander in Chief in the period prior to Girón;[1] Fidel's success in clarifying the situation in face of the plans to intimidate the people through psychological means, using a whole arsenal of methods and propaganda techniques of subversive warfare; Radio Swan, the lies and the rumors—completely unethical, brazenly cynical, and malicious—such as those that promoted the campaign around child custody, which was designed to trample on the most cherished values of the Cuban family.[2]

---

1. In other testimony during the trial, José Pérez Fernández of Cuba's Ministry of the Interior reported that between 1959 and 1999, there were 637 attempts on the life of Fidel Castro. As confirmed by a U.S. Senate committee report in 1976, as well as numerous other U.S. government documents released since that time, many of the assassination attempts against Castro were organized by the CIA at the instigation of the White House.

2. The Swan Islands (Islas Cisnes) are two islands in the Caribbean off the coast of Honduras taken over by the U.S. government in 1863. Following the triumph of the Cuban Revolution, Washington used the Swan Islands to make counterrevolutionary radio broadcasts to Cuba. In 1971 Washington agreed to recognize Honduran sovereignty over

From a strategic and tactical point of view, the concept of the operation was not flawed. They chose an area where they could disembark, where there was an airstrip and buildings, and that was separated from solid ground by a swamp, across which there were only three roads, on which they were to drop paratroopers.

In Illustration 1[3] we can see the swampland, as well as the three access roads—one of them running from Jagüey Grande to Australia, Pálpite, Playa Larga, and then Girón; another running from Covadonga to San Blas, Helechal, and then Girón; and the third one running from Yaguaramas to Horquitas, San Blas, Helechal, and then Girón. All three roads, it should be noted, were built by the Revolution in a region that beforehand remained isolated, in the most dire poverty, its inhabitants thoroughly exploited, with no access to health care, schools, or communications, living a life of bare survival.[4]

What we have said about the adequacy of their choice

---

the islands, although the U.S. maintained its radio station.

From November 1960 to October 1962, the U.S State Department, working with the Catholic Church hierarchy, organized a campaign against the revolution by spreading rumors that the Cuban government intended to take children away from their parents. Simultaneously they launched Operation Peter Pan, which sought to encourage Cuban parents to send their children to the United States. Under the program, over 14,000 were sent. Many were separated from their parents for years.

3. See pages 145–66 for the illustrations.

4. The majority of residents of the Zapata Swamp at the time were charcoal makers. The revolutionary government quadrupled the price per pound of charcoal these superexploited workers received. In addition to roads, the new government built hospitals, schools, and tourist facilities, and helped the charcoal workers form fourteen cooperatives. These measures dramatically raised living standards and quality of life in the area.

for the zone of operations is valid. It is confirmed in many declassified U.S. documents; we knew it previously and the documents have reconfirmed it. This is corroborated by José Pérez San Román, leader of the mercenary brigade, in his book *Respuesta: La verdad sobre Girón*: "The goal of the Cuban mission was to assure this beachhead and establish itself on a portion of free Cuban territory on which to immediately bring in the broadly representative Cuban Exile Government, to convert it into a Cuban Government in Arms that would be granted international recognition . . . along with the accompanying political, economic, and military support already arranged by the U.S. government and a number of Latin American countries."

The mercenaries came well organized, well armed, and well supported. What they lacked was a just cause to defend. That is why they did not fight with the same passion, courage, conviction, valor, firmness, bravery, and spirit of victory as did the revolutionary forces.

Hence the surprise at the scope of the Cuban people's victory. This must have surprised the U.S. government, which expected a different result. The outcome can be explained only by the courage of a people who saw the January 1 triumph as the genuine opportunity to determine their own future.[5] This is why they proudly wore the militia uniforms and were on alert, and willing to fight, with the firm conviction they would win.

The men and women, the people who in early January 1959 cheered Fidel Castro in his triumphant tour of nearly the entire island, were the same ones who on April 17, 1961—convinced of their cause, rifles in hand, conscious of

---

5. January 1, 1959, marks the victory of the Cuban Revolution. On that date U.S.-backed dictator Fulgencio Batista was forced to flee Cuba in face of an advancing Rebel Army under the command of Fidel Castro and a popular insurrection led by the July 26 Movement.

the declaration of the socialist character of our revolution—were determined to resist and repel the U.S. attack.

Over that brief period, the Revolution's work, and Fidel's words in particular, reached deeply into the hearts of the Cuban people, who identified with the ideas of national sovereignty, social justice, equality, and dignity. The Revolution had resolved the land question. It was taking sure, tangible steps to put an end to racial discrimination and the discrimination against women. It was assuring access by the masses to employment, education, health care, sports, and culture. The goal of eradicating all forms of corruption took hold in the collective consciousness, a concrete manifestation of the economic and social gains made in such a short period of time.

Fidel personally led the fight against the imperialist attack at Girón. This aggression was waged by the mercenary brigade and saboteurs, by bandits in the countryside and CIA agents, by reactionaries and traitors of all stripes who had sold themselves to the empire. In this fight, the Cuban people knew what they were defending, and they did so with a sense of patriotism and revolutionary fervor. Their firm support of the Revolution and Fidel was a decisive factor in the lightning-quick victory over the mercenary invasion.

Compañero president, compañeros of the Court, my testimony on the events at Girón will be based on the following:

First, the events I participated in, or that I personally witnessed.

Second, the firsthand reports of my subordinates during and immediately after the battle against the mercenary invasion.

Third, what I learned through the statements of the prisoners we captured during and immediately after the battle.

Fourth, the statements of U.S. president Kennedy, who said that the invasion was his complete responsibility.

Fifth, the books and articles that have been published on the subject, especially in the United States. Some of these contain firsthand accounts by many of the invasion's organizers and top U.S. officials involved, or contain statements from persons who in some way participated in those events.

I would like to point out six sources, in particular:

First, the little-known book *Respuesta: La verdad sobre Girón*, which I would be willing to provide the Court if it does not have a copy, written by José Pérez San Román, who commanded the mercenary brigade that invaded the country on April 17 at Playa Girón. It was printed in Miami in 1979 by Carlos Miami Press, 223 S.W. 17th Avenue, Miami, Fla.

Second, *The Bay of Pigs: The Leaders' Story of Brigade 2506*, co-authored by U.S. writer Haynes Johnson together with Manuel Artime, the political leader of the mercenary brigade; José Pérez San Román, brigade commander; Erneido Oliva, second in command of the brigade; and Enrique Ruiz-Williams, second in command of the mercenaries' heavy gun battalion. All of them were taken prisoner.

Third, *Operation Puma: The Air Battle of the Bay of Pigs* by Edward B. Ferrer, one of the pilots recruited in the United States by the CIA. Ferrer was in Guatemala during the entire training there and participated in the air attacks on Cuba during the battle. Previously he had also participated by dropping weapons, communications equipment, and other supplies to the counterrevolutionary bands, especially in the Escambray mountains.[6]

---

6. In the early 1960s small bands of counterrevolutionaries armed and financed by Washington—popularly known in Cuba as the bandits—based themselves in the Escambray mountains in south-central Cuba. The bandits carried out sabotage and other operations against the revolution. In December 1960 and January 1961, some 40,000 militia members from throughout Cuba were mobilized in what became known as a "cleanup" operation to wipe out these bands through an encirclement operation. The big majority of the bands functioning at the time were eliminated in the effort. By the opening months of 1965 the counterrevolutionary bands had been eliminated.

Fourth, *Bay of Pigs: The Untold Story* by Peter Wyden, published in 1979 in New York. This is one of the most meticulous studies ever done on the subject.

Fifth, *La batalla inevitable: La más colosal operación de la CIA contra Fidel Castro* by Juan Carlos Rodríguez, published in Cuba in 1996. It is a highly informative analysis of the battle, of the events and conditions leading up to it, as well as how the battle developed.

Sixth and last, an account above any doubt or question, the report of Lyman Kirkpatrick, then CIA inspector general, who gives a detailed analysis and evaluation of the history of every aspect of the project.[7]

A brief review of facts and events

As quickly as I can, I would like to lay out for the Court the sequence of events taken from Kirkpatrick's report. This will give an idea of the chronology of events leading up to the invasion, of some of the preparations for the landing of the mercenary brigade.

It begins with a meeting with then-President Eisenhower on March 17, 1960. That's where Kirkpatrick's report begins, in the famous meeting also attended by the vice president, the chairman of the Joint Chiefs of Staff, and several other people. It was at the end of this meeting that the president of the United States, with the hypocrisy characteristic of the empire's leaders, stated, according to notes taken by Gen. Goodpaster in the meeting summary, that no one could say or know that the president had participated in it—that he

---

7. Kirkpatrick's report is available in *Bay of Pigs Declassified: The Secret CIA Report on the Invasion of Cuba*, edited by Peter Kornbluh (New York: The New Press, 1998). The book also includes a reply at the time by Richard Bissell, the CIA's director of covert actions, who was in overall charge of the operation for the agency, as well as related documents and a chronology.

should appear uninvolved in the matter, even though he knew of "no better plan" to confront the Cuban Revolution.

That meeting agreed on several measures: organizing the exiles, launching a propaganda offensive against Cuba, creating a clandestine apparatus inside Cuba, and developing a military force outside Cuba with which to confront the Revolution.

Initially, a budget of $4 million was earmarked for this operation. Over the course of the operation, the budget eventually multiplied by as much as twenty times the initial amount.

The concept was classic: the hand of the U.S. government was not to be seen. According to Kirkpatrick himself, the CIA personnel in contact with Cuban exiles would have documents identifying them as private U.S. businessmen.

At a CIA meeting in August 1959, a series of studies were presented and a new airline was even created to support the action against Cuba. Information was requested from the entire intelligence community in the region, which resulted in a three-volume study on Cuba.

By December 1959 the CIA was preparing small groups of Cuban exiles to be military instructors to train people in Cuba to act against the Revolution. In January a special group of 40 people was formed to deal with the Cuban problem, which had 18 people in the Florida office, 20 in Havana, and 2 in Santiago de Cuba.

At the same time, a study was made of the Cuban leaders, the Cuban politicians who were abroad, and there were plans to have them form a front.[8] A meeting was held in Massachusetts. Other operations were carried out. A plan was adopted to create an underground newspaper. In March there were new discussions of a plan and possibilities for covert action.

---

8. On May 11, 1960, at Washington's instigation, a number of diverse Cuban exile groups formed the Democratic Revolutionary Front (FRD).

In fact, says Kirkpatrick, the CIA efforts against Cuba had become an important activity with authorization at the highest political level. From a 40-man operation, the CIA's Cuba Task Force, in short order—by April 1961—had grown to 588 people, larger than other CIA divisions.

Funding was supplied, and people were sent to train in various places, including Fort Gulick, Panama. A communications center was opened under the cover of the U.S. Army at the former Richmond Naval Air Station, which was under lease from the University of Miami.[9] Even though a front had been formed, its leaders could not agree on whom to elect as its president.

In July 1960 an air training program was begun. In August the president was briefed. That same month 500 people were expected to be undergoing military training.

The first idea was to train these people and form groups of 20 agents plus one radio operator and get them into Cuba. Later the idea evolved, and the plan was to organize uprisings in Pinar del Río, the Escambray, and the Sierra Maestra. A second phase envisioned attacking and seizing the Isle of Pines. A third phase called for a landing in Havana.

Later, these plans gradually changed. Radio Swan was set up.

At the end of September 1960 there was simultaneously the first maritime operation and the first parachute drop of cargo in Cuba. The maritime operation proved successful, while the parachute drop was the first of a series of setbacks.

The CIA, meanwhile, reported that the Rebel Army was being strengthened and that more forces would be needed. Later, the Nicaraguan president offered Puerto Cabezas as an air base.

Later, the magazine *Bohemia Libre* was created, financed

---

9. Located in Dade County, twenty miles south of Miami.

by the CIA. The Democratic Revolutionary Front was stuck at an impasse; only when they were told that their support would be withdrawn if they did not come to an agreement did they finally elect a president.[10]

In early 1961 feverish activities began to prepare the landing strip in Nicaragua. On November 29, 1960, Eisenhower gave authorization for air strikes, which later did occur, but with the impending change of administration he felt the authorization of the new president was also necessary. Thus the idea was conceived and the new president took office.

It is noteworthy that on March 13, according to Kirkpatrick, the armed LCI[11] owned by the CIA named *Barbara J*, which later participated at Girón, successfully landed and picked up a sabotage team involved in an action against the Texaco refinery in Santiago de Cuba. In other words, it was a vessel owned by the CIA, under the direction of the CIA, that carried out the action, an act of aggression against our country.

On April 15 the famous "defection" of the b-26 took place. This was the sham in which a Cuban exile pilot, Mario Zúñiga Rivas, flew from Nicaragua to Miami, after riddling his b-26 with .50 caliber machine-gun bullets. In Miami he declared that he and several other Cuban air force pilots had risen up and were responsible for the attack that morning on the air bases in San Antonio, Ciudad Libertad, and the Santiago de Cuba airport. He was the one who caused United Nations Ambassador Stevenson—believing Zúñiga had told the truth—to be discredited by Raúl Roa, our representative

---

10. On March 22, 1961, Cuban exile politicians formed a Cuban Revolutionary Council, with José Miró Cardona as president. The agreement came four days after the former CIA station chief in Havana convened the exile politicians in Miami and threatened them with a cutoff of support.

11. LCI stands for Landing Craft, Infantry.

at the UN. Stevenson displayed a photograph to try to prove these were planes of the Cuban Air Force, unaware that the planes of the mercenary forces had been painted with the insignias, colors, and flag of the Revolutionary Air Force.

The three attacks on the airports were carried out by eight B-26 aircraft. The group that attacked Ciudad Libertad was code-named "Puma," the one that attacked San Antonio was code-named "Linda," and the one that attacked Santiago de Cuba was code-named "Gorilla."

At the same time, plans were made for a group of about 160 men to land in the vicinity of Baracoa, in what was called Operation Marte. This was intended as a diversion—a decoy force to divert the attention of the government and Revolutionary Armed Forces to that region, in order to facilitate the main attack to be carried out at the Zapata Swamp. The ship they used for this attempted landing was the *Santa Ana*.

Meanwhile, Radio Swan was transmitting a total of 16 hours a day on short wave and 18 on medium wave. After the landing, it began broadcasting over 14 frequencies, transmitting a daily total of 26 hours on short wave and 55 on medium wave. It could be heard throughout the Americas.

According to Kirkpatrick—and we know this to be true, since it is corroborated by the books *Respuesta: La verdad sobre Girón* written by San Román, head of the mercenary brigade; by *Operation Puma* by Edward B. Ferrer; and by *The Bay of Pigs* by Haynes Johnson—the invasion set sail from Puerto Cabezas on the night of April 16 and headed toward southern Cuba. The ships took different routes so as not to resemble a convoy. They consisted of two CIA-owned infantry landing craft (LCIs), one U.S. Navy LSD, which stands for landing ship dock, containing within it 3 multiple-use landing craft (LCUs), 4 vehicles and personnel landing craft (LCVPs)—all of them loaded with supplies—and 7 chartered cargo vessels. Inside the ships were 36 sixteen-foot aluminum boats. According to Kirkpatrick, all of these vessels participated in the attack, with the exception of three cargo vessels that were to arrive later with backup supplies for the land and air forces. These ships were armed with .50 caliber machine guns. Mounted on the LCIs were 57 mm. and 75 mm. recoilless guns and twin 20 mm. antiaircraft guns. They also possessed a 40-mile radar system. (See Illustrations 2 and 3.)

The troops were also heavily armed with personal and support weapons: 4.2 mortars, heavy machine guns, automatic rifles, 60 mm. and 81 mm. mortars, 57 mm. and 75 mm. recoilless rifles, rocket launchers, and flame throwers. There were also 5 tanks and 12 heavy armored trucks, 1 tanker truck for air fuel, 1 mobile crane, 1 bulldozer, 2 large water trucks, and numerous small trucks and tractors.

The brigade was made up of 1,511 men, all of whom landed by sea, except for 177 from the paratroop battalion, who were dropped in the places I will be mentioning in my description of the battle.

The troops were transported over three days by air, from Guatemala to Puerto Cabezas in Nicaragua. Another two ships were to arrive two days after the landing.

In the early morning hours of April 17, demolition crews arrived at the beach, to mark the landing area—using frogmen, under U.S. command, according to Kirkpatrick—and to create the conditions for the landing. The paratroopers were dropped at dawn.

I should mention that by dawn the Cuban air force, on orders from Fidel, was in the air heading to attack the invading fleet.

Kirkpatrick goes on to say that the first attacks by the revolutionary forces were on Red Beach—i.e., Playa Larga.

He says—and here he offers some hardly encouraging news for the mercenary attackers—that of the eleven mercenary B-26s attacking the revolutionary forces in the landing area on April 17, four were shot down, four were forced to land in other countries after sustaining damage or for some other reason, and only three returned to base.

On the afternoon of April 18, as well, they attacked the revolutionary forces. These are the events I will describe when I present my account of the battle.

Allow me, if I may, to briefly discuss the book by San Román.

He starts out by giving his personal history. He was recruited by the CIA in May 1960—he says so himself—and thereafter he underwent training at Fort Gulick, Panama, and in Guatemala at Base Trax. He was appointed commander of the brigade by the U.S. instructors who were training and leading it, and he was the field commander of the Bay of Pigs invasion.

On page 19 San Román states that President Kennedy met with him in December 1962, in the presence of Kennedy's family, personally explaining to him the reasons for the administration's conduct toward the brigade. Kennedy accepted full responsibility for the events.

On page 22 he says that State Department officials reviewed the plans for the invasion of Cuba at Girón, and that the president assumed ultimate responsibility.

On page 23—and I repeat what I read earlier—he states that the mission of the brigade was to occupy an area of Cuban territory on which to establish a government that would then receive economic, political, and military support. He says that in order to carry this out, the U.S. government had made agreements with various Latin American countries.

Hence the urgency and wisdom with which Fidel called on us to immediately crush the landing because of the danger it represented—not because of the landing itself, but because of the possibility that it was one element that could unleash an intervention in Cuba by outside forces.

San Román says that from midnight April 17 until 1700 hours on April 19, "I was in contact with the U.S. advisory group in the war room (i.e., the operation control room), through Grayston Lynch, who is a CIA agent and who retransmitted from aboard the U.S. Navy aircraft carrier *Boxer*."

The book *Respuesta: La verdad sobre Girón*, written by the mercenary San Román, nominal head of the invading brigade, is a lament in which the author admits that the members of the brigade, starting with himself, were recruited by the CIA, and that the brigade was organized, armed, and led at all times by officials from the CIA and the U.S. armed forces. It is a lengthy attempt to explain and justify the unjustifiable.

In the book *Operation Puma* written by Edward B. Ferrer, the mercenary pilot who admits he was a participant, Ferrer briefly says that from the beginning he was among the forces in Guatemala that were being prepared for use against Cuba. He recounts the air drops of weapons and equipment over the Escambray—how they marked them, how they missed, their failures as a result of the struggle being waged by the militias and Rebel Army against the mercenary bands. He recounts the bombing of the airports in Santiago de Cuba, San Antonio de los Baños, and Ciudad Libertad. He mentions the U.S. agents by name and pseudonym.

On page 165 he mentions Marine Col. Jack Hawkins as the commander of Brigade 2506. It's not us saying that—Ferrer says it in his own book, which I also make available to the Court should it be necessary to provide as evidence.

On page 207 of this book, Ferrer says that of the group of six planes that attacked the revolutionary forces on the afternoon of April 18, two of them had U.S. pilots, one of them named Simpson and the other Doug, and that both of them attacked the motorized column heading from Playa Larga to Girón. He also says that they took off from Puerto Cabezas at 2:00 p.m. that day.

He shows the mercenary aircraft with the flag, initials, and colors of the FAR, and the photos also depict the LSD, the ship named the *San Marcos* that was carrying the tanks. To round out what I said previously about Mr. Ferrer, the book's foreword is written by Admiral Arleigh Burke, chief of U.S. naval operations at the time, and an active participant in the U.S. government decisions in organizing and carrying out the invasion of Cuba.

The book *The Bay of Pigs*, co-authored, as I mentioned previously, by Johnson, Artime, San Román, Oliva, and Ruiz-Williams, describes the entire operation and coincides with Kirkpatrick's report, as well as the other books I've mentioned. This book, I repeat, has the credential, among others, of having been written by the leaders of the mercenary brigade.

Johnson says that on March 3, 1963, President Kennedy stated—and this was published in the U.S. press—that the pilots who died in the plane shot down at the Australia Sugar Mill "died while serving their country." He is referring to the U.S. pilots killed during the mercenary invasion.[12]

Johnson also says that on the morning of April 19, a c-46 landed at the Girón airport with rockets, munitions, and other support materials for the brigade. He says that the pilot of this plane was the mercenary Navarro, accompanied by a North American flight navigator named Bob, apparently an instructor of the brigade.

Preliminary conclusions

Compañero president, compañeros of the Court:

Given everything stated up to this point, and based not only on my personal knowledge but also on direct reports, statements by the CIA inspector general as well as participants and leaders of the brigade, a number of things have

---

12. A number of members of the Alabama Air National Guard flew combat missions for the mercenary forces at the Bay of Pigs. Four of them were shot down and killed.

been corroborated. (I leave aside mentioning all the places where these books coincide with each other. For reasons of time I have omitted mentioning them, although they are at the disposition of the Court.)

First: Operation Marte, which was to have been carried out at Baracoa, was organized from the United States. Training for the mission was done in Louisiana and it left from Louisiana for its attack on Cuba.

Second: President Eisenhower approved the "Program of Covert Action against the Castro Regime," which Eisenhower himself admits in his autobiography. He also approved the plans at various stages.

Third: Fort Knox, the main site for tank training in the United States, was used to train the tank operators who participated in the invasion.

Fourth: The Belle Chase Army ammunition depot in New Orleans was the place from which the LSD containing the tanks that landed in Cuba on April 17 set sail along with the rest of the brigade.

Fifth: Fort Benning, a U.S. infantry division base in Georgia, was used for training the mercenary brigade, as were other installations in U.S. territory.

Sixth: Installations in Florida, including Useppa Island and others, were used for recruiting, examining, and training the mercenary brigade.

Seventh: Members of the U.S. Armed Forces—Army, Air Force, Navy, Marines, and National Guard—were the instructors of the mercenary brigade and, in fact, gave direct orders to the brigade and its ships during the battle.

Eighth: Several of those members participated directly in the aggression, with some of them losing their lives. In one case, a body was recovered by the revolutionary forces.

Ninth: Bases in various locations in the United States, Puerto Rico, Panama, Guatemala, and Nicaragua were used for the attack on Cuba.

Tenth: The CIA organized and was involved in obtaining, through purchase or loan, numerous weapons, as shown in these documents. I will list the weapons and equipment obtained:

• Fighter and transport planes.

• Ships owned by the U.S. Navy, armed LCIs, LCVPs, LSDs and the armament mounted on them, their munitions and accessories.

• M-41 tanks of the U.S. Army.

• Recoilless cannons of the U.S. Army.

• The U.S. armed forces participated in the operation—for example, the planes on the aircraft carriers carrying out reconnaissance, protection, and harassment missions.

• The U.S. Navy protected the sea crossing, gave support, and later attempted to evacuate the brigade.

• Col. Hawkins was the real leader of the mercenary brigade.

• As the date of the attack on Cuba neared, Gen. Doster, the coordinator of Pentagon activities, personally inspected the mercenaries' air base in Nicaragua and gave the orders to move the planes and pilots to Puerto Cabezas.

• The ship *Atlántico*, which was part of the mercenary fleet and carried a mercenary battalion, had two injured members on board. The U.S. destroyer *Eaton* approached the *Atlántico* during the night of April 16 with a doctor and evacuated the injured.

• During combat on the afternoon of April 18, the U.S. destroyer *Murray* approached the *Caribe*, a ship in the invading fleet, and transferred U.S. technical personnel to it in order to repair the radio equipment on board the *Caribe*, which had been damaged by Cuban air attacks.

Who conceived the invasion of Cuba, who organized, armed, and led it, is clearly shown in the books *Respuesta* by San Román, *Operation Puma* by Ferrer, and *The Bay of Pigs* by Johnson, San Román, Artime, Oliva, and Ruiz-Williams, as well as in Inspector General Kirkpatrick's report.

To sum up, compañeros of the Court, the U.S. government not only enlisted the participants in the ill-fated adventure, but also organized, trained, paid, and transported them, and it planned the operation. In fact, the leadership of the Cuban brigade—according to what San Román says in his book—did not even know where or when they would land in Cuba until they were already on the ships.

Additionally, in related activities during the period immediately preceding the invasion—all of them organized by the United States in support of the mercenary brigade—the following events, among others, took place:

• The CIA networks and those operating inside Cuba were reinforced, specifically in Havana.

• Landings with explosives and armaments were planned in order to blow up bridges and carry out other acts of sabotage.

• The bands in the Escambray, which were scattered, were told to support the landing. (As an aside, I would add that compañero Fidel—anticipating precisely this a few months earlier—organized an operation involving tens of thousands of militia members during which the counterrevolutionary bands in the Escambray were practically annihilated, with their remnants in most cases dispersing and fleeing.)

• There was an increase in air drops of weapons, food, and communications equipment in the Escambray.

• Radio Swan and other stations increased their hostile transmissions inciting action against the Revolution.

• Acts of sabotage were carried out in Havana, such as the one at the El Encanto department store.[13]

• Assassination attempts on leaders were planned.

• Attacks were carried out against militia members guard-

---

13. On April 13, 1961, a fire set by counterrevolutionaries destroyed the large nationalized department store El Encanto in Havana.

ing key objectives, or walking through the streets, simply for being dressed in militia uniforms, or against people openly known as militia members.

• Conditions were created for all the networks and the entire counterrevolution in Havana to carry out actions and, if possible, to paralyze Havana, in order to give assistance to the landing and subsequent actions.

Many of these efforts were thwarted through energetic measures taken by our people. Through the action of the Committees for the Defense of the Revolution, State Security, and the people in general, almost all the CIA networks were taken into custody and dismantled, and the counterrevolutionaries were detained and neutralized.

Brigade 2506

So far, compañeros of the Court, I have gone over the climate that had been created, the actions that had been carried out, and the participation in this action against Cuba by the various agencies and highest authorities of the U.S. government.

We will now take another look at Illustration 1, which indicates the landing site, an area of solid ground surrounded by swampland, with access to it by three roads.

The next illustration is copied from a book published in the United States. In this illustration we can trace the cycle of preparations for the invasion over a period of months— initial recruitment, lie detector tests, interrogations in Miami and surrounding areas, followed by final enlistment. Then transportation to the training bases in Guatemala; transfer to Puerto Cabezas in Nicaragua; and from there to the invasion of southern Cuba by those who were recruited for that purpose. The book containing this illustration is *The Bay of Pigs* by Haynes Johnson, Artime, San Román, Oliva, and Ruiz-Williams, whom we have already mentioned. (See Illustration 2.)

Illustration 3 is more complicated. I call to your attention that we have followed the book to the letter in reproducing these maps—including the symbol of Brigade 2506, its logo. (See Illustration 4.) Several pages of this book by Johnson, San Román, Oliva, Ruiz-Williams, and Artime show these maps, with the logo in various places, to explain the invasion. This map, prepared by them and not by us, also shows how the tanks left New Orleans, as well as all the movements of the fighter planes, the bombers, and the fleet that transported the mercenary brigade.

Illustrations 3 and 2 show the places where the training bases were located in Guatemala—in Helvetia; in Retalhuleu, the air base; and in Garrapatenango. (See Illustration 5.)

Illustration 6 shows the structure of the brigade, which is given in more detail in Illustrations 7 and 10.

There was a commander with 1,511 men, organized in 7 battalions: 5 infantry battalions, 1 paratroop battalion, 1 heavy gun battalion, 1 tank company, and other smaller units involved in command and support.

In each infantry battalion there were three companies of infantry and one of heavy guns. The latter company was equipped with 81 mm. mortars and 57 mm. recoilless guns.

The brigade's heavy gun battalion had companies equipped with 4.2 inch mortars, 75 mm. recoilless guns, and .50 caliber heavy machine guns. In addition there was a company of M-41 tanks. (See Illustrations 10 and 11.)

These were the combat units, as well as those of command and support, of the mercenary brigade that invaded us at Playa Girón and Playa Larga on April 17, 1961. (See Illustration 6.)

I would like to point out—although we will come back at the end to the question of the social composition of the brigade—where the 194 former military officers and henchmen in command of the brigade came from. All the main leaders were military officers. Morales Cruz, Varona, Ferrer Mena, Trinchería—these are well-known names of former military figures in the tyranny's army. This is the command structure of the brigade: G-1 dealt with personnel; G-2 dealt with intelligence, using U.S. terminology; G-3 dealt with training and operations; G-4 dealt with logistics; and G-5 dealt with the civilian government in occupied territories.

On the upper right-hand corner of Illustration 7 we see other leadership bodies: the engineering corps, medical and sanitation, communications, etc., along with the names of those in charge. In Illustration 8 we can actually see the names even of the chaplains; I remember personally interrogating one of them named Lugo, a Capuchin.

Illustration 9 gives a more detailed picture of the mercenary brigade's support units, among other information it contains.

I call your attention to the existence of groups belonging to Operation 40. Operation 40 had the "honorable mission" of taking charge of the civilian government, supervised by G-5, seizing the government and party archives, as well as the "honorable mission" of "eliminating all party and government leaders who might be dangerous," according to the words they themselves use. (See Illustrations 9 and 10.)

It was made up of a large number of personnel, headed by Col. Vicente León León, a former army colonel. He landed together with part of his unit. The rest of them did not disembark; they remained on the ships that retreated from the coast, as we'll see later. After the brigade dispersed on April 19, the group from Operation 40 fled into the woods.

I don't recall whether it was on April 20 or April 21 that Vicente León was caught by surprise together with four or five accompanying him. He did not surrender and put up resistance. He was killed in the exchange of fire.

I would like to emphasize that the revolutionary forces—the militias, the Rebel Army, the police—were strictly respectful of the traditions of the Mambí Army[14] and the Rebel Army. No prisoner was mistreated. No one wounded was denied assistance. No one was left to go hungry or thirsty, to the best of our possibilities. The utmost respect was shown throughout the operations, in spite of the character of the enemy's actions.

Illustrations 12 and 13 contain the names of the commander of each battalion and company:

The 1st Battalion was commanded by Alejandro del Valle, who escaped by boat and died at sea.

The 2nd Battalion was led by Hugo Sueiro, who was taken prisoner—both of them former officers.

The 3rd Battalion was headed by Noelio Montero, known as "Light Weight." Rebel Army combatants know him well, since he was part of the tyranny's army in the Sierra Maestra. His battalion didn't do much fighting, and on April 19 he was removed as battalion commander.

The 4th Battalion was commanded by Valentín Bacallao, another ex-army officer. Below his name are those of S-1, S-2, and S-4 (on a battalion level they use "S," while on the brigade level they use "G"). Then come the heads of companies—all of them former officers. Then come those second in command of each company—all of them former officers, too.

In Illustration 13 we have the 5th Battalion, which was under the command of Ricardo Montero. That was the battalion that had come on the *Houston*, which was damaged by Cuban air force fire and ran aground on the western shore of the Bay of Pigs. This battalion did not fight, but rather landed and upon seeing the situation at Playa Larga, refused to come to the aid of the reinforced 2nd Battalion,

---

14. *Mambí* was the name taken by fighters in Cuba's wars of independence from Spain in 1868–78 and 1895–98. Many of these fighters were freed slaves or agricultural workers.

which was the one fighting at Playa Larga.

Also shown in the illustration is the 6th Battalion, led by Francisco Montiel.

Finally, it shows the heavy gun battalion, which was commanded by Roberto Pérez San Román, the brigade commander's brother; the second in command was Henry Ruiz-Williams, one of the co-authors of the book I've mentioned.

How the invasion unfolded

Illustration 14 shows the combat zone. This map is a faithful reproduction of one brought along by the mercenaries. What appears in this illustration does not contain a word or a letter written by the patriotic side; it was written by the Yankee and mercenary invaders and shows how they envisioned operations.

Their plan was to occupy the area up to the top of this map—dropping paratroopers on the Yaguaramas road, on the Covadonga road, and on the road leading to the Australia Sugar Mill. Doing so would seal off access by the revolutionary forces to the beachhead as well as to the area south of the Australia mill and to Pálpite. This would enable the brigade to also drop paratroopers outside this zone—slightly to the east, as well as in the vicinity of the Australia mill.

Based on everything I've said earlier, on the numerous comments in the press, as well as other information that reached Cuba by different means, we knew an invasion of Cuba was being prepared. But we had no precise information as to when, where, and by what means the invasion would come, or how many men would be involved. So the utmost vigilance was required.

Fidel had been through these areas on several occasions. On Christmas Eve 1959 he had visited a group of residents of the Zapata Swamp.

I had never been to the swamp; rather, I had been there only once. That was shortly before the invasion, when I was returning with the Commander from the Escambray on the Yaguaramas road. We went through Girón, continuing on to Playa Larga, and ending up at Jagüey Grande. We were returning from operations in the fight against the bandits.

To restate what I have said: We had no exact idea what was going to happen, what forces the enemy would use, the moment they would pick, or the place they would select to attack the homeland.

I will now turn to describing how the invasion unfolded.

At around midnight on April 16, 1961, strange noises began to be heard, and mysterious lights began to be seen, both by a group of militia members at Playa Girón led by Mustelier, and by groups at Punta Perdiz and Playa Larga. The militia members at Playa Girón figured it was a lost boat.

Shortly thereafter the operation began to unfold. A shadow was spotted by militia members at Playa Larga—by compañero González Suco and five others. They yelled, "Halt" and opened fire. An invasion force was coming ashore equal in size to the one that had landed at Playa Girón. Thus began the battle of one small unit of Cuba's 339th Battalion, and they notified their command.

When the mercenary leaders landed, they took over the radio installations, which were at the construction sites of the Ministry of Construction and were part of a network the ministry had. The militia unit at Girón sent a messenger to Covadonga, while the unit at Playa Larga communicated with Australia. Through various channels, news of the invasion got out. The commander of the 339th Battalion in Australia moved the unit into action. Lacking transport vehicles, he first sent a platoon to fight near Playa Larga. Then he took with him additional troops from the battalion to the front. They engaged the mercenary landing in combat, but the superiority of the invasion force forced them to retreat.

The 339th Battalion took a large number of casualties in

the fighting: 16 killed out of about 500 men.

Already that morning, as I said previously, compañero Fidel had told Capt. Raúl Curbelo, who was coordinating the actions of the Air Force, that a number of fighter planes should be in the air before dawn, heading to attack the enemy fleet.

Compañero Fidel ordered them to attack the ships bringing the mercenary brigade. At the time there were several alternatives: attack the ships, engage the mercenary air force, protect our land forces, or attack the enemy's land forces.

Fidel's decision was absolutely correct: attack the ships of the mercenary brigade.

Having come under attack, the ships retreated from the coast and moved farther offshore. At that point, the landing cordon was cut, along with the flow of supplies. The mercenaries who had landed at both Girón and Playa Larga were left without the logistical support that was now no longer coming. The code name for Playa Larga was Red Beach; Playa Girón was Blue Beach; and Caleta Buena—where they never landed—was Green Beach. These were names given by the mercenaries, and that's how they sometimes refer to these locations.

Fidel was at Point One (the command post)[15] when he received confirmation there had been an actual landing in force, and a bit later he received confirmation there had been a paratroop drop as well. At one point, when Fidel—who seemed to be in a thousand places at the same time—called the Covadonga Sugar Mill (known today as "Antonio Sánchez"), the militia member answering the phone reported he could see paratroopers falling. Fidel told the militia members at the Covadonga Sugar Mill not to let it fall into enemy

---

15. Point One, established in December 1960, was the general command post in Havana of all military units in Cuba, under the direction of Commander in Chief Fidel Castro.

hands, as the mercenaries were in the immediate vicinity.

The news from Covadonga convinced Fidel that the landing in that area was the principal one.

Among other reasons, he assumed the paratroopers were meant to occupy the access points that the revolutionary forces would need to use in order to get to the landing zone. By getting to the landing zone, the revolutionary forces could prevent the mercenaries from reaching solid ground and could keep them bottled up in the swamp. In that case the mercenary brigade would be destroyed, pushed into the sea, or taken prisoner.

On the basis of that sound and very clear judgment, Fidel concluded that this was the main line of attack.

After immediately ordering the aircraft to be in the air before dawn, Fidel began calling various units. He called Column 1 of the Rebel Army in Cojímar, and told them to assemble the unit for action. He ordered Matanzas to mobilize the 219th, 223rd, and 225th battalions from Jagüey Grande, Unión de Reyes, and the surrounding area.

Fidel also mobilized the Militia Leadership School in Matanzas—of which I was director at the time—which was a good unit in every sense. It was a select unit of militia leaders composed of workers and student youth. These were individuals who had proven themselves and been chosen for training as officers in the militias. This unit had already been in training for several months, and I would venture to call them, if not the best-trained unit in Cuba at the time, then certainly one of the best.

Fidel called me at the School of Cadets in Managua, Havana province, and told me to take command of the unit. He ordered me to repulse the landing through the direction of the Australia Sugar Mill and Playa Larga, in other words, to attack from that direction. He did so because he had already received information that part of the mercenary forces had landed at Playa Larga; that report came from compañero

Maciques, who was head of development in that zone.

I repeat, from a strategic and tactical point of view, the enemy's idea was well-conceived. What they did not take into account were other factors.

When the mercenary leaders landed, they found the radio units turned off but still hot. They concluded that our high command had been informed of the landing, that it was no longer a secret.

In the meantime, a lot of inexact information was coming in. Point One received reports of the threat of a landing in Mariel. In Punto Alegre, north of Ciego de Ávila, it was said that a landing was threatened or already under way. A landing was reported at the lighthouse in Moa, now in Holguín province; in Baitiquirí; another in Trinidad; and yet another on the beach at Rosario, south of Havana. In the very midst of the ceremony paying tribute to those who had fallen in the attack on Ciudad Libertad on April 16, there were even reports of a landing in Havana.

In spite of all this, once Fidel learned that the paratroopers had landed where they did, in the region of the Zapata Peninsula, he deduced that the enemy was making its principal assault in that direction. This enabled Fidel to make the correct decision, ensuring that the invasion would be met promptly, firmly, and vigorously. There was no confusion, and we were able to rapidly mobilize the needed forces and equipment in the direction of Playa Larga and Playa Girón to destroy the landing.

A firsthand account

Compañeros of the Court, since I have stated that my main source of information is what I saw and what I directly participated in, permit me to explain my own situation and responsibilities at the time.

I was in charge of several schools in Havana and Matanzas: the School of Militia Battalions in Guanabo; another in

La Chorrera; one in El Esperón; the Cadet School in Managua; and the Militia Leadership School in Matanzas, where the second course for these leaders was under way. These courses, as I've already explained, were for compañeros who had been specially selected.

Fidel has always been rigorous and demanding. Whenever possible, he tests people before giving them a responsibility. In this case, after the students had passed the first course, he proposed that they should climb the Turquino Peak three times.[16] A total of 534 had graduated, and these students were sent to me after they had climbed the Turquino Peak. At the time of the invasion, more than 900 students were taking the second course.

Fidel called me between 2:00 and 3:00 a.m. and told me to go to Matanzas, as I said before. I want to give you an idea of how Fidel conducted himself in this situation. I was asleep, as is normal at that hour. The burial of the victims of the aerial bombing had taken place the previous morning. After Fidel gave me my orders, I began to get dressed, ordered the driver to fill up the jeep and check it over, and called a group of four officers to accompany me.

Before I had finished dressing, Fidel called me again.

"What are you doing?"

"I'm just finishing getting dressed, Commander." I continued dressing and, with the greatest urgency, doing everything else I had to do.

Ten minutes later: "Why are you still there?"

I went downstairs—my room was on the second floor of the School of Cadets—and began looking for the maps. The officers weren't there yet, but the jeep was waiting.

Fidel called again: "Why haven't you left yet?"

Well, I was looking for the maps, which were locked up in

16. Turquino Peak, the highest elevation in Cuba, is located in the Sierra Maestra mountains.

118 / JOSÉ RAMÓN FERNÁNDEZ

a room and someone else who lived in Managua had the key. I thought, "The Commander is going to think I'm refusing the operation, or that I won't leave." So, I ordered the door to be broken down, grabbed the maps, and left.

As soon as I arrived in Matanzas, Fidel was on the phone: "Has the school been assembled? What are you doing? How is the morale? Is the school organized?"

On April 16, the day before the invasion, after the burial at which Fidel made a historic memorial speech and declared the socialist character of the Revolution, Sergio del Valle, who was then chief of the General Staff, called me and said: "Fidel says that no matter what happens, your job is to continue training people. You're not to do anything else."

One day before this, on April 15, right after the bombing of our air bases, I had been sent to the Matanzas Militia Leadership School in Managua. I organized the students there into a combat unit with heavy machine guns and two 82 mm. mortar batteries. In short, we restructured the school, organizing it for combat, utilizing for this purpose the weapons in the school that had been there for instructional purposes. So when Fidel called and asked, "Is the unit ready?" I could answer him, "It's ready."

There were no transport vehicles at the Militia Leadership School in Matanzas. In accordance with the rules of warfare, we had to begin requisitioning, on a temporary basis, all the trucks that passed by on the main road and some local roads. The school had only one truck, which was totally inadequate for moving more than 700 men. Twenty-five to thirty were needed. So the trucks going down the main road in both directions were stopped, the cargo was unloaded from them, and we put together a transport column to go to Australia–Playa Larga.

Fidel called again: "When are you going to leave?"

"I'm leaving right now. The unit is formed up. Everything is fine. I've checked everything and morale is good."

While I was still there, Fidel called a second and a third time. He was following the operations step by step.

I left for Australia. In order to get there, it's necessary to leave the main road and take other roads. It's possible to go by way of Jovellanos, or else through Perico or Colón. When I got to Jovellanos, there was a captain standing along the road, and I told him to let me pass. "No, Fidel is on the phone," he told me.

"How are things going? What do you see?"

"Well, I don't see anything. I don't know anything."

"OK, when you get to the Australia Sugar Mill, go to the manager's office; there's a telephone there. Leave it off the hook, and whenever you pick it up you'll have a direct line to me at Point One. What route will you take to get to Jagüey Grande?"

I didn't know. I had only been there once. I was like most Cubans—nobody went to the Zapata Swamp. Before the Revolution, there was no way to get there; it was very difficult. I'd been there only once before, a few weeks earlier, with Fidel. So I asked for the map and said, "I'm going in through Colón. From Colón to Agramonte, then Jagüey Grande to the Australia mill."

"OK, that's fine."

Soon I was very happy, because as I left Colón heading toward Agramonte, I saw a b-26 flying overhead. "Great!" I said. "Our planes are in the air!" I didn't know it was an enemy b-26 painted with Cuban markings. I didn't actually see the markings, since it was about 1,500 or 2,000 meters in the air. But I felt very satisfied.

As soon as I arrived at the sugar mill, I informed Fidel. He was assembling units, taking care of numerous things. We spoke about the paratroopers.

"What's your strength?" he asked.

"There are eight militia members in the sugar mill. I'm going to send them on a scouting party to see if they can locate the paratroopers."

"When will the school arrive?" Fidel asked.

"I'm waiting for it. I expect it any time now."

A few minutes later part of the 223rd Battalion, together with its commander, arrived at the Australia Sugar Mill. Also included with it were elements from the 219th Battalion, made up of militia members from Jagüey Grande, Calimete, Colón, and other villages and towns in Matanzas. These were very good people, but poorly armed. Some had just a rifle with 20 cartridges. Others, I dare say, had never fired a shot at that time. I sent them to advance on Pálpite, to defend the road as we waited for the battalion to arrive from the Militia Leadership School.

Later we learned that the 223rd Battalion's movement along the road prevented the road's capture by a company of mercenary paratroopers that had landed south of the Australia Sugar Mill and a little east of the road. Faced with the large number of troops the mercenaries saw, they decided not to risk attacking the road. This mercenary company remained hidden in the woods and was not located until days later. It did not put up resistance.

I recall that when the Militia Leadership School arrived at the Australia Sugar Mill, I did not let the men get out of the trucks. I climbed up on the cab of one of the trucks and spoke to them, laying out the mission to capture Pálpite.

Earlier that morning Fidel had told me insistently (he was calling every ten minutes), "Take Pálpite." Why Pálpite? Even I didn't understand very well. Pálpite is here; it's a beachhead on solid ground. *(He points to a map: Illustration 16.)* While Fidel was still on the phone, I started looking for it on the map.

"Commander, there's no Pálpite on my map."

"Look more carefully. It has to be there."

"Commander, it's not here. Where is this Pálpite supposed to be?"

You can imagine the tension at that moment. The Commander in Chief knew this marsh like the back of his hand; he had been there dozens of times. The problem was that the old map of Cuba I had with me didn't say "Pálpite"; it said "Párrite." Finally, a militia member standing next to me overheard what I was saying and said no, there's no such place as Párrite—*that's Pálpite*. So I said to Fidel, "OK, where is this Pálpite? Is it between where I am now and Playa Larga?"

"That's the one. Take it!"

I ordered the battalion from the school to take Pálpite, which they did without much trouble. Around noon I called Fidel, who had sent a plane to protect us as we crossed the swamp from Australia to Pálpite. "We've taken Pálpite," I told him.

"Wonderful!" he said. "They may not realize it, but they've lost the war!"

Fidel hung up and then called again. "Listen," he said, "we sank one ship, two boats, we did this and that . . ."[17] And he went on with all the spirit, energy, and optimism that characterize compañero Fidel. "Now go on and occupy Playa Larga," he added. In other words, now that we were in Pálpite, we should go forward and take Playa Larga.

There was an important concentration of enemy troops at Playa Larga. It wasn't the largest—that was at Playa Girón. The reason for this, according to testimony by some of the U.S. strategists, was they expected our main attack to come not along the Jagüey–Australia–Playa Larga road, but at Yaguaramas–Playa Girón, which is closer to the base of the Central Army. The distance from Jagüey Grande to Playa

---

17. By the end of the first day, the Cuban air force had sunk the two transport ships, the *Río Escondido* and the *Houston,* and one landing craft; it had also damaged another ship and three freighters. Four mercenary B-26s were shot down, and two were damaged. The Cuban air force lost one Sea Fury and one B-26.

Girón is about 70 kilometers.

The Commander in Chief had ordered Sector 4, under the command of Osmany Cienfuegos—one of the four defense sectors Havana was divided into—to prepare to join the battle. What was sent were several battalions from Sector 4, a bazooka company, Column 1 of the Rebel Army, some troops from the Central Army, forces from Matanzas, the tanks that were ready in Managua, the artillery that was ready to be deployed, and the antiaircraft artillery needed to provide protection. All these units were beginning to move from Havana to the Australia and Covadonga sugar mills. That's a distance of almost 200 kilometers from the Granma army base, and a little over 150 kilometers from Havana itself. So it would take several hours for a unit to get there.

The principal concentration of tanks was in Managua, and they were now on the move. You can see in Illustration 15, taken from the mercenaries' book, how they viewed the action, the planes, the ships that were sunk, the other ships, etc., and the territory they intended to take.

Day 1: April 17
Illustrations 15 and 16 show the situation as of 6:00 a.m., April 17.

A part of the 339th Battalion had been fighting the mercenaries opposite Playa Larga until dawn. We did not yet have forces at the other fronts.

By 6:00 p.m. April 17, the mercenary forces were bottled up. (See Illustration 17.) We did not yet have the beachhead under our control; they still occupied the area up to Pálpite. There was still fighting along the Covadonga road, and up to Yaguaramas on the other road. But they had not been able to establish another beachhead, a protected base, inside the landing zone.

To summarize the situation, of the three roads leading into the territory occupied by the mercenaries, one was in our hands—the road from Australia to Pálpite and Playa Larga—and two were in the enemy's hands, the Covadonga and Yaguaramas roads. But the mercenaries were already blocked off from any action outside the landing zone.

A little after noon on April 17, we ordered the Militia Leadership School to attack Playa Larga. During their advance, the mercenary aircraft attacked. Our troops confused these planes with our own aircraft because of the markings, and therefore waved to them. On their second pass, the enemy planes attacked the Militia School with machine guns and rockets, causing many casualties.

Our initial attempt to take Playa Larga failed. When I reached Australia earlier in the day, Fidel had ordered me to stay there at the command post, next to the telephone. I was about to ask permission to leave and proceed to Pálpite when Fidel arrived at the command post. I had just been listening to a report on the enemy air attack, and Fidel said: "Don't worry, the tanks, antiaircraft guns, and other artillery are on their way." He began to assess the situation.

Fidel told us about the ship we had sunk early on—the *Río Escondido*. (See Illustration 15.) This ship was carrying 145 tons of munitions, 38,000 gallons of vehicle fuel, and 3,000 gallons of airplane fuel. Later we sank the *Houston*, which was carrying 160,000 pounds of foodstuffs, drinking water, 150 gallons of gasoline for vehicles, five tons of light arms ammunition, eight and a half tons of explosives, and a ton and a half of white phosphorus.

The antiaircraft guns, other artillery, and tanks all arrived while Fidel was at the Australia command post. He stayed until evening, or at least until very late afternoon, and then left for Pálpite.

Fidel's strategy had been to move the heavy artillery and tanks—which are easily identifiable from the air, and have little defense against air attack—and concentrate them in Jovellanos. Then, under cover of night, move them into the combat zone. Later in the battle, some of these forces were moved in daylight hours as well, although as a general rule they should be moved at night. As soon as it started to get dark, Fidel gave us permission to transfer our base of operations to Pálpite and from there organize the attack on Playa Larga. We were protected by antiaircraft guns, five tanks, three batteries of 122 mm. howitzers, two or three batteries of 85 mm. cannons, and a battery of 120 mm. mortars.

The same thing happened in these directions (*pointing on the map to the Covadonga and Yaguaramas roads*). The troops in those areas were reinforced with artillery, antiaircraft guns, and tanks. This involved moving several battalions from Havana: the 117th Battalion came via the Covadonga road; the 113th Battalion came via the Yaguaramas road; and the 326th Battalion entered eastward along the coastline—on a trail, not a road coming from the direction of Cienfuegos. In the case of the latter of these battalions, right from the beginning Fidel—believing in victory, and in a rapid victory at that—ordered this battalion into a containment position, so that when the mercenaries started to flee from our attacks we would be able to capture them.

That night we again attacked Playa Larga. There is a fork in the road at Playa Larga that helps form a triangle of about 100 meters on each side, with a depression about a meter below ground level. (See Illustration 17.) A good portion of the mercenary forces were concentrated in this depression, as well as behind a wooded area near the coast. There they had tanks, antitank guns, machine guns, rocket launchers, and over a battalion and a half of men. That's why they were able to repulse our nighttime attack.

Before this, a little after dark, Fidel had arrived in Pálpite. Every few minutes shells from the enemy's artillery at Playa Larga—only four kilometers away—were falling on Pálpite. We were very worried about Fidel's presence in the vicinity of enemy artillery bombardment and insisted he leave the area. As has always been Fidel's bent when this comes up, he refused.

Fidel ordered the 111th Battalion to advance through Soplillar, then Jiquí, until it reached Cayo Ramona, with the objective of coming up behind those advancing on Covadonga, cutting off those forces from the ones at Girón. This operation began during the night of April 17. Commander Borges was in charge of the battalion, and the guide was Maciques. This operation was not successful.

After what seemed to us like an eternity, Fidel left and returned to the command post in Australia after he finished organizing things, issuing orders, and attending to details. The command post was where we had telephone contact with Havana. A little after midnight, Fidel sent me a written message saying that urgent matters forced him to return to Havana.

The urgent matter was the following: A number of reports were coming into Point One in Havana about landings in the area west of Havana. Fidel remained convinced that the main attack was the one under way at the Zapata Swamp. But information kept coming in about a new landing closer to Havana, of considerable size. Given the potential danger this represented, it had to be confronted immediately.

Fidel was uncomfortable with having to leave the area. Before going, he asked for verification of the attack in the Havana region, and they said yes, it was true, there had already been contact with the enemy. Had this not happened, I'm sure Fidel would never have left the Australia–Playa Larga area of the Zapata Swamp. He sent me a note that said, "I have to leave for Havana immediately." That document is now in the museum.

But in face of evidence of contact with the enemy, Fidel went to Havana. In fact, the whole thing turned out to be just another diversionary operation north of Havana.[18] Given the confirmation of contact with the enemy, however, this constituted a greater potential danger than the landing at Girón and Playa Larga, which are 200 kilometers from Havana. Additionally, the enemy forces by now were cornered without any exit from the zone they occupied.

Day 2: April 18
That night, as I said, our attempt to take Playa Larga was repulsed, notwithstanding the efforts by the battalion of the Militia Leadership School and other units that reached enemy positions. The school took numerous casualties. The enemy too suffered important losses, despite the advantageous positions it was holding, and despite its favorable firing position overlooking the road—a road that any attack was compelled to use. But the force of the attack by the Militia Leadership School had an impact on the enemy. The mercenaries were incapable of awaiting the offensive launched the following morning, withdrawing at dawn back toward Playa Girón.

At dawn, Commander Augusto Martínez, who had stayed at the command post in the Australia Sugar Mill—our only source of communication with Havana (remember, we had no radio, no communications except by messenger on motorcycle, truck, or car)—forwarded a message to me from Fidel. The message contained orders to send a battalion to the coast at Caleta del Rosario. The order had been written in Havana at 4:40 a.m. and reached my hands in Australia just after 5:00.

I ordered the 144th Battalion, which was just arriving from Havana, to prepare to carry out the mission. It had to march through the open country, since there were no roads,

---

18. The CIA operation off the coast of Pinar del Río province, near Bahía de Honda, involved sending ships toward the Cuban coast, setting off sounds and explosions that simulated a full-scale landing.

only footpaths used by charcoal makers. I found a guide and explained the mission to the battalion. When they came out on the coast at Caleta, I told them, they were to organize the defense both toward the west and toward the east, cutting the enemy in half. That was Fidel's plan, to divide the enemy. The 111th Battalion would cut off the enemy units north of San Blas from those at Playa Larga. The 144th Battalion would cut off enemy units in Playa Larga from those at Girón. Divided in three groups, the enemy could be wiped out more quickly.

I'm convinced that if we had been able to do this, Girón would have fallen on April 18. Unfortunately neither the 111th Battalion nor the 144th Battalion carried out their tasks. Fidel was upset by this. The guide I had sent for the 144th Battalion disappeared. At 7:00 a.m. the enemy forces fled Playa Larga. At a little after 6:00, I could have sent troops, but there were 18–20 kilometers of open country to cross. Had we moved more energetically, more quickly, with more foresight, then perhaps we would have succeeded in this operation to divide and isolate the enemy forces at Playa Larga.

But the operation was not successful. The enemy in Playa Larga fled and—now united with the principal force—contributed to the powerful resistance put up by the defenders of Playa Girón. We had to fight them again on April 19 at Playa Girón. We had to go up against the enemy's 2nd Battalion reinforced by additional units and its 4th Battalion.

To sum up. By 6:00 a.m. on April 18 we had a beachhead at Pálpite inside enemy territory that was securely in our hands. There was fighting on the roads from Covadonga to San Blas, and from Yaguaramas to San Blas, where the two roads forked. And we had blocked the enemy from fleeing toward Cienfuegos. The invaders were bottled up and could not advance. (See Illustration 18.)

According to the Haynes Johnson book, the enemy's evaluation of the situation at that time can be seen in Illustration 19. It depicts the real situation, more or less, and shows how combat activity was proceeding.

The principal units that participated in the staggering defeat of the mercenary brigade that invaded the homeland at Playa Girón and Playa Larga were the following battalions: the 339th, 111th, 113th, 114th, 115th, 116th (a light infantry battalion attached to the Revolutionary National Police battalion), 117th, 120th, 123rd, 144th, 164th, 180th, 219th, 223rd, 225th, 227th, 326th, 329th, and 345th. Also participating were the Rebel Army's Special Columns 1 and 2, the battalion of the Revolutionary National Police, ten 12.7 mm. "cuatro bocas" antiaircraft guns,[19] one 37 mm. antiaircraft gun, two batteries of 122 mm. cannons, four batteries of 85 mm. cannons, three batteries of 120 mm. mortars, twenty-four batteries of 82 mm. mortars, five IS-2M tanks with 122 mm. cannons, ten SAU-100 tanks, ten T-34 tanks with 85 mm. cannons, a small patrol of the Revolutionary Navy, and an especially noteworthy role played by the Air Force.

Altogether, at Girón we had approximately 10 percent of the forces located in the western part of the country. Notwithstanding all the units I've mentioned, some 90 percent of our forces remained in Havana or its outskirts. In other words, the enemy did not fool us. Our potential forces for confronting an attack from another direction were nine times greater than what we deployed at Playa Girón in terms of artillery, tanks, infantry, antiaircraft defense, and troops.

The struggle against the enemy did not let up for an instant. We gave them no rest day or night. We subjected them to constant attack and pursuit.

That was the situation as of 6:00 a.m. on April 18. At that

---

19. *Cuatro bocas*, literally "four mouths," was the popular term in Cuba for the four-barreled heavy machine guns Cuba had recently obtained.

hour combat was occurring in San Blas. It had not been captured, but our troops were fighting there, and they linked up with the troops coming from Yaguaramas, who were attacking the same objective as those coming south from Covadonga. A little after 8:00 a.m., Playa Larga was captured by the forces advancing from the west. (See Illustration 18.)

At about 8:00 a.m. that day we took Playa Larga. Our forces then advanced as far as Punta Perdiz, eleven kilometers west of Girón. The other front continued fighting in the San Blas area. (See Illustration 19).

By this point, the enemy's defeat was imminent. Demoralization was setting in, even though they continued fighting. They were desperately issuing calls over the radio begging for aid of any kind from anybody.

The mercenaries sent their 3rd Battalion and two companies of their 4th Battalion to reinforce their troops in San Blas. In the morning, the 2nd Battalion moved into the reserve, while the 4th Battalion—which was defending Girón from the west—was reinforced by the 2nd Battalion. So they had two and a half battalions defending Playa Girón against our forces that were advancing from the west. Located in San Blas were the mercenaries' paratroopers and their 3rd Battalion—almost two battalions plus some smaller units, tanks, recoilless cannons, and mortars. The remaining mercenary forces at Girón were now concentrated in the western part, except for some small units that defended the eastern part.

During the morning hours of April 19, the revolutionary forces advanced from the direction of Playa Larga to within two kilometers of Girón. The police battalion that had arrived in the middle of the night had taken its place at the front, together with some militia units, the light infantry company of the 116th Battalion, and some smaller units.

By the late afternoon of April 18, the plan to cut the enemy in two between San Blas and Girón had not been car-

130 / josé ramón fernández

ried out. On the other hand, Fidel was unaware that we had taken Playa Larga, and he still had the idea of cutting the enemy in two, so he ordered some units to infiltrate the zone between Soplillar and the coast east of Playa Larga. This operation was canceled when Fidel heard that Playa Larga was in our hands.

The final day: April 19
On April 19 fighting was occurring in San Blas. Fidel, who was present on the San Blas front, organized our combat operations. At 11:00 a.m., San Blas fell. During the entire day fierce combat was taking place nonstop on the western front of Playa Girón.

At 11:00 a.m. on April 19, as I just said, the revolutionary forces advancing from Covadonga and from Yaguaramas linked up with each other, and the village of San Blas was captured.

It's worth saying that of the 176 deaths suffered by the revolutionary forces overall—150 of these suffered by the forces engaged in combat on April 17–19—more than 100 were suffered by the forces advancing from Australia–Playa Larga to Girón. The breakdown is as follows:

339th Battalion: 16
Militia Leadership School: 21
Revolutionary National Police battalion: 23
Special Column no. 1: 16
Antiaircraft batteries: 4
123rd Battalion: 15
144th Battalion: 1
111th Battalion: 1
219th Battalion: 6
225th Battalion: 2
227th Battalion: 2

There were a few more deaths in other units. The rest of the combat deaths came primarily on the San Blas front, where there was equally intense combat.

Meanwhile, Fidel had made the decision to protect all the bridges between Havana and Matanzas, along the Central Highway and on the Vía Blanca road. We also took measures to keep the roads open by protecting all the culverts and all the areas where the road between Australia and Playa Larga could possibly be cut.

That afternoon, Fidel ordered an artillery bombardment of Playa Girón with 122 mm. artillery located in the Covadonga area. He indicated that some rounds should be fired long, into the sea, and the rest right on Girón itself. With our three batteries of 122 mm. howitzers and one of 120 mm. mortars, we also opened fire on Playa Girón.

The night before, San Román had sailed ten kilometers out at sea to ask for help. He cursed the officers and crews of the mercenary brigade's ships, which had moved far off the coast and were providing no support.

It's important to point out that despite our accumulation of forces in the area, not all of these could be fully deployed. We were often operating in terrain where we had only thirty to forty meters to spread out our forces, since aside from the road and embankment all the rest was swamp. Under those conditions, it didn't matter if we had a thousand troops behind us, the only ones who could fight were those in front. We faced the same problem with tanks and armored vehicles. The artillery had a little more flexibility, since it could redirect its fire on the enemy without changing location.

I would remind the Court that in those days we had only recently begun receiving Soviet technical assistance, including tanks, artillery, mortars, and machine guns, although we had not yet received any aircraft.

We even had tank gunners who reached enemy positions but didn't fire their cannons because they didn't know how. Some combatants learned to fire their weapons along the road from Managua to Australia and then Playa Larga. It

132 / JOSÉ RAMÓN FERNÁNDEZ

normally takes several weeks, or even months, for a soldier to learn how to fire this kind of weapon.[20]

The artillery crews were a little better trained, but we had no communications equipment, which is essential for artillery. Artillery units need information from observers who can tell them where their shells are landing. The battery then has to make corrections on the basis of that information—more to the right, more to the left, farther, closer, and so on.

At Playa Girón our artillery belonging to the units advancing from the west used an unorthodox technique—one improvised for the particular situation of not having communications equipment enabling us to observe the results. We had eighteen pieces that we lined up next to each other, in parallel formation. There is a technical method of aiming these so that each cluster falls 20 or 30 meters from the next, enabling us to cover almost half a kilometer. We lined all the weapons up in one direction and at one angle of elevation, fired three times, then increased the range of all the guns 100 meters, fired three times, and so on, until we had increased the range by 500 meters. Then we moved our line of fire 300 meters to the right, fired three times again, then 600 meters to the left, and fired three times again. And we continued that way, since we couldn't see where the shells were landing. Although a bit unorthodox, the technique paid off, since it enabled us to find out where

20. In a 1996 speech on the thirty-fifth anniversary of the victory at Playa Girón, Fidel Castro explained the crash training the Cuban armed forces had organized in 1960–61 in preparation for the imperialist assault they knew was coming: "There were a few Czech and Soviet instructors, and when they saw how things were, they said, 'This is impossible. They need at least two years to train all these people.' . . . That's when we invented something, which was to ask the trainees to teach in the afternoon what they had learned in the morning in regard to tanks, artillery, antiaircraft weapons, whatever. And that's what they did."

the enemy was. Remember, the important thing was to defeat the enemy rapidly. This method allowed us to pound them quite effectively.

We practically exhausted the usable life of an entire battery of howitzers during the battle. Each individual cannon has a usable lifespan of "x" number of bursts, and less if fired at maximum range. We were firing at intermediate range, since we were four or five kilometers from our target. We first deployed these pieces west of Pálpite, and then moved them into the area around Girón. And we virtually exhausted the usable life of those weapons over the three days of the battle.

Meanwhile, Pedro Miret, who was stationed in the Covadonga area, was firing 122 mm. artillery shells at Girón, at the area occupied by the mercenaries next to the sea, trying to prevent them from escaping. The firing kept up even after we had entered Girón, and even after compañero Fidel himself arrived there. The problem, as we said earlier, was that there was no communications equipment, and Miret had not received the order to cease fire. He didn't know Girón had fallen. He stopped firing only after a messenger arrived giving him the order to halt.

Anyway, that afternoon Fidel, who was at the San Blas front, issued the order that Girón had to be taken before nightfall. We arrived at Girón from the west at 5:30 p.m. (1730 hours), and immediately afterward the troops from the north—that is, from San Blas—also arrived. (See Illustration 20.)

The previous evening, at Helechal, Fidel had prepared the assault and positioned several tanks, with a commander in each one. He had been notified of an antitank barrier along the road to Girón, and he ordered our tanks to overrun the barrier and take Girón. As a captain in one of the tanks said, "Fidel ordered me to get the treads soaking wet in the sea." This happened shortly after we took Girón. We heard the sound of a tank coming from the north and initially thought it was an enemy tank. When it was a short distance away, however, we managed to establish radio contact. The captain got down from the tank, and Rodiles and I told him we had already taken Girón.

"No, no," he answered. "I have orders from Fidel to get the treads soaking wet in the sea, and I'm not stopping til I get there."

"You're going right up to the sea?"

"I'm carrying out Fidel's orders."

We consider the example set by Fidel—his presence, his orders, his leadership—to have been decisive on all fronts in the assault against the mercenary brigade, which we engaged in battle and defeated in a matter of 68 hours. I'll return to this question.

Once Girón was captured, we concentrated all our efforts on encircling the area completely and capturing the mercenary brigade.

Earlier I explained that warplanes attacked our forces on the afternoon of April 18, when the 123rd Battalion was about halfway between Playa Larga and Playa Girón. Three planes were involved in the assault, dropping napalm. According to Ferrer's book, the planes were carrying 6,000 pounds of napalm bombs, in addition to rockets and ammunition for machine guns.

As far back as 1868, the Declaration of Saint Petersburg, issued in Russia, "fixed the technical limits at which the necessities of war ought to yield to the requirements of humanity."

Later the Hague Convention of 1907 said it was impermissible "to employ arms, projectiles, or material calculated to cause unnecessary suffering," as well as to use the type of bombs banned by the Saint Petersburg Declaration. In short, it is forbidden to use weapons, projectiles, and materials designed to cause that kind of harm contrary to the normal laws of humanity. But those were precisely the type of bombs used by the armed forces of the United States.

I should also point out once again that the planes attacking our troops were flying with the flag, colors, and insignia of our Revolutionary Air Forces.

We saw this with our own eyes, and Ferrer confirms it in his book, *Operation Puma*. This is a violation of Article 39 of the Supplemental Protocol of Geneva, issued August 12, 1949. This article, under Point Three, establishes that "it is prohibited to make use of in an armed conflict of the flags or military emblems, insignia or uniforms of adverse Parties while engaging in attacks or to disguise, or in order to shield, favour, protect or impede military operations."

So both these aspects of the April 18 air assault are banned by international conventions or agreements.

Moment of the defeat

I also want to refer to something that demonstrates the degree of involvement by the armed forces and government of the United States.

We took Girón at 1730 hours (5:30 p.m.) on April 19. There were two reasons this happened at 5:30 rather than earlier.

First, although we were in position to make a final assault on Girón by 2:30 or 3:00 p.m., we held off since the Revolutionary Air Force had scheduled a bombing of enemy forces at 3:00 p.m.

The second reason is something I was an eyewitness to, which produced one of the tensest moments of the whole battle. It's related to what's depicted in the map in Johnson's book, which shows the situation at 4:00 p.m. as seen through the eyes of the enemy forces. This appears in Illustration 21.

We were about one and a half kilometers from Girón, on the side of the road, when an officer who was with me pointed out two enemy warships approaching the coast. I looked through binoculars and saw two U.S. destroyers—

according to Kirkpatrick, these were the USS *Eaton* and USS *Murray*—which were protecting the mercenary fleet. At that moment, they were moving toward our coast and had penetrated our jurisdictional waters.

Seeing them come directly toward us, I issued the order to halt offensive actions and position all the cannons, tanks, and other weapons toward the sea.

Right at that moment a battery of 85 mm. guns arrived under the command of Dow, later to become a colonel. This unit had been with me at Pálpite. There were about 20 guns, and I ordered all of them, too, positioned toward the sea. We couldn't use the howitzers, since they were a kilometer and a half inland in the woods; they had been placed there for cover, in a zone where their shells could reach Girón.

I continued to observe the destroyers, with our cannons ready and aimed toward the sea. I could see the sailors; I could practically see the faces of the crew. The ships began lowering rowboats that headed for the coast, while rowboats and other craft from Girón began heading for the ships.

I sent off a message to Commander Fidel. I had to send it by way of a messenger to Australia, from there by telephone to Point One in Havana, and from Point One to Fidel's position at the front. I don't regret the message, although on a certain level I'm embarrassed by it. "Send me a battalion of infantry and a battalion of tanks," I wrote, "because another landing is under way." Our aircraft had also judged it to be a landing and advised Fidel to the same effect.

An hour and a half later, after all the fighting was over, Fidel's response came: "They're just trying to escape from you. Grab them!"

I was witnessing all this firsthand. Fidel was at another sector of the front to the north from which the ocean wasn't even visible. But he saw clearly what the destroyers were up to. He understood the operation they were planning. I must admit that I overestimated the enemy's combat will at that point. They had fought tenaciously to defend their positions at Girón. But Fidel knew that San Blas had fallen to us; that our forces were two kilometers away; that the enemy was bottled up on a beachhead now just four kilometers east-to-west and at most seven kilometers north-to-south, without any prospect of success. Under these circumstances, Fidel knew it would have been a serious error for the enemy to land another battalion or brigade, with the revolutionary forces facing them and carrying out nonstop, vigorous offensive operations, with complete domination of the situation.

So we were wrong about the landing. But in this case we were glad to be wrong. It's a little embarrassing, but that's the truth about what happened.

I should add that while the two destroyers were attempting to rescue the brigade—which we interpreted as a new landing—we fired on the rowboats and other landing craft with everything we had, thinking that this was an attempted reinforcement. We did not fire on the U.S. destroyers, however, although that's what many of our combatants wanted to do, inflamed by the battle and thinking about all the losses we had suffered. While we were firing on the small boats, with the aid of our air force, the destroyers set sail for the high seas, retreating—as far as we know—without rescuing the crews on a single one of the boats.

You can imagine how difficult it was to forbid our troops to fire on the real invaders. While that decision might look to my subordinates like an act of weakness, however, I knew it was what had to be done. It was what the Revolution needed. Firing on the destroyers could have resulted in an attack by the United States. Try to imagine how alone I felt, what was going through my mind, without anyone to share it with, thinking that the wrong decision could cause irreparable harm to the Revolution and the country.

I said earlier that I would come back to the social composition of the brigade. According to Kirkpatrick's report, the brigade consisted of 1,511 men, of whom the revolutionary forces took 1,197 prisoners.[21] As to the social composition of the brigade, the breakdown included: 194 ex-military personnel and henchmen; 100 owners of large landed estates; 24 large property owners; 67 landlords of buildings; 112 large merchants; 179 idle rich; 35 industrial capitalists; and 112 lumpens. That was the landing force, a few of whom were technicians. All of them were Cubans who had left the country.

The brigade had 16 B-26s, 6 C-46s (a transport plane), 8 C-54s (another transport plane); and two PBYs, known as Catalinas, a plane that can land on either water or land. The mercenary force had six times as many pilots as the Cuban air force, and three times as many warplanes.

The brigade's commanders had current photos taken by U-2 spy planes of the zone of operations. This included photos of the three roads across the swamp that had been built by the Revolution: Jagüey–Australia–Pálpite–Playa Larga–Girón; and Covadonga–San Blas–Bermeja–Helechal–Girón; and also Yaguaramas–Girón. San Blas didn't even exist on our maps, but they had it on theirs.

Compañero president, compañeros of the Court:

The planes of the mercenary air fleet that strafed our trucks that were evacuating civilians, causing deaths of innocent civilians—men, women, and children from our villages, as well as troops and installations—came with the markings, insignia, and numbers of our Revolutionary Air Force, and with the colors of the Cuban flag painted on their tail wings. As I already pointed out, this is in violation of the Supplemental Protocol of the Geneva Convention of 1949. In sev-

---

21. In addition to those captured, 114 mercenaries were killed, and about 150 either never were part of the expedition, were unable to disembark, or were picked up by a CIA crew of frogmen over the next few days from beaches and coastal islands and brought back to the United States.

eral cases, these planes were flown by U.S. pilots.

The bombing of villages like Pálpite; the attack on groups of civilians being evacuated; the mistreatment and killing of children, women, and others who had nothing to do with the fighting; the use of napalm—all these aggravated crimes are the responsibility of the U.S. government. It was the U.S. government that created, recruited, mobilized, trained, and armed Brigade 2506. It was the U.S. government that directed the invasion, participating with its own military personnel and equipment in several cases. It was the U.S. government that provided the support weapons, gave protection to the brigade during its journey to Cuba, and attempted to rescue the mercenaries after they had been defeated, using U.S. Navy destroyers. It was U.S. Navy planes that carried out scouting flights and attacks on our troops, and it was U.S. Navy helicopters that flew low over the ground, in an effort to prevent the capture of fleeing members of the defeated brigade.

They tried to rescue Brigade 2506 once it had been defeated and was in flight, and they used U.S. Navy destroyers to do so. This added one more element of risk to the situation they themselves had created.

I also want to highlight the effectiveness of the Revolutionary Air Force in destroying the enemy transport ships, the *Río Escondido* and *Houston*, as well as many landing craft. Our air force brought down enough enemy aircraft to cause their fleet to be decimated; more than half their planes were shot down. Our pilots also protected our land forces and attacked the enemy troops. The compañeros who carried out these missions by the air force—Carreras, Bourzac, Ulloa, Silva Tablada, Alberto Fernández, and others—played a decisive and heroic role.[22]

---

22. During the battle the pilots of the Revolutionary Air Force, flying its ten planes, conducted seventy combat missions. Despite the merce-

140 / JOSÉ RAMÓN FERNÁNDEZ

The testimony of eyewitnesses; the oral statements of the invaders; the books I have referred to by direct participants in the military actions; the report by former CIA Inspector General Kirkpatrick describing the plans leading up to the invasion—all these clearly reveal the goals of this campaign and the direct participation of the U.S. government, the CIA, and the U.S. armed forces. The mercenary invaders were confident they would have U.S. support.

It is amply demonstrated by the mercenary's own declarations that the objective of the invasion was to destroy the Revolution and install a U.S. puppet government. To accomplish this goal, they didn't care if they killed children, women, and innocent civilians or combatants defending their homeland.

What we are showing here and testifying to is that during the preparation and carrying out of the mercenary invasion of Cuba, the U.S. government—utilizing the CIA, its armed forces, and its entire political and military potential conceived, inspired, financed, organized, and carried out this crime. It is a crime that brought death and grief to Cuba, causing our people the deaths of 176 of our sons, with 300 wounded, of whom 50 were permanently disabled.

That is my declaration, compañero president, compañeros of the Court.

✳

PRESIDENT: Does the plaintiff have any other requests it wishes to make?

ATTORNEY: I think the witness's statement has fully answered the questions we put to him.

---

naries' vast superiority in aircraft and trained pilots, Cuba's air force achieved supremacy of the skies, shooting down nine B-26 bombers, sinking two troop transport ships, three LCIs, and five other landing craft, all the while hounding the mercenaries' land forces.

PRESIDENT: Does the witness have anything else he wishes to state for the Court?

FERNÁNDEZ: Yes, I don't think I can pass up the opportunity to recognize the patriotism and courage displayed by the Rebel Army, the Revolutionary Air Force, the Revolutionary National Police, and the Revolutionary National Militias, which made it possible for us to defeat the enemy in less than 72 hours.

In addition, a crucial task was shouldered by the Committees for the Defense of the Revolution, the Ministry of the Interior, and the entire population in taking into custody and disabling the counterrevolutionary organizations and fifth-columnists inside the country, thus protecting our rear guard and making any enemy action impossible.

All of them—loyal followers of the patriotic and combative traditions of the Mambí Army, the Rebel Army, and the long struggles for our homeland's independence—are a true example for the new generations of Cubans.

We pay tribute to those who fell fighting the enemy. With our most profound admiration and respect, we honor them as "Eternal Heroes of the Homeland."

History will recognize the place in this struggle of Fidel, our Commander in Chief. His firm and wise leadership of operations against the mercenary invaders, his prompt and sound decisions, his timely measures, his firmness and personal example in the combat zones during that glorious action were elements that made the victory possible.

Maps & charts

ILLUSTRATION 1
Map of isolated area mercenaries intended to occupy

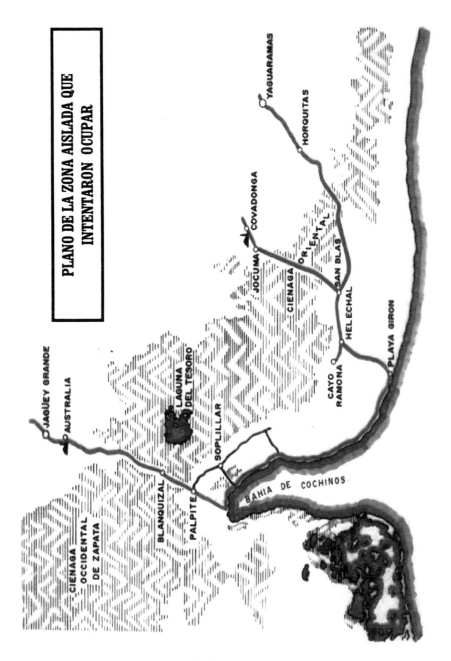

ILLUSTRATION 2

Cycle of Brigade 2506 recruitment, training, departure from Puerto Cabezas, and landing on Cuban shores

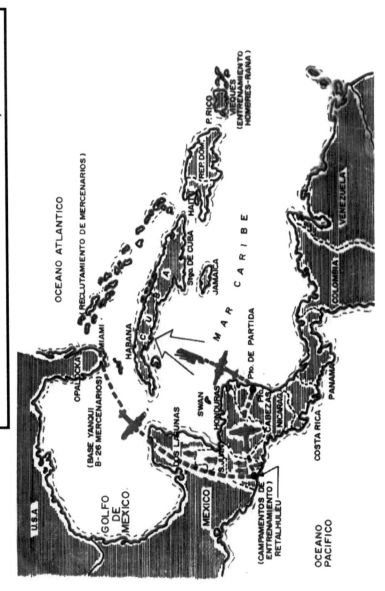

ILLUSTRATION 3

Cycle of recruitment and assembling of mercenaries, as well as routes followed to attack Cuba

(CICLO DE CAPTACIÓN Y UNION DE LOS MERCENARIOS Y DE LAS RUTAS SEGUIDAS PARA EL ATAQUE A CUBA)

ILLUSTRATION 4

Brigade 2506 logo

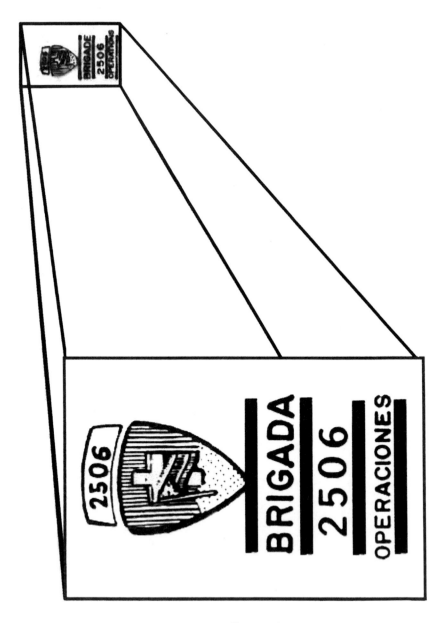

ILLUSTRATION 5

Mercenary training areas in Guatemala

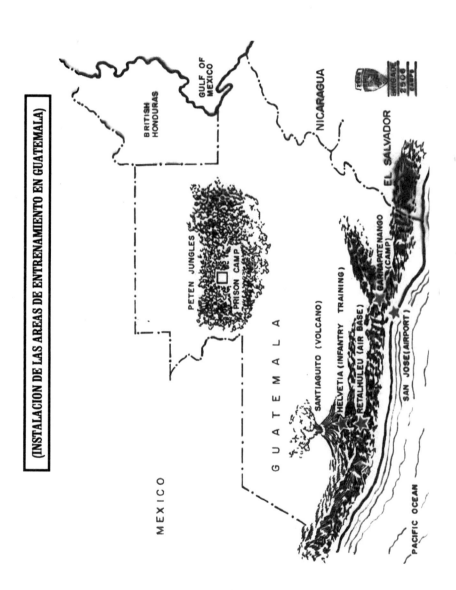

ILLUSTRATION 6
Structure of mercenary brigade

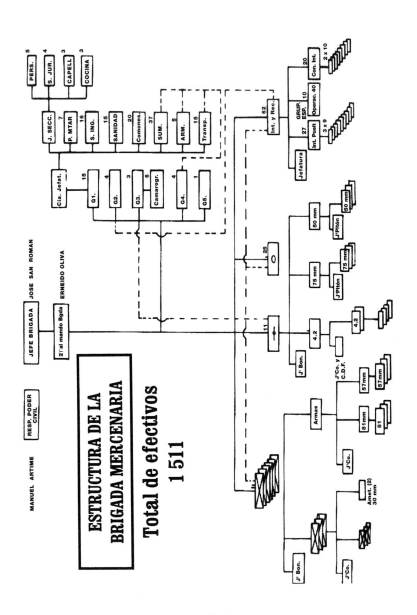

ILLUSTRATION 7

Structure of mercenary brigade

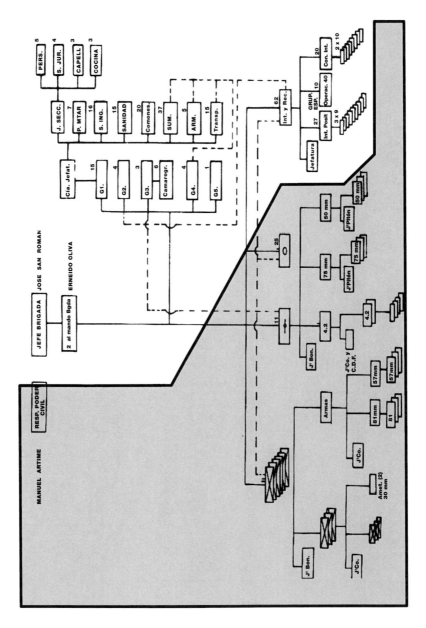

151

ILLUSTRATION 8

General staff of mercenary brigade and some of its main cadres

ESTADO MAYOR DE LA BRIGADA MERCENARIA Y ALGUNOS DE SUS CUADROS PRINCIPALES

LEYENDA

G1: José Morales Cruz
    SDO: Osvaldo E. Rojas
G2: José R. Varona Glez. (Yayo)
    SDO: Aurelio Pérez L. (Yayo)
G3: Ramón Ferrer Mena
    SDO: Juan A. Santamaria G.
G4: Roberto Pertierra Raymat
    SDO: José I. Trincheria D.
G5: José Andreu Santas
JEF. SEC.: Rubén De Quesada
    Río Seco
P. MTAR.: Ramón L. Piñeira

S. ING.: Mirto Collazo Valdés
SANIDAD: José Almeida Glez.
COMONES.: Enrique Falla Crabe
SUM.: Felipe S. Toledo Miebla
ARM.: Pedro Lucio Cabrera
TRANSP.: Geraldo Silva Perdomo
CAPELL.: Segundo de la Neras
    (Cabo)
    Tomás Magno Castillo
    Fermín Isla Polo (Lugo)
INT. y REC. (JEFATURA): Vicente
    León León

ILLUSTRATION 9
Command and supply structure of mercenary brigade

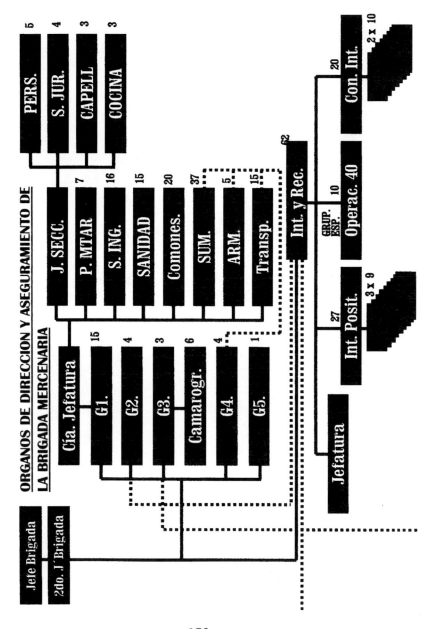

ORGANOS DE DIRECCION Y ASEGURAMIENTO DE LA BRIGADA MERCENARIA

Jefe Brigada

2do. J´ Brigada

PERS. 5
S. JUR. 4
CAPELL 3
COCINA 3

J. SECC. 7
P. MTAR 16
S. ING. 15
SANIDAD 20
Comones. 37
SUM. 5
ARM. 15
Transp.

Cía. Jefatura 15
G1. 4
G2. 3
G3. 6
Camarogr. 4
G4. 1
G5.

Int. y Rec. 62

GRUP. ESP. 10
Operac. 40
Con. Int. 20
2 x 10

Int. Posit. 27
3 x 9

Jefatura

ILLUSTRATION 10
Structure of mercenary brigade

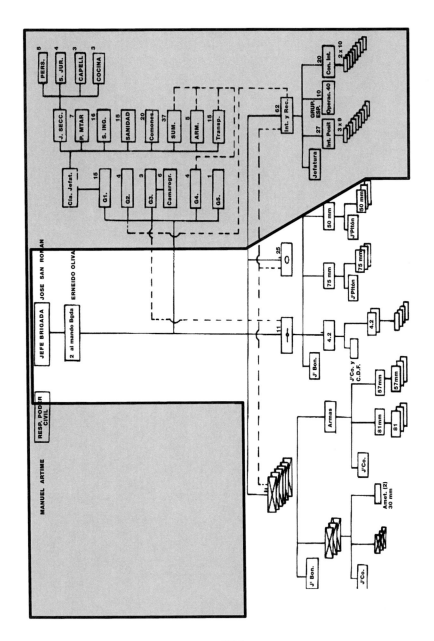

ILLUSTRATION 11
Combat units of mercenary brigade

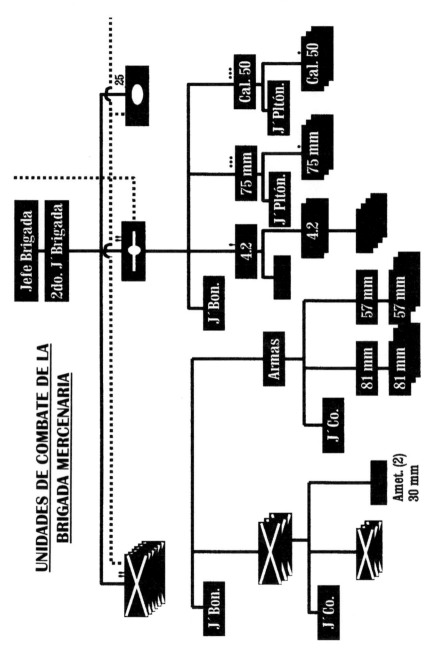

ILLUSTRATION 12

Command of mercenary brigade units

MANDO DE LAS UNIDADES

	BON. 1	BON. 2	BON. 3	BON. 4
JEFE	Alejandro del Valle	Hugo Sueiro	Noelio Montero	Valentín Bacallao
2do.	Pedro Vera	Napoleón Vilaboa	Dagoberto Darías	Antonio Iglesias
S1	Caballero Parodi	Antonio Gómez	Pelayo Cuervo	Curbelo
S2	Jorge Soulaay	Porfirio Bertot	Pedro Amaus	————
S4	Amando López	José González	Esteban Escobar	Jorge Fernández
JEFE CO. INF.	(A) Tomás Cruz	(E) Oscar Acevedo	(I) Juan I. Peruyedo	(1) Miguel Battle
2do. M.	Freddy Izquierdo	Eulogio Lavandeiro	Salón	Virginio Cuellar
JEFE CO. INF.	(B) Juan Quintana	(F) Máximo Cruz	(J) Tomos Vargas	(2) L. Orlando Rodríguez
2do.	Giraldo Pentón	Arturo Sánchez	Serafin González	René Gómez
JEFE CO. INF.	(C) Nestor Pino	(G) Pedro Avila	(K) Pedro Delgado	(3) Angel R. Mojica
2do.	Manuel Cazaña	Alexis Aguado	Félix Serrano	Miguel López
JEFE CO. ARMAS	(D) Sixto Pérez	(H) R. Rodríguez	(L) Rafael Crenter	(4) Luis E. Martinez
2do.	Juan de la Cruz	Luis Morse	José Casals	José Raúl Beltrán

ILLUSTRATION 13
Command of mercenary brigade units

MANDO DE LAS UNIDADES

	BON. 5	BON. 6	BON. AP.	
JEFE	Ricardo Montero	Francisco Montiel	Roberto Pérez San Román	
2do.	Félix Pérez	Félix Urra	Henry Williams	
S1	Roberto Collado	Miranda	Pérez Marquez	
S2	Cesar Noble	Raúl Granda	José Millán	
S4	Rafael González	Jesús Sosa	Edilio Pereira	
JEFE CO. INF.	(Q) Irenaldo Padrón	(V) José Luis González	Arturo Comas	4.2 "
2do. M.	Aguedo Hernández	José Bacallao		
JEFE CO. INF.	(R) Alfredo Barrera	(U) Hugo Samar	Heberto L. Morales	Cal.. 50
2do.	Hildo Pérez	Luis Pino	Eduardo B. Valdés	
JEFE CO. INF.	(S) Francisco Padrón	(Y) Antonio Padrón	José Angel Pomares	75 mm
2do.	Cruz de la Torre	Luis Chinea	Hilario Montoto	
JEFE CO. ARMAS	(T) Pedro Sánchez	(Z) Miguel A. Padrón	Rodolfo Díaz	Tanques M-41
2do.	Julio Soto	González Ferrebal	Elio Alemán	

ILLUSTRATION 14

**Copy of map seized from invading brigade,
giving their conception of the operation**

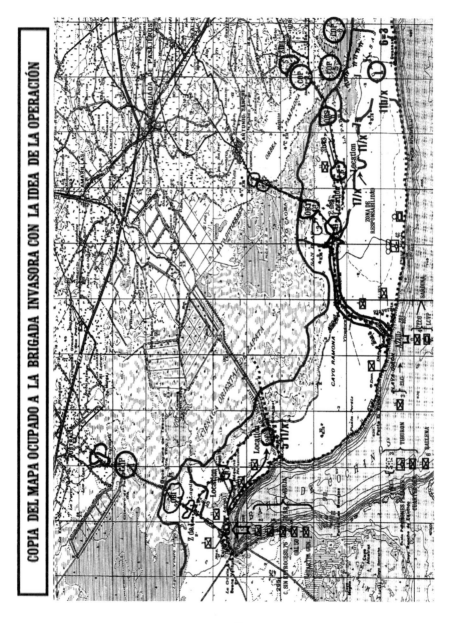

ILLUSTRATION 15

Route followed by mercenary forces for their attack on Cuba, 6:00 a.m., April 17, 1961

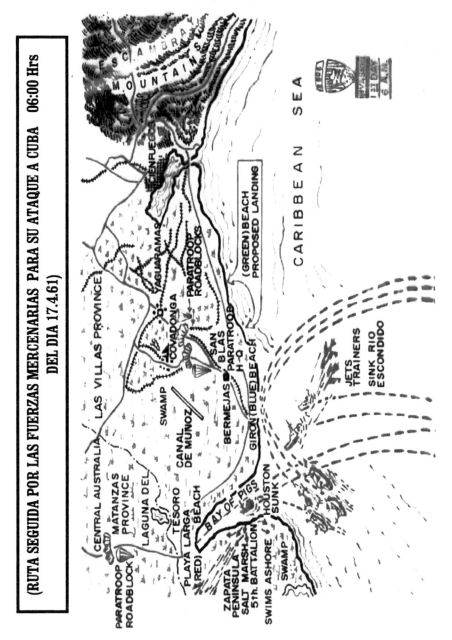

(RUTA SEGUIDA POR LAS FUERZAS MERCENARIAS PARA SU ATAQUE A CUBA   06:00 Hrs
DEL DIA 17.4.61)

159

ILLUSTRATION 16
Situation as of 6:00 a.m., April 17, 1961

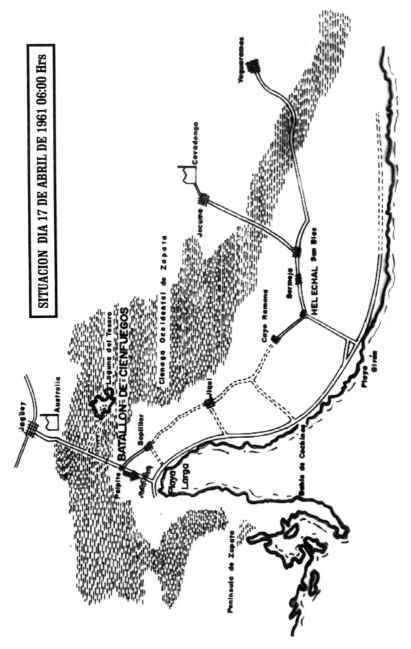

ILLUSTRATION 17

Situation as of 6:00 p.m., April 17, 1961

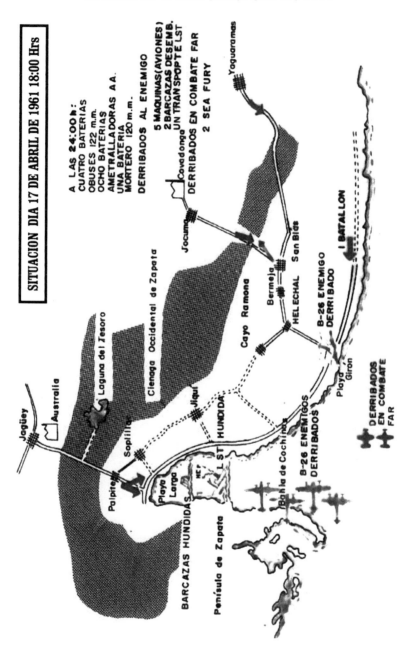

ILLUSTRATION 18
Situation between 6:00 a.m. and 6:00 p.m., April 18, 1961

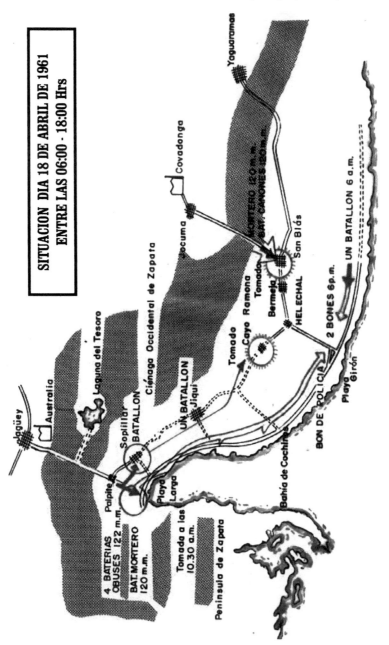

ILLUSTRATION 19

Situation as of 8:00 p.m., April 18, 1961

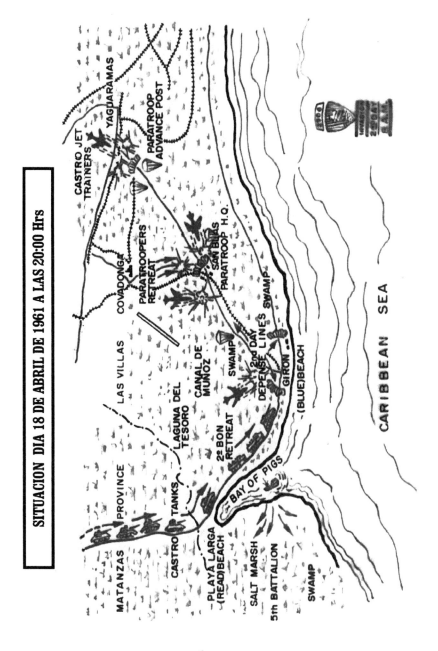

ILLUSTRATION 20
Situation as of April 19, 1961

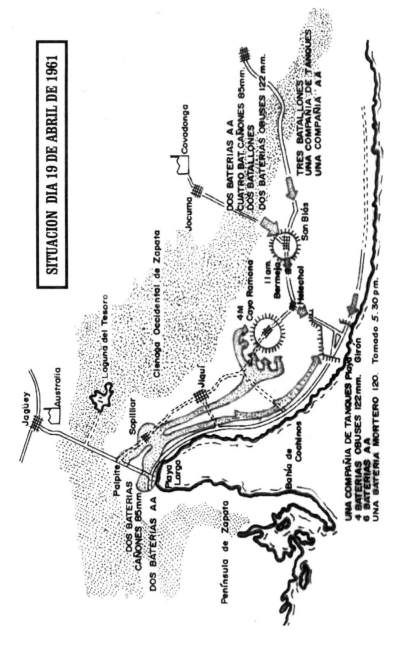

ILLUSTRATION 21

Combat activity at time of the defeat

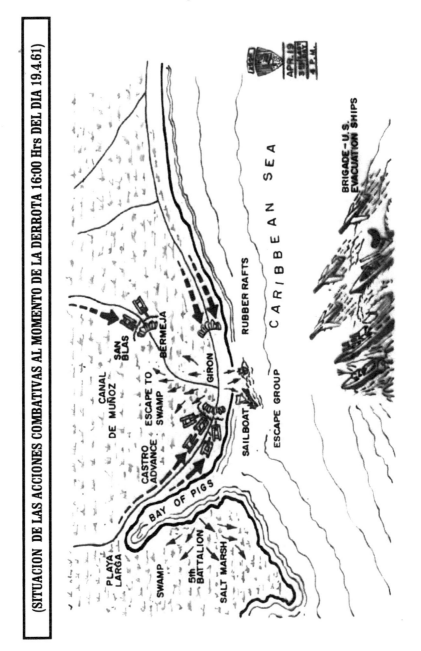

(SITUACION DE LAS ACCIONES COMBATIVAS AL MOMENTO DE LA DERROTA 16:00 Hrs DEL DIA 19.4.61)

165

ILLUSTRATION 22

Route of boat in which a group of mercenary leaders and soldiers were able to flee

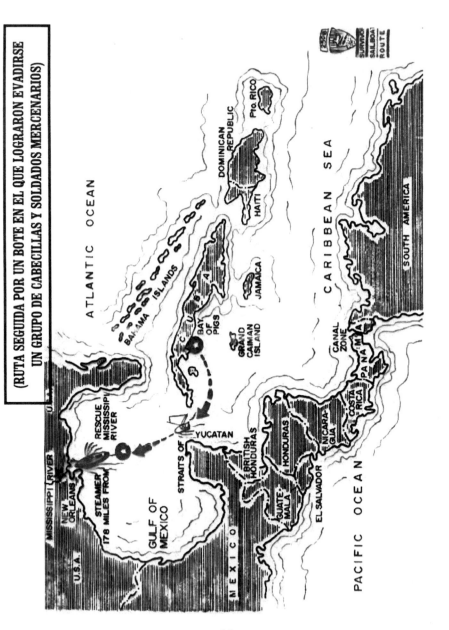

Imperialism relied on cannons and tanks, we began with a revolutionary people

Fidel Castro
April 23, 1961

Four days after the defeat of Brigade 2506 at Playa Girón, Fidel Castro, in a broadcast carried live by all of Cuba's radio and television stations, reported on the victory to the Cuban people. Roughly half the speech provided a day-by-day account of the three-day battle, which is treated in the July 1999 testimony by José Ramón Fernández before the Provincial People's Court of the City of Havana. Reprinted here is the bulk of the remainder of Castro's televised address.

Report to the Cuban people on the victory at Playa Girón

Fidel Castro

The people are already familiar with most of the facts, and have already heard various reports on the way the attack took place. Partly this comes from the reports issued by our General Staff and by information subsequently printed in the newspapers. In addition, there was the testimony spontaneously offered by the prisoners. So the public has been furnished with a large quantity of data on the invasion and its organization, as well as how it was crushed.

We will now make some general comments, as well as provide a more detailed account of how the enemy's whole plan developed. We will also review the revolution's plan and how it unfolded within the zone of operations.

In the first place, it had been known for some time, for almost a year, that an expeditionary force was being organized to attack our country. Ever since the triumph of the revolution, we have been living under threats, dangers, and perils. In other words, the revolution has had to constantly confront a series of possible attacks.

There were many different approaches on the part of the revolution's enemies, that is to say, on the part of imperialism, which is the only enemy with the strength and capacity to organize this type of attack. We always had to foresee different possibilities of action by imperialism against the revolution. One of these was some sort of indirect aggression—which is what they finally carried out, although it wasn't so indirect. It was indirect only in the sense of the individuals who personally participated in the invasion. It was a direct aggression insofar as these individuals were obeying orders from, and had received training in camps organized by the North Americans, using naval and airborne equipment furnished by the North Americans. The invading convoy was even escorted by U.S. Navy units; and even more, it had the direct aid and participation of the U.S. Air Force at one point. This is quite important.

That is why this was not your typical indirect aggression. It was rather a mixture of indirect and direct aggression. In other words, it was a mixed affair; not a direct aggression carried out by U.S. marines, their planes, and their military forces; neither was it a purely indirect aggression lacking participation by their military units. This means that they organized the invasion force primarily on the basis of using mercenaries, while they supported the invasion very directly with their navy and air force.

So we always considered the following possibilities: an indirect attack, an attack through the Organization of American States, or a direct attack.

The classic type of indirect attack was the one carried out in Guatemala against the Arbenz government.[1] It was an

---

1. Seeking to crush worker, peasant, and student struggles in Guatemala accompanied by a limited land reform initiated by the regime of Jacobo Arbenz, mercenary forces organized by the CIA—and nominally led by Col. Carlos Castillo Armas—invaded the country in June 1954. Ar-

organization of mercenaries too, although it has been said—
and subsequent experience has shown it to be true—that a
number of U.S. planes from U.S. aircraft carriers participated in the operations against Arbenz. Generally speaking,
however, this is viewed as an indirect attack.

We also considered the possibility of some action based
on the exertion of U.S. pressure on the Organization of
American States, assembling a majority of Latin American governments to launch some kind of collective action
against Cuba.

We considered the possibility of a direct attack, as well.

The U.S. government, in fact, has always been practicing
and threatening all three types of actions. It began preparations for indirect action right away, of course. It also ma-
neuvered to organize some type of collective action against
Cuba, which did not get very far. It did not get very far
largely because of public opinion in Latin America favorable
to the Cuban Revolution. This support has been and will
increasingly become an insurmountable barrier to the U.S.
government. It has forced certain hesitating governments
in Latin America to maintain a firm stance against the U.S.
moves, together with other Latin American governments that
have held a firm stance all along. In this sense, the Mexican
government has steadfastly opposed intervention in Cuba.
The same is true of the regime of [Brazilian President Jânio]
Quadros and the government of Ecuador.

In a word, the United States has encountered powerful
resistance on the part of the governments and the peoples
of Latin America in their attempt to organize an aggression
with the help of the Organization of American States.

Who could they rely on? Well, the United States has had
to maneuver with the most corrupt, most discredited re-

---

benz refused to arm the population and resigned. Several weeks later,
mercenary forces entered Guatemala City, unleashing a bloodbath.

gimes in Latin America. At first they began by conniving with Trujillo, and for a time the organization of aggression against Cuba seemed to be originating in Santo Domingo.[2] Subsequently, with the hypocrisy characteristic of an imperialist government, they began a new maneuver to enlist the support of a certain type of government in Latin America, the so-called representative democracies, in order to find a fig leaf to conceal their filthy policy. They then began to present themselves as enemies of Trujillo, inclining more toward a specific group of Latin American rulers who were not as discredited as Trujillo.

That was the period when the Costa Rica conference was held in which a declaration was jointly issued that—when all is said and done—didn't do much. But it evoked a response by that mass rally in Havana, and it elicited a big reaction among public opinion within Latin America.[3] On that occasion U.S. policy went in that direction, trying to condemn Trujillo, utilizing it as a pretext to attack us. In other words, a government that had been supporting Trujillo's regime and had promoted that type of government in Santo Domingo, suddenly appears to abandon that policy, for purely hypocritical reasons, and presents itself as Trujillo's enemy.

The governments of Nicaragua and Santo Domingo both

---

2. Rafael Leónidas Trujillo was dictator of the Dominican Republic from 1930 until his death in 1961. See chronology, August 13, 1959.

3. At a meeting in San José, Costa Rica, in August 1960, the Organization of American States (OAS) approved a declaration, aimed at the Cuban Revolution, censuring any government in the hemisphere that accepted aid from the Soviet Union or China. In response, a mass rally of one million was held in Havana on September 2, approving by acclamation what became known as the First Declaration of Havana. This ringing condemnation of U.S. imperialism and its domination of Latin America was echoed and expanded by the Second Declaration of Havana of February 1962. Both documents can be found in *The First and Second Declarations of Havana* (Pathfinder, 1962, 1994, 2007).

"The people who in January 1959
cheered Fidel Castro were
the same ones who—convinced
of their cause, rifles in hand,
conscious of the declaration of
the socialist character of our
Revolution—were determined to
resist and repel the U.S. attack."

—*José Ramón Fernández*

Working people pour into streets to welcome Fidel Castro (profile to
camera) and other Rebel Army leaders as they arrive in Havana,
January 8, 1959.

ANTONIO NÚÑEZ JIMÉNEZ

"The Cuban people identified with the revolution's work, its ideas of national sovereignty, social justice, equality, and dignity."

—*José Ramón Fernández*

BOHEMIA

GRANMA

Toilers in Zapata Swamp were among those who had gained most from the revolution. **Facing page, top:** Fidel Castro with peasants in Jagüey Grande, 1959; **middle:** Family in Zapata region learning to read during 1961 literacy campaign; **bottom:** September 1960 demonstration in Havana supports nationalization of U.S. banks. Sign says, "Blow for blow: For two planes, 20 Yankee banks." **This page, top:** Charcoal workers donate crocodile to Agrarian Reform Fund. Fidel Castro at right; **bottom:** New road through the swamp being built by revolutionary government.

"We ask the solidarity of the peoples of the Americas and the world."

—*Fidel Castro*

EASTFOTO

GRANMA

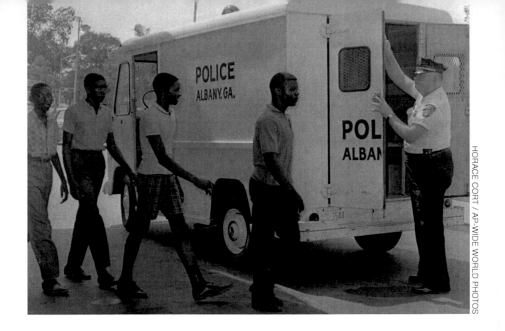

HORACE CORT / AP-WIDE WORLD PHOTOS

COURTESY MATILDE ZIMMERMANN

Cuban Revolution drew strength from and gave impetus to revolutionary struggles around world. **Facing page, top:** Beginning in the late 1950s, Vietnamese revolutionaries used Ho Chi Minh Trail to transport supplies; **bottom:** U.S. soldier assaults youth planting Panamanian flag in Canal Zone. Such attacks in 1959 sparked further protests demanding canal's return to Panama. **This page, top:** Black youth in Albany, Georgia, are arrested for sitting at "white" lunch counter, 1962; **bottom:** Nicaraguan revolutionary Carlos Fonseca speaks at meeting of Federation of Cuban Women, 1961. Inspired by example of Cuban Revolution, Fonseca and others founded Sandinista National Liberation Front that year.

> "The invasion was the culmination of a stage of the U.S. effort to destroy the Cuban Revolution, a stage whose final outcome was the defeat of Brigade 2506 on the sands of Playa Girón."
>
> —*José Ramón Fernández*

GRANMA

RAÚL CORRALES

This page, top: Canefields in Matanzas aflame after terrorist attack, April 1960; **bottom:** Members of peasant militia capture counterrevolutionary bandits (second and third from right), early 1960. **Facing page, top:** El Encanto department store after April 13, 1961, arson attack; **bottom:** After October 1959 strafing of Havana, bus drivers call for arms to defend revolution.

PHOTOS: GRANMA

RAÚL CORRALES

"The U.S. government conceived, inspired, financed, organized, and carried out this crime."

—*José Ramón Fernández*

Facing page, top: President Kennedy with military advisers, including General Lyman Lemnitzer (at left) and Admiral Arleigh Burke (standing at right), May 1961; **bottom left:** Marine Col. Jack Hawkins, U.S. commander of Brigade 2506; **bottom middle:** Grayston Lynch, CIA agent who landed with invaders and fired first shot; **bottom right:** CIA's Richard Bissell, "covert actions" chief responsible for operation. **This page, top:** CIA training camp in Retalhuleu, Guatemala; **bottom left:** Brigade recruits get medical exam at Miami CIA recruitment center; **bottom right:** Manuel Artime (left) and José Pérez San Román, top "civilian" and military leaders of invasion force, respectively.

BOHEMIA

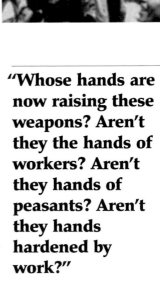

"Whose hands are now raising these weapons? Aren't they the hands of workers? Aren't they hands of peasants? Aren't they hands hardened by work?"

—*Fidel Castro*

RAÚL CORRALES

Above: Castro points to socialist character of revolution at April 16, 1961, rally honoring victims of previous day's attacks. **Facing page, top:** Airfield in Santiago de Cuba after April 15 bombing; **middle:** Adlai Stevenson, U.S. ambassador to United Nations, falsely claims planes that bombed airfields were Cuban; **bottom:** Cuba's foreign minister Raúl Roa, speaking at UN two days later, displays U.S. weaponry captured from invaders. **This page, bottom:** After April 15 attack, Cuban pilots took turns between cockpit and sleeping under the wing of their planes, ready to respond to attack.

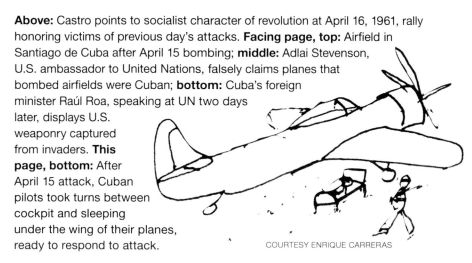

COURTESY ENRIQUE CARRERAS

"**From a strategic and tactical point of view, the U.S. operation was not flawed . . . The outcome can be explained only by the courage of a people who saw the revolution as the genuine opportunity to determine their own future.**"

—*José Ramón Fernández*

This page, top: Aircraft carrier USS *Essex*. U.S. escort fleet waited offshore to aid Brigade 2506; **bottom:** Woman and child killed by invaders' bazooka fire. **Facing page, top:** Cuban troops and militia volunteers arrive near battlefront in buses and other requisitioned transport; **middle:** Members of Cuban armed forces on patrol; **bottom:** On first morning of battle, Cuban air force, with only ten planes, sank brigade transport ships *Houston* (shown here) and *Río Escondido*.

RAÚL CORRALES

GRANMA

Top: Fidel Castro in command at Playa Girón.
Bottom: Cuban artillery units in action. Some combatants learned to fire their weapons along road to battle.

"This revolution
is not defended
with mercenaries;
this revolution is
defended by men
and women
of the people."

—*Fidel Castro*

GRANMA

Top: Napalm attack on advancing militia forces; **middle:** Castro beside downed mercenary plane painted with counterfeit insignia of Cuban air force (FAR); **bottom:** Riley Shamburger, one of several Alabama Air National Guard pilots who flew bombing missions during invasion. He and three other U.S. pilots were killed during the operation.

"If we had not been well armed, the imperialists would have hurled themselves on our country long ago. But they know we prefer to die a thousand times over rather than lose this homeland we have today. That is why they are forced to think."

—*Fidel Castro*

Facing page, top: Cuban militia members celebrate victory; **bottom:** Cuban tanks reach Playa Girón. **This page, top:** José Ramón Fernández (front left), with captured mercenaries; **middle:** To indemnify damage inflicted on Cuban people, U.S. delivers $53 million in food, medical equipment, and drugs, and in December 1962 Cuban government frees 1,113 Brigade 2506 mercenaries; **bottom:** Eisenhower stands with Kennedy after defeat.

Counterclockwise from top left: Young Socialist Alliance leader Peter Camejo speaks at Union Square rally of 5,000 in New York. Actions elsewhere around the world included Egypt, United Kingdom, and Bolivia.

"Let the world know that
the peoples, the workers,
the students, the intellectuals,
and the peasants of Latin America
are on Cuba's side."

—*Fidel Castro*

"The workers now are not
subject to domination
of any exploiting class."

—*Fidel Castro*

May Day rally in Havana, 1961. Banner says, "Workers in power."

have the same origin, coming out of the U.S. military occupation of those countries. Military forces were organized that later maintained their dominance, allied to U.S. monopolies and local reaction. Notwithstanding that these regimes had the same origin, the United States, while condemning Trujillo, strengthened its alliance with Somoza in Nicaragua and Ydígoras in Guatemala.[4]

In the end, the U.S. government was isolated in its plans of aggression against Cuba. It remained linked and associated with the governments of Guatemala and Nicaragua, which are the two governments most typically corrupt and despotic, and are reactionary enemies of the interests of the workers and peasants of those countries. These are the instruments Washington has been able to count on. The United States could not count on a government like Mexico's for a maneuver of this type, nor could it count on the government of Brazil. In short, it could not even count on other Latin American governments that were not willing to go so far in connection with U.S. moves against Cuba.

In other words, the U.S. partners in this adventure to bring about indirect aggression have been the most reactionary and most corrupt governments of Latin America, primarily the governments of Guatemala and Nicaragua.

On certain occasions we have been under the threat of a direct attack, too. That threat has always been hanging over our heads, and more than once this idea picked up steam within U.S. ruling circles. One of those moments, during which we seemed to be on the verge of that type of direct

---

4. A reference to the Somoza dictatorship in Nicaragua, ruled at the time by Luis Somoza, and to Gen. Miguel Ydígoras, the military strongman in Guatemala. Both regimes allowed their territory to be used as staging grounds for the mercenary invasion of Cuba. Ydígoras was overthrown in March 1963.

U.S. military forces had occupied Nicaragua in 1912–25 and 1926–33, and the Dominican Republic in 1916–24.

aggression, was late last December and early January, that is, in the closing days of the Eisenhower administration.

We have been speaking out at the United Nations and everywhere else against the possibility of such an aggression, against the possibility that they might look for a pretext, that they might organize or prepare a "self-aggression," something the United States has done under various circumstances every time they have wanted to carry out a plan of military aggression. They have always managed to invent or fabricate a pretext. That is why we have followed an extremely careful policy with respect to the naval base at Caimanera.[5] We have always followed a very cautious policy to avoid giving the United States a pretext to attack our country. In the United Nations, during our visit to the UN, one of the points we raised was our concern that the North Americans would stage a "self-aggression" at Caimanera. And we declared that we would never try to retake Caimanera by force. We said we will always follow a legal road of demanding, by legal means and through international bodies, the return of this piece of our territory. Our aim was to not provide them even the slightest pretext to carry out a direct attack against our country.

Our frame of mind as to the possibility of a direct aggression has always been perfectly clear: we are determined to resist to the last man! That is our determination. Naturally,

---

5. Caimanera is the port on Guantánamo Bay in southeastern Cuba where the U.S. naval base is located. That base was set up shortly after the U.S. military occupation of Cuba in 1898. Since 1959 it has been held in defiance of the demand of the Cuban government that it be returned.

The phrase "self-aggression" refers to U.S. attempts to stage a provocation at the naval base as a pretext for an attack on Cuba. At a high-level meeting at the White House in early January 1961, for example, Secretary of State Christian Herter had suggested to Eisenhower staging an attack on the naval base and blaming it on the Cuban government.

however, we are interested in avoiding that aggression. No nation can remain indifferent to the destruction of resources and lives such an event would entail. Hence our interest in avoiding that type of aggression. That is why we have made every possible effort to keep them from having the slightest pretext. We have always been alerting the world as to our position in this respect, so as to make it as difficult as possible for them to take a step of that nature.

On the other hand, if such a direct aggression against our country were to take place, they know now what they will encounter here. They will encounter a determined resistance on the part of our people. And they will simply smash up against the resistance of our people, even in the event of a direct aggression. . . .

Imperialist domination

Prior to the revolution our economy was based around exports to a single market, and on the production of a single item: sugar. Our economy was based on the cultivation of a single crop. It was based on the export of that crop to a single market, the U.S. market. Our economy was completely dependent on the United States.

That is why the watchword of economic independence has been repeated so often in our country. And that's why nearly everybody kept repeating the slogan that "there is no political independence without economic independence." That was simply a fact recognized by everyone. We did not have economic independence. Why not? Because we were entirely dependent, above all on the U.S. market. In addition, our imports came almost exclusively from the United States.

Moreover, our country's economy was also in the hands of U.S. monopolies. The banks, the main industries, the mines, the fuel, the electric power, the telephones, a large portion of our best arable lands, the most important sugar mills—all these belonged to U.S. monopolies. Our economy was totally dependent on the United States. That's why we could not call ourselves a truly free country, because we were not economically free.

That was the situation when the revolution came to power. It immediately began to introduce a series of reforms and revolutionary laws designed to transform the country's economic structure. These revolutionary laws brought about an immediate clash with the monopolistic interests in the United States. And a clash with the monopolistic interests in the United States means a clash with the ruling circles in the United States. Because when all is said and done, in the United States the monopolies and the government are one and the same thing.

No other government had run into problems with the United States, simply because no government had enacted a single revolutionary law in the interest of the people, a law that at the same time might harm or jeopardize the monopolies' interests in Cuba. Naturally there are governments in Latin America that maintain excellent relations of friendship with the United States. Why is that? Because they don't enact revolutionary laws. Because they have not nationalized their oil. Because they have not nationalized their mines, which is something demanded by the peoples. Because they have not carried out an agrarian reform. Because they don't have a truly sovereign policy.

When the government of Arbenz attempted to carry out a land reform in Guatemala, affecting the land holdings of the United Fruit Company, this automatically produced U.S. aggression against that country and the ouster of the government.

Direct intervention had been the U.S. method in the 1920s and 1930s. Under the Roosevelt administration, this type of direct U.S. intervention in Latin America was discontinued and replaced by indirect intervention, which is what they applied in Guatemala. They did not send the marines to Guatemala; they sent Castillo Armas and a mercenary army that, in connivance with Guatemala's professional army, took over the country and are making it suffer what it is enduring right now. They have a gentleman there who is a mere tool of the United States. There is terrible hunger and widespread unrest throughout Guatemala today, under a gentleman who organizes mercenary armies there, like the one that attacked our country.

Such is the sad fate to which the Guatemalan people were led by those mercenary hordes that attacked this country at the instigation of the U.S. government.

The people in arms

In our country, when a series of social and economic reforms began to be enacted, we too clashed with U.S. interests. In this case, however, the imperialists did not have—as they had in other countries, such as Guatemala—a professional army trained and led by their embassies that could be utilized against the people's government. In Cuba the professional army had been destroyed, the old army was destroyed, and the weapons were totally in the hands of the peasants and the workers, who were the ones that made up the ranks of the Rebel Army. The weapons were in the hands of the people.

The U.S. Military Mission had been operating in Cuba until the very day of Batista's fall. There's an interesting anecdote about this. When our troops arrived at Ciudad Libertad, formerly Camp Columbia, they found the members of the U.S. Diplomatic Military Mission there, following their daily routine. They were there waiting for us, waiting for us to tell them: "Start training us. Up until yesterday you trained Batista's army so they could kill us. Now we want you to train us."

But what we told them instead was: "Well, the best thing

you can do is go home as soon as possible, because we don't need you." [*Applause*] I remember very well that I met those officers there, in a small drawing room, and I told them: "Well, you trained Batista's army, and Batista's army lost the war. Meanwhile we, whom you didn't teach a thing, have won, routing Batista and his men. So you are trainers of losers, and we don't want you to teach us anything." [*Applause*] We therefore asked them to leave.

So there was no more Military Mission. They no longer had an instrument here to use for establishing relations with the military high command who could be utilized in face of some political conjuncture. The situation they found themselves in here in Cuba was a bit more complicated. It was not the same as in Guatemala, because they could not rely on a professional army, or on a Military Mission. Instead they had to deal with an entirely new army, led by men who had been in the war and were in no way connected with them. In fact, it was commanded by men whose class interests were diametrically opposed to those defended by the former professional army.

In other words, they could not count on an army in Cuba to carry out a coup d'état. The government had enormous popular support. The revolutionary government had a brand new army whose members came from the ranks of the people. So what could they do? . . .

U.S. economic warfare

That's when the economic aggression, the plans of harassment began. . . . They carried out that aggression against a country that was, first of all, an underdeveloped country. Secondly, a country that was accustomed to a number of luxury items and imports that in recent years had exceeded our exports. So one of the first things the revolutionary government did was to adopt a policy of austerity, of frugality. It was not a policy of austerity at the expense of the workers or peasants, because the peasants were not the ones who drove Cadillacs, the peasants and the workers were not the people who took trips to Paris or the United States. The peasants and the workers were not the ones who consumed those luxury items. But the country as a whole was spending—I believe the imports of automobiles alone amounted to about $30 million a year. And the spare parts for these cars amounted to a fantastic sum, too. Meanwhile, only about $5 million a year was spent on agricultural implements.

There were extensive areas of uncultivated land covered with marabú.[6] These lands were completely abandoned, while tens and hundreds of thousands of families were without work, going hungry, totally dependent on the sugar harvest, which gave them three months of work—three months that in general were devoted to paying off the debts they had incurred during the "dead season."[7]

That was the situation in our countryside.

So the revolution adopted, to start with, a set of policies in the interests of the people. It lowered rents, it cut public utility rates, it gave idle lands to the cooperatives, it developed agriculture. It invested tremendous resources in farm implements, to give employment to everybody. It initiated a policy that, on the one hand, greatly benefited the people, and on the other hand, restricted the import of luxury items so those funds could be used not to purchase luxury cars but to buy farm implements and industrial machinery.

Thus, by means of that policy of frugality, the government was achieving an extraordinary rise in our foreign

---

6. Marabú is a dense, thorny shrub that grows wild in Cuba and other tropical climates.

7. The dead season was the nine months of the year between sugar harvests. During this period tens of thousands of sugarcane workers were left without steady work or income.

exchange reserves. That was just the opposite of what the imperialists thought would happen. When they speak to Latin America of an austerity policy, they are referring to an austerity policy that sacrifices the people, sacrifices the workers and peasants, that freezes wages, and a whole series of measures that don't affect in the least the standard of living, the spending, the tastes, or the income of the economically dominant classes, to whom that sort of austerity policy never entailed any sacrifice. We, on the other hand, adopted an austerity policy that affected the social classes that were precisely the ones who spent the most on luxuries, on expensive items and trips. In other words, we refused to turn over all the dollars requested by those ladies and gentlemen for travel expenses; we gave them a limited amount. In the old days they used to take their Cuban pesos to the bank and ask for $10,000 for trips to Paris. But when the revolution triumphed, things changed. We said: you can have a greatly reduced number of dollars for trips to Paris.

An austerity policy was established that did not affect the people, it affected the dominant economic classes only. That policy was designed precisely to obtain agricultural equipment, to build factories, to raise educational levels, and to improve housing and health conditions for those classes that work for a living.

In Latin America they advocate an austerity policy based on sacrifices by the workers and peasants of the country, with no sacrifices by the dominant classes. The revolution, on the other hand, established an austerity policy that benefited the workers and peasants, while calling for sacrifices by the economically dominant classes.

They saw the results of that policy. They saw Che arrive at the National Bank and have complete success in his work. And that brainy fellow whom everybody considered a great wise man on economic questions packed up and left the country after he had been dismissed from the National Bank.[8] They assumed that without the aid of these "brainy" gentlemen the country would fall apart.

The opposite occurred, because those extremely brainy gentlemen were really at the service of imperialism, not the people. We replaced them with compañeros who are intelligent and who went there to work not for imperialism but for the people.

So our foreign exchange reserves kept growing. At that point, as it dawned on them what was happening, they took another step of aggression: they began with oil. Everybody remembers how they attempted to leave us without oil.[9]

Being very much interested in selling our products in other markets, we had signed an agreement to sell a certain quantity of sugar to the Soviet Union in exchange for buying oil from them. We were using our sugar to buy oil.

Before that happened, we had to pay for oil in dollars, acquiring it from countries that did not buy any of our sugar. Given the country's interest in saving foreign exchange so that it could be invested in industrial and agricultural machinery, it was to our benefit to sell sugar to other markets and receive in payment articles that previously had been paid for in dollars. So we sold sugar to the Soviet Union and purchased oil from them.

When we told the U.S. oil companies that a portion of our crude oil requirement was going to be acquired from

---

8. On November 26, 1959, revolutionary leader Ernesto Che Guevara was appointed president of Cuba's National Bank, with responsibility for the country's finances. He replaced Felipe Pazos, a bourgeois economist who opposed the government's revolutionary course.

9. In June 1960 three major imperialist-owned oil trusts in Cuba announced their refusal to refine petroleum bought from the Soviet Union. The Cuban government responded by taking control of refineries owned by Texaco, Standard Oil, and Shell.

the Soviet Union, they decided not to refine any Soviet petroleum here. They would not refine it unless the oil came
from the wells controlled by them in other countries of the
world. Such a setup brought them fabulous profits, because
they controlled both the refineries and the extraction of oil
in other countries. They are typical monopolies. They own
the oil wells. They own the oil pipelines. They transport
the oil through the pipelines. They refine the oil. And they
handle distribution of the oil. That's a monopoly.

When they were told that part of the fuel we would be
consuming was going to come from other sources, they refused to refine that oil. Why did they refuse? Because they
thought, if Cuba takes any measures against us, then we'll
leave them without oil; and if a country is left without oil,
it will go through a tremendous crisis as a consequence of
lack of fuel, and this would inflict a harsh blow to the revolution.

What we did was to take over those refineries. And the
Soviet Union made a tremendous effort to supply us with all
the oil we needed. This effort bore fruit, and we withstood
that aggression, which would have left the country without
oil—thanks to the effort by the Soviet Union to maintain
the supply of oil, so that we have not lacked it up to today.
Moreover, the oil is cheaper, much cheaper, than what we
used to pay to the U.S. monopolies. Not to mention the fact
that we don't pay for it in dollars, but in accordance with
the trade agreements we have signed with other countries;
that is, we pay for it with sugar. Moreover, while we buy
oil, we sell other things; previously we bought oil but did
not sell anything.

So we overcame that situation. They saw the revolution's
success in confronting that aggression involving oil. At the
same time, they saw our foreign exchange reserves keep
going up, enabling us to forge ahead with our economic development plans. So they decided to take another step. What

did it consist of? They canceled our sugar quota, that is, they shut us out of the U.S. market.[10]

It would have been extremely difficult for any government, under normal circumstances, to withstand that kind of blow. An aggression of that type can be withstood only by a revolutionary government, with the support of a revolutionary people. That aggression meant our country would be deprived of the hundreds of millions of dollars we received for our sugar in the U.S. market.

In the old days, when Cuba sold its sugar on the U.S. market, the most important sugar mills and the most productive sugarcane-producing lands were owned by U.S. interests. In other words the trade was really trade among themselves. They grew the cane, which was then harvested by our workers for a miserable wage, working only part of the year at that; the cane was processed at U.S.-owned sugar mills; and the sugar was sold to the U.S. market.

Consequently, there was no profit for our country. Who got the profits? The oil monopolies, the public utility monopolies, the sugar monopolies.

When the country carried out the agrarian reform, we organized cooperatives to give employment to those peasants on a year-round basis and to have them diversify their production. Not only would they grow sugarcane, but all types of foodstuffs they needed. Just at that moment, when our people were beginning to receive the benefits of the work in the fields and in the factories, they deprived us of the U.S.

---

10. The sugar quota was first established in 1934 to protect wealthy U.S. sugar interests during the Great Depression. It set the amount of Cuban sugar Washington allowed to be sold in U.S. markets. At the time of the revolution, sugar exports accounted for about one third of Cuba's total national income and represented about 80 percent of its export trade. In July 1960 Eisenhower cut the quota by 95 percent, and in March 1961 the Kennedy administration banned any remaining imports of sugar from Cuba.

market, and they deprived our country of hundreds of millions of dollars it used to receive.

What was the aim? To make the revolution submit, to force the people down on their knees, to make our people surrender. They said: "We are going to deprive you of that income. Let's see how you get along. Either you surrender or we ruin you. We'll blockade you through hunger." But our people reacted to that policy with the determination to press ahead.

In face of the imperialist aggression, once again the Soviet Union, together with the other socialist countries—despite the fact that they were heavy sugar producers and did not need all that sugar—made a great effort to acquire from us four million tons of sugar. They did this so our revolution could withstand the U.S. economic aggression.

A clause barring economic aggression had been approved by the Organization of American States—that is to say, by this "hemispheric system" that the U.S. government talks so much about. This clause provided that no country could resort to economic pressures or economic aggression in order to achieve an internal political objective in another country, to influence in any way, change, or intervene in the internal affairs of another country.

Such economic aggression was expressly prohibited by an agreement of all the countries of this hemisphere. Nevertheless, our country was brutally attacked economically. And while this economic aggression was going on, what do you think happened? The representatives of the Latin American countries held a meeting in Costa Rica, not to condemn the United States, not to condemn the aggressor, not to condemn the victimizer, but to issue a declaration against the attacked, to issue a declaration against the victim.

The powerful country had violated international law, it had carried out an act of economic aggression in order to influence our internal policy. And when the moment came

to condemn the shark, the sardines got together not to condemn the shark, but to condemn another sardine. It so happened, however, that this other sardine was not a sardine
any more; we had ceased being a sardine. [*Applause*] We had
ceased being a sardine and had become something like a sea
urchin, an urchin that's extremely difficult for the Yankee
shark to swallow!

That's what happened when our country was the victim
of economic aggression. And some people wonder why we
distrust the OAS. Given that experience, given what happened to us, how could we not distrust it! As if we hadn't already experienced what happens to all the countries of Latin
America—of the number of times the shark has tried to devour a little Latin American sardine! And the other sardines,
despite their distress, tolerate the shark devouring some other
sardine, for fear it may devour still more of them.

When our country was the target of economic aggression, the hemispheric system had no protection for us, no
guarantee, no defense. They just canceled our sugar quota,
which constituted a brutal aggression against the economy
of a country that had been entirely dependent on that market. But that was not enough.

Thanks to the efforts of the Soviet Union, the Chinese
People's Republic, and the other socialist countries, we were
assured of the sale of four million tons of sugar, at a higher
than world market price. Once again the revolution, though
at the expense of effort and sacrifice, was able to keep moving forward, despite the imperialist aggression.

What did they do then? They took further steps and prohibited all exports of raw materials and spare parts to our
country.[11] What did that mean? Simply that all the factories

---

11. In an effort to paralyze Cuban industry by depriving it of spare
parts and raw materials, on October 19, 1960, Washington suspended
all trade with Cuba except for medicines and food.

in Cuba, almost all of them, almost all the transportation system in Cuba, almost all the moving equipment—in the construction industry, in agriculture, in industry—in short, some 95 percent of the industrial equipment and machinery in our country used to come from the United States.

Many factories even used raw materials that were produced only in the United States. Not satisfied with taking away our market, they instituted a ban on those exports. Why? To leave us without raw materials or spare parts for all our transport industry, our construction industry, our agriculture, and our factories.

Some of those factories require thousands of different spare parts, because they use a wide assortment of different types of parts that are extremely difficult to obtain in other markets. So they took a further step and stopped exports of those items.

As if that were not enough, they took still further steps. Now they were no longer just blocking our export of sugar, but also our exports of other products, such as sugarcane molasses, for instance. Our molasses had already been sold to its traditional market—the U.S. market—because the law they had enacted there against Cuba did not say anything about molasses; so some U.S. companies had already purchased our molasses. And through pressures exerted by the State Department, they took away from our country the $15 million it was going to receive from the sale of molasses.

To sell molasses in other places is more difficult. Why? Because it requires special storage facilities and a certain type of ship to transport it. It is not easy to get a sufficient number of such vessels.

In short, what was involved was one step after another designed to blockade us, drive us to shortages, to a difficult economic situation.

Why did they do this? Simply to defeat the revolutionary government, which was enacting laws in the interests of the working people. They wanted to bring back to our country government by the bootleggers, the gamblers, the racketeers, the embezzlers, governments that served the interests of the electric company and the telephone company. They wanted to bring back governments that, whenever the telephone company might want a new, more advantageous, contract, raising rates by a nickel for each additional call, would say, "Yes sir!" A government that, when the mining companies wanted concessions, would say, "Yes sir!" A government that, faced with any request for concessions in our markets, in transportation, or anywhere else, would say, "Yes sir!" They wanted a government, in short, that would hand over our country's economy and our people's interests to the monopolies.

They wanted to replace the revolutionary government with a government of crooks, swindlers, embezzlers, and murderers. They wanted a government of ignorance. They wanted to overthrow a government that sends teachers to the remotest corners of the country, that creates jobs for hundreds of thousands of peasants without work, that increases the number of construction workers from 30,000 to nearly 90,000—in short, a government that stands up to the aggression. Because the revolution's merit is that all the work being done is occurring in the midst of one aggression after another. First with oil refineries; next, the sugar quota; then the blockade barring all exports of raw materials and spare parts, followed by the blockade of all other products.

Yet imperialism is not satisfied with taking away our sugar quota and blocking our sales to the United States. They also pressure other countries they have influence over to prevent us from selling to them. And while all these attacks are going on, the revolution is building houses, developing cooperatives, raising agricultural production, constructing beach facilities, carrying out reforestation plans, engaging in an educational campaign throughout the country. This gives an idea of what this country could have done had they not taken away our sugar quota, had they not attacked us economically.

Campaign of terror

But that was not enough. Cuba kept resisting. So they started to organize terrorists and saboteurs, who were specially trained in the United States to become experts in handling inflammable materials and explosives. They began a campaign of destruction against our stores and factories.

There was the case of the electric power company, which never had any trouble when it belonged to a U.S. monopoly. After it became the property of the people, its rates were cut and its earnings no longer wound up in the coffers of U.S. banks. At that point a campaign of sabotage was launched against it.

The El Encanto department store used to be for the rich, and its profits benefited some rich man and no one else. Back then that store had no problems. But as soon as the big industries became the property of the people, the Yankee Central Intelligence Agency—the same one that organized this clumsy piece of bungling [*Laughter and applause*]—began campaigns of sabotage to destroy our industrial plants, our factories, and our sugar production.

The Hershey Sugar Mill was never set on fire when it belonged to Mr. [Julio] Lobo, who had, I believe, fourteen sugar mills and fifteen thousand caballerías of land [some half million acres]. But that changed when that same sugar mill became the property of the nation, when Lobo's lands became the property of the people's cooperatives—you should see how different the peasant's life is there now; you should see how the peasant lives in those cooperatives, compared to how he lived in the past. So they come to destroy that wealth, which they would never have thought of destroying before, when it belonged to a gentleman who owned fourteen sugar mills. They come to destroy it now that those lands belong to twelve or fourteen thousand families, who are the cooperative members working those lands.

It seems that for imperialism—that gang of sanctimonious liars and hypocrites—what's fair is for one man to own fourteen thousand caballerías of land, while fifteen or twenty thousand families go hungry. What's unfair, for them, is for the former owner not to own land. What's unfair, for them, is for 15,000 families to have land, a house, a job, food, and a school all year round. According to the imperialist gringo mentality, the imperialist conception of justice, one thing is fair and the other thing is unfair.

So they organized sabotage raids against our sugar mills, against our wealth, they organized the burning of our canefields. As you will recall, they began with planes that came openly from U.S. territory, though in the end such activities created such a scandal that they changed their tactics and methods for setting our canefields on fire.

But that was not enough for them. They began to organize groups of counterrevolutionaries, for which they recruited former military men, deserters, lumpens, the worst types. And the very worst were those who commanded the so-called Second Front of the Escambray, whose history is well known to you all.[12] Utilizing all those elements, they organized groups of counterrevolutionaries at the service of imperialism, and sent more and more weapons.

You have seen at the Civic Plaza the enormous quantity of arms and ammunition they had sent. Think of it: during the revolution, after sixteen months of fighting, we had only

---

12. The Second National Front of the Escambray was an anti-Batista guerrilla group that functioned largely as a group of bandits during Cuba's revolutionary war, refusing to collaborate with the Rebel Army. Most of its leaders openly joined the counterrevolution after 1959.

a hundred and sixty weapons. Our armament had grown from twelve to a hundred and sixty pieces. These had been wrested from the enemy, one by one, in small skirmishes or in full-fledged battles, such as the battle of El Uvero.[13]

What was our ammunition reserve? The bullets dropped along the road by columns of passing soldiers. Because out of three hundred men passing by, there's always one who will drop his cartridge belt, another a magazine, and a third may leave a sack of ammunition on a stray mule. The peasants used to go along the country roads gathering up the bullets dropped by the enemy columns, and then take the ammunition to us to fight with.

These *gusanos* here had received, in one week alone, a thousand weapons via parachute drops. We, on the other hand, during the entire war, managed to get only two bazookas. At the Civic Plaza you can see the antitank guns, mortars of all kinds, bazookas, automatic weapons, ammunition, communications equipment, all in enormous quantities, and they kept sending them. They sent them by air, by sea, by every possible means. We've captured them and are still capturing them; in the last few days we've been seizing some of the weapons they brought with them for these plans.

So our country has been subjected to a continuous and systematic campaign of harassment and aggression. These include economic attacks, such as the moves against our oil and our sugar. They include the halting of exports from the United States, in order to leave us without spare parts and raw materials, the blockade of other Cuban exports not only to the United States, but to other countries as well. There were also the sabotage campaigns and the organization of groups of counterrevolutionary guerrillas. . . .

---

13. On May 28, 1957, the Rebel Army overran a well-fortified army garrison at El Uvero in the Sierra Maestra. It was the largest battle of the revolutionary war up to that time.

Solidarity and intransigence

What happened in Latin America [in response to the Bay of Pigs invasion]? What an awakening of solidarity! How many young workers and students have lost their lives fighting, in almost all the capitals of Latin America, because of their solidarity with us! The world will not, under any circumstances, go along with the spectacle of a country like the United States launching that type of criminal, brutal, and cowardly aggression against Cuba.

I am convinced that such aggression would mean the suicide of imperialism and the end of imperialism. I am certain of this. [*Applause*]

With that certainty we must resist even if they sweep us away with atomic bombs. For even if they swept away a part of the country, there will be another part left. There will always be men left to fight. With that certainty we must resist, with that sense of loyalty and faithfulness to the men who have fallen up to today.

Because many compañeros have fallen in the struggle in the Sierra Maestra, in the clandestine struggle, in the struggle after the triumph of the revolution. They have already paid their tribute, they did their part; and we have the same obligation to do our part, to be ready to do so when we are called upon, with the same sense of duty, with the same sense of loyalty and solidarity as those who have fallen. None of us has the right to try to save his own skin.

Our determination to resist at all costs is firm, and must remain firm. In any event, that situation is imposed on us by circumstances that do not depend on us. Because the historic reasons for the formation of that powerful empire next to our country have not depended on us. In fact, all Cubans should feel truly satisfied, all Cubans should feel proud. Before we were the last card in the deck, we were the last wheel on the cart; today we are among the first cards in the deck of the world. [*Applause*]

A demonstration of 200,000 people took place in Mexico. In Chile the workers declared a general strike. The peasants in one region of Chile called a strike in support of Cuba. In Peking 600,000 people gathered, and 100,000 people congregated in a city in the Soviet Union. All this gives an idea of how in every corner of the world, an extraordinary echo of solidarity with our country has been heard, which is an echo of denunciation and condemnation of the government of the United States.

The world has risen in our favor. After what? After the victory. That is what strengthened this faith around the world—admiration at how the Cuban people destroyed the mercenary invasion in less than seventy-two hours, an invasion prepared by the Pentagon, an invasion meticulously prepared with all the techniques and tactics of war. The United States placed great faith in that invasion, it placed its prestige on the line, and it has been discredited.

Think of how much care they took, and how well they planned, and how all the "great brains" of the Pentagon and the U.S. government were employed. Yet their plans were destroyed in less than seventy-two hours. That is what they don't want to accept. They went looking for this problem, because it was they who created this situation, who fell into this absurdity, who fell into this ridicule. It was their own fault.

Ah, but now they can't put up with the consequences. Now they threaten direct intervention, because they were incompetents. Does anyone doubt this, given that they were capable of such an act of craziness? Couldn't they commit an even bigger one? Who has any doubts? If they were capable of making this mistake, why not an even bigger one? We should believe that they are capable of making another mistake, but a mistake that will cost them not only their prestige, but their very existence and will cost them—no one knows what it would cost humanity. The fact is that they are acting as bullies threatening the whole world, as killers threatening the whole world. They have become a gang of killers threatening world peace, threatening the world with war, threatening Cuba with intervention, threatening Latin America into defending them. Through doing so, they think they'll revive the right of intervention here.

We who are soldiers in this trench therefore have a duty as soldiers to defend it. Today we should concentrate all our spirit, all our thoughts, all our energy, on this historic minute the world is living through, in the effort to defend this trench and defend our homeland. Above all, today we are defending the world. We are defending world peace, because this willingness of ours to defend ourselves will perhaps make these gentlemen reflect.

Perhaps they imagine they'll drop a few bombs and everyone will start running. What if the opposite happens, as happened here, and no one starts running? What trouble they'll be getting themselves into if they make an attack of this type, sending their mercenaries, their soldiers to commit a felony, an act of shamelessness by invading our country.

First they'll have to wipe us off the map—that must be our attitude. They'll have to wipe us off the map before they can conquer the resistance of our people, the resistance everywhere, in the mountains, in the swamps, in the plains, in the cities—all over. Because even if they captured and destroyed all the cities, there would still remain the resistance throughout the rural areas. That's assuming they capture the cities, because we'll see if they can capture them. We'll see if they can capture Havana, for example. We'll see.

So we must be very conscious of all these things. These are the conclusions we must draw from experience. We should not rest on our laurels. We should not sit down and think there are no more risks for our country. Because imperialism has received a very harsh blow, and it's like a furious beast.

That's the situation of the ruling circles. It is a beast in-furiated by the failure and the ridicule it is subject to before the world. We must be fully conscious of their threatening statements, of their haughty attitude. Let's see whether they reevaluate or not. You've seen how that man there [Kennedy] has acted. When our country was in danger of direct aggression and mobilized, awaiting the presidential inauguration and thinking that this man might do something different—because we couldn't understand why a man assuming the presidency of the United States would want to bear the guilt for someone else's mistakes. On his first day, he himself said: "Let's start anew." But he didn't start anew, he started with the old.

Not only did he follow his predecessor's policy, but he was even more aggressive against our country. He followed the same line, and adopted an even more aggressive stance against us. The mercenaries themselves have said that until the day this man took office they had Germans and others instructing them. As soon as he took office, they began being trained by U.S. officers.

This gentleman has brought the problem on himself through lack of common sense, and he has committed even greater mistakes. He himself has brought about this discredit. What did this man do in face of our attitude, of our hopes for a change of policy in the United States, of our demobilizing, of our telling the people to wait? He intensified even more the attacks against us. In face of our wait-and-see attitude, an attitude of confidence that there might be a change because they were Democrats, because there was a certain shade of difference between the Democratic and Republican adminis-trations, and in this case it was a Democratic administration. But no, what this gentleman did was heighten and intensify the degree of aggression against our country.

And now he will probably not do what he should: recog-nize his error. He will probably not do what he should, which is to fire Mr. Allen Dulles, because the CIA has made the U.S. government look ridiculous before the world. The least he could do in this situation was disclaim the responsibility and fire the head of the CIA. Why didn't he do this? Simply because he too was implicated! [*Applause*]

In fact, it was one of the most ridiculous things that has ever occurred in the history of the United States. And they have only themselves to blame, because all we did was defend ourselves against the aggression. We were obviously not going to let the mercenaries get settled there in order to please Mr. Kennedy, or Mr. Allen Dulles. What did we do? Well, we pushed them into the sea. [*Applause*] Because this invasion of mercenaries, organized by the United States, was a sort of Normandy that didn't end with a Dunkirk.[14] That is, when it was all over, they were not even able to reembark.

That is what happened, and it was their own fault exclusively, because they were seeking something. Now they are enraged, furious, they threaten. What are we going to do in face of Mr. Kennedy's threats? Get scared? No, we are going to smile at Mr. Kennedy's threat of intervention. Why? Because we have many thousands of men with weapons in their hands and in the trenches. Once again we have to return to the trenches, we have no alternative. Once again we have to wait and see what happens with the crisis, watching the events, ready to defend ourselves.

That is the first thing I wanted to speak about today.

The expedition of the mercenaries should prove to us that these people make a lot of mistakes, and that they are capable of committing the greatest stupidities. As far as we're concerned, we cannot prevent these people from doing something stupid. We do everything possible to prevent them from

---

14. In May–June 1940, after the German army's conquest of France, 300,000 British and other Allied troops were evacuated by sea at Dunkirk on the French coast and taken to Britain.

doing something stupid. We do so, among other things, by preparing ourselves, defending ourselves, entrenching ourselves, all to make them think about it. But if they make a mistake, it's not in our hands to prevent it.

Our duty is to maintain our position firmly and to defend ourselves. To be ready to defend ourselves seriously and calmly, without boasting or anything like that, just as so many of our comrades went to fight and die, in a natural way, with absolute calmness, and with great confidence in the future of their homeland. No one has the right to preserve himself, like a seed, or anything of the sort. We all have exactly the same obligations, and we must be very conscious of these obligations, above all after we have just waged a bloody battle where a large number of compañeros and brothers of the people have fallen.

That was the first thing we wanted to speak about.

Imperialism's plans

We also wanted to explain to the people how the mercenary invasion was destroyed, what their plans were. Even the mercenaries, when they speak on television—you've seen them, they've all said it, and tomorrow we're going to take the television cameras there, so you can see what all of them say about the Americans, they're saying all sorts of things about the Americans. [*Shouts of "To the wall!"*]

Naturally, those lackeys who made up that government, that counterrevolutionary council, had so much faith that the Yankee plans could not fail that they sent their own sons. That's proof of how sure they were of success. I'm going to explain why they believed they would be successful, what they based their hopes of success on, what the strategic plan was, how they intended to carry it out, and why they were inspired with such great confidence that they sent their own sons.

Now the imperialists are promoting a campaign to ask

for clemency [for the captured mercenaries]. They are doing so before people in Latin America take to the streets to condemn the cowardly and criminal aggression against our country. They are doing so before it is condemned in the OAS as a violation of all international norms, of all laws in Latin America. That is, in face of the ridicule, in face of the blow they've been dealt, certain Latin American rulers are now making moves and organizing not to demand condemnation but to demand clemency.

Very well, we are going to tell those gentlemen to ask the U.S. government, to ask the Yankee Central Intelligence Agency, to ask the sponsors of the aggressions against Cuba, to first demand clemency for the children murdered here by their bombs. [*Applause*] To demand clemency for the victims of their bombings, to stop sending arms to Cuba, to stop supplying arms used to murder and kill, to stop supplying explosives and incendiary materials used to destroy our wealth, our factories, and the lives of our workers. They should ask them to stop their activities if they want clemency. But if they don't stop their aggressive activities against us, then it is completely absurd for them to stage the farce of asking for clemency for the mercenaries.

That is what some so-called government leaders in Latin America are now doing. These consummate hypocrites, instead of asking for condemnation of the aggression, are now expressing worry about the perpetrators of the aggression. Instead of defending the victims of the aggression, they are now concerned about the perpetrators of the aggression. That is the situation.

We shall now analyze the imperialist plan of attack against Cuba, why they landed there, why they didn't land elsewhere, what their intentions were.

In the first place, they exaggerated the number of mercenaries they say were recruited. They spoke of four or five thousand mercenaries, and they couldn't even get that many.

Those who landed here were the groups they had in Guatemala. They have another little group of mercenaries over in the Caimanera naval base, but it is much smaller and much more poorly armed than the ones who came.

Their elite troops, the elite of the mercenary army, was the part that was in Guatemala, trained in camps there, one of them Retalhuleu. They were receiving training there in two or three camps, although part of the personnel had also received training on Vieques Island in Puerto Rico,[15] and in New Orleans, in the United States. That has already been stated by all of them, it is perfectly well known. They had a small group of mercenaries in the zone of the naval base, headed by one Nino Díaz, and it's not known why that group did not land.[16]

There was an attempted landing in the Baracoa zone, but they were awaited with antitank guns and a whole series of things, as well as planes flying overhead; it may be that they retreated. But the fact is that the group of mercenaries they had at the naval base zone—some 400–500 mercenaries— did not land.

The bulk of the mercenaries, the group that had received the most training, the group that had air support and very powerful weaponry, was the mercenary army that they organized in Guatemala.

At the beginning, so it seems, imperialism's aim was to seize the Isle of Pines, to take control of the Isle of Pines and release all the war criminals and counterrevolutionaries

15. The U.S. Navy took over the island of Vieques, Puerto Rico, at the start of World War II to use as a base and target range. In face of growing opposition from the Puerto Rican people, the base was closed in 2003.

16. Subsequently it has become known that the Nino Díaz group trained in New Orleans and departed from Key West for their abortive landing. See the April 15, 1961, entry on this operation in the chronology at the back of this book.

who were imprisoned there in order to immediately fill out the ranks of the invading army and seize a piece of the national territory, an island. It would have been difficult for us to retake this island, given the naval and air resources at our disposal.

Under those circumstances they directed their efforts toward seizing a piece of the national territory, in order to establish a "provisional government" there. Because imperialism's greatest difficulty is not having a piece of territory here. So they must operate from Guatemala or Nicaragua, they must use foreign territories, which involves violating a number of international norms and creating quite a scandal. Because the establishment of military bases in foreign territory to attack our country is contrary to international law.

This is simply an act of piracy, of international filibustering,[17] which imperialism has perpetrated using its lackeys in Guatemala and Nicaragua. But it creates a problem for them: first, distance, then the violation of all international norms and the scandal it causes.

They needed a piece of our territory to operate more freely in. Then they could send ships, planes, men, everything, in order to begin a war of attrition. Their belief was that the economic blockade and cancellation of the quota, plus a war of attrition with daily bombing taking off from within the national territory itself—with lots of planes and war matériel furnished by them—would create a difficult situation

---

17. Filibustering was the name given to efforts by various expansionist adventurers in the United States in the early to mid-nineteenth century to seize control of countries in Latin America and the Caribbean. Most such expeditions were organized by proslavery elements from the U.S. South seeking to add future slave states to the Union. These efforts reached their peak during the 1850s, when William Walker was able to briefly seize control of Nicaragua. Filibustering expeditions were also waged against Cuba, then under Spanish colonial rule.

for the revolution.

Almost all counterrevolutions throughout history have made an effort to seize a piece of that country's territory. The Spanish civil war began, as you will remember, with the occupation of a piece of the territory—an island—by the forces that rose up against the republic. Once they had a piece of territory within Spain, the fascists and Nazis sent them ships, planes, tanks, and even troops.[18]

Hence their interest in seizing a piece of the territory. For this reason, at all costs we had to prevent the enemy from seizing a piece of the country's territory, wherever it might be.

The Isle of Pines was the most tempting spot for them at the time, because the war criminals and counterrevolutionaries were imprisoned there, and it was distant from our coast. It therefore lent itself to the establishment of a base within the national territory, which would open the way for them to receive imperialist aid openly, without having to incur all those violations, or the scandal caused by using the territory of other countries to attack ours.

What did we do in response? We filled the Isle of Pines with battalions, cannons, tanks. We established a force on the Isle of Pines that made it invulnerable to any attack. Faced with that situation, they had to desist from attacking the Isle of Pines, since before they attacked it we had already sent all the reinforcements there we would have needed had it actually been attacked. For a number of months we had

18. The fascist-led military uprising in Spain, organized by Gen. Francisco Franco, began in the Spanish colony of Morocco in July 1936. The fascists rapidly seized the Canary Islands and several of the Balearic Islands, and from there went on to occupy up to a third of the country over the following week. In their bloody, nearly three-year-long civil war against the workers and peasants of Spain, Franco's Falangist forces received the military and political backing of the fascist-led regimes of Adolf Hitler in Germany and Benito Mussolini in Italy.

been strengthening our positions on the Isle of Pines, sending more equipment, more arms, more units, strengthening more defensive positions, so that the Isle of Pines truly became invulnerable; it would have to be attacked with an enormous army. Now the mercenary army could no longer attack the Isle of Pines.

Then, for a period of time they tried to strengthen the groups in the Escambray, until they were swept out of there, and could no longer count on using this territory to try to establish a base, making use of the Trinidad Airport. The Escambray, too, became well defended. . . .

Assault on Cuban airfields

[On April 15] we were at the General Staff, waiting for news, when at 6:00 a.m. a B-26 flew by very low. Almost immediately, a few moments later, we felt the explosion of bombs and antiaircraft fire. We looked out and saw that it was a bombing attack, of a military character, on Ciudad Libertad, over the location of the Artillery School, over the airfields. Another B-26 came right away.

In the face of such a brazen and open air attack of a kind that had not taken place before, we concluded this was unmistakable evidence that we were facing the aggression. "This is the aggression," we said.

We tried to make contact immediately with the San Antonio airfield, so that their planes would take off, and we also got in touch with Santiago de Cuba. They were simultaneously attacking San Antonio and Santiago de Cuba. Our antiaircraft guns at the airfield opened fire immediately on those planes. We saw one plane make only one circle; the other one flew by, and on its second pass, the antiaircraft gunners made a direct hit and the plane retreated in a curtain of smoke, and we could also see flames. So that plane may have been one of those that got back, or it may have been one of those that crashed on the way.

A similar thing occurred at San Antonio de los Baños. Those planes, too, encountered heavy antiaircraft fire and got shot up. In Santiago de Cuba they also encountered antiaircraft fire.

We had calculated that wherever the attack might be, whether at the Isle of Pines . . . We had taken measures at the air base ever since the first steps were taken in connection with defending the Isle of Pines.

We have few planes, and in fact, we had fewer pilots than planes. These were planes left over from the Batista days: B-26 bombers, jets, and Sea Furies. But we were being very careful with those few planes; we were concerned about not letting them be destroyed. Because we had calculated that the first thing they would do, in case of an attack, was to destroy what little air power we had. That this would be the first thing they would do.

What did we do? Orders were given to the air force, to the base, to disperse all the planes; that order had been given months ago. No two planes could be together. Absolutely all the planes had to be spread out over a large area. Planes that were out of service were to be placed together, more or less. We established a decoy system in the air field. We placed the planes that were out of service together, in groups of twos and threes, with others spread out. All the planes were placed in this manner, so no one could tell which planes were good and which were out of service. They were completely dispersed. Furthermore, they were protected by 24 antiaircraft multiple machine guns. That was the protection they had, at the time. Later, more protection was sent. So if they think this is not much, they'll be quickly disillusioned! [Applause]

Result of the attack on the airfield? There were no planes there, only planes that were grounded. They were fired upon, and two of their planes left full of holes, with one giving off smoke.

They went to attack San Antonio, and at San Antonio exactly the same thing happened. At San Antonio they managed to destroy a transport plane and a fighter plane, but it was a minimal thing: one fighter plane. At Santiago de Cuba they destroyed another fighter plane, a Cubana Airlines plane, several other types of planes there, civilian planes. Because at Santiago de Cuba the airfield is smaller, and as a result the planes were closer to each other, so they did more damage there.

But they destroyed a total of two fighter planes.[19]

They attempted to destroy our air force on the ground. It was a classic military operation, a classic general staff move, a classic move accompanying every act of aggression. At Pearl Harbor, for example, what the Japanese did was try to destroy the air force on the ground. Whenever the Germans attacked, whenever they invaded a country by surprise, the first thing they did was try to destroy the air force on the ground. When Egypt was attacked by British imperialism, the first thing done was to destroy—or try to destroy—Egypt's planes on the ground.[20]

So all imperialist aggressions, all of them, in modern times, have been characterized by an attack on the air force, in order to immobilize it and destroy it on the ground.

Our air force was very modest, very small. But the few planes we had, we planned to use well, and we had confidence in the few pilots we had.

When the attack on the San Antonio base took place, the

---

19. Two of the Revolutionary Air Force's B-26 bombers were destroyed in the raid, leaving in flying condition 4 B-26s, three T-33 fighter-trainers, and three Sea Fury fighter-bombers.

20. British and French imperialism, together with Israel, launched military assaults against Egypt in 1956 in an attempt to reverse the nationalization of the Suez Canal by the government of Gamal Abdel Nasser. Nasser had taken this measure against British and French interests in face of mounting anti-imperialist sentiment and mass actions in Egypt. By November 1956 Egypt secured its control over the canal.

reaction of the antiaircraft gunners was formidable. There were even some gunners who opened fire before the planes did. The antiaircraft gun batteries are composed of fellows all under twenty; they are very young, very enthusiastic, with very good vision, very good health, and they've received a lot of training. And those boys responded immediately to the fire, planes were enveloped in smoke, others damaged, all forced to withdraw and they only destroyed one plane on the ground.

The pilots, for their part, reacted very well. The fellows who were sleeping left just as they were. They got into the planes without parachutes, without life preservers, without anything. [*Prolonged applause*] They reacted and gave pursuit; they were going toward Miami, they were unable to continue the pursuit because that would have involved entering the United States. But it had been a formidable reaction on everyone's part.

At Santiago de Cuba the antiaircraft gunners also attacked the planes very hard, forcing them to retreat.

As a result, the first step of the aggression—that is, the destruction of our planes on the ground—failed. The next day we reinforced the antiaircraft batteries, and took even more precautionary measures. They did not return. They had attacked with six B-26 bombers: two at Oriente, two at San Antonio, two at the airfield at Ciudad Libertad.

What happened? Some planes did not return to their base, and those that returned were damaged, completely perforated. So the first impact they received was the impact of our antiaircraft batteries that caused them losses, damaged their planes, and proved to them that they could not fly over our antiaircraft batteries with impunity. That is the first thing that happened: they were dealt a blow.

Second: our air force remained intact. There were still more planes than pilots, even though they had destroyed two fighter planes. The air force was intact and ready, and among the compañeros of the air force there was a desire to avenge that cowardly, surprise attack that they had launched at dawn.

That took place Saturday. All the forces were immediately mobilized, put on a state of alert. On Sunday the burial took place. The burial was guarded by our air force planes, watching over the skies during the burial of the victims of the air attack.

At the Ciudad Libertad base, one of the enemy projectiles had hit a truck that was transferring ammunition that day; during the morning some ammunition trucks were parked there. One of them caught fire and the ammunition began to explode, but just as had happened at the *La Coubre* explosion, the people displayed extraordinary courage. They even unloaded boxes from trucks that were on fire; that is, they unloaded boxes from trucks that were burning, with projectiles flying. [*Applause*]

There were other trucks full of ammunition that were also emptied by our compañeros with great courage in the midst of the explosions of those trucks, and there were victims. Obviously, there shouldn't have been trucks loaded with ammunition parked there at that time. Those things are impossible to foresee, because a transfer of the items was taking place, and those in charge of the transfer left the truck parked in the middle of the field. That was an error, and should not have been committed. But the fact remains: because of not always taking all precautions, they had left some trucks waiting overnight to continue the transfer. They had left trucks loaded with ammunition in the middle of the field, a field that could be the object of an attack at any time. But the compañeros there overcame that difficulty; they removed the trucks that had not exploded, and, as I said before, they even unloaded boxes from trucks that were exploding.

On Sunday the funeral procession for the victims of the

air attack took place. We were on the alert during those days; we had adopted the habit of sleeping during the afternoon and not sleeping at night. We were waiting.

Because of the scandalous nature of the attack, a true international scandal—the fact that planes came in to bomb, fire rockets, and strafe our positions—we deduced that the attack could not be merely harassment. Because if they had wanted to harass, to commit sabotage, they could have attacked other industrial locations, to try to cause damage. We concluded that it was an air attack—notwithstanding the scandal it was sure to cause—with a military objective, and the military objective was to destroy our planes.

We therefore drew the conclusion that the attack would occur in a matter of hours. What we have not been able to find out thus far is why they didn't land that same day; why they attacked two days earlier. From a military point of view, this was an error, because it placed everyone on a state of alert. We had already been on a state of alert, but now we reinforced the measures taken and adopted new ones, certain that the attack would come any minute. We mobilized all the combat units.

So they attack with their air force two days early. They commit an error. Sunday went by and nothing happened.

On Monday morning [April 17] at 3:15 a.m.—that night I had laid down, because we had held the demonstration—I and the other comrades were told that fighting was occurring at Playa Girón and Playa Larga, that the enemy was landing, and that platoons on watch in that area were putting up resistance.

We ordered that the information be verified; in this type of thing you must always be certain. Otherwise you start having ships at this place and that place. Then we received news reporting with absolute certainty of the first wounded men, reports that an invading force was giving heavy fire with bazookas, recoilless cannons, .50 caliber machine guns, and seaborne artillery, that Playa Girón and Playa Larga in the Zapata Swamp were coming under heavy attack.

There was no longer the slightest doubt that a landing was taking place there, and that it was strongly supported with heavy weapons.

Our people there immediately began to put up a heroic resistance. The shortwave stations at Playa Girón and Playa Larga established communication, and they gave information on the attack, until the very moment when, as a result of the attack itself, the radio stopped functioning. Between 3:00 and 4:00 a.m. news about Playa Girón and Playa Larga stopped coming in over the shortwave stations established there, since communications had already been silenced.

Zapata Swamp

By then we were facing this situation.

Look, [points to a map] this is the Bay of Pigs, this is Cienfuegos Bay. We had considered this zone as one of the possible sites for a landing.

At that time, there was a battalion from Cienfuegos posted at the Australia Sugar Mill. There were various platoons of armed charcoal makers, throughout the zone of Cayo Ramona, Soplillar, and Buena Ventura, small groups that immediately joined forces with those guarding these positions. They were the first to confront the aggressors.

This other map is bigger, [goes to another map] Playa Larga is here, Playa Girón over there.

I am going to go back here to explain something. [Goes back to the first map.] The Zapata Peninsula has the following characteristics: It is a region of solid ground right next to the shore: there is solid ground for several kilometers away from the coastline. It is rocky and wooded up to here. But north of this solid ground is an absolutely impassable swamp.

This is an absolutely impassable swamp. Previously there

were no means of communication whatsoever; there was a narrow gauge railroad from the Australia Sugar Mill to the Bay of Pigs, and from Covadonga to Girón. So it was a completely impassable place; the residents of this zone had only a single narrow gauge railroad for communication.

The Zapata Swamp is one of the places where the revolution has worked hardest. It has built three main roads that cross the swamp; these are the points of access for anyone going there. The charcoal workers of the swamp—thousands of people live here, and they used to live under the worst conditions imaginable. They were paid 80 or 90 cents for a bag of charcoal, and had to pay rent for a bit of land, and then the middleman who took the charcoal out through here, through this narrow gauge railroad, sold it at a price two or three times higher.

That is, it was the poorest and most forgotten population in the country. And the Zapata Swamp is one of the places where the revolution has done the most. It has built tourist centers at Laguna del Tesoro, Playa Larga, and Playa Girón; communication routes have been built; not only this highway, but more than two hundred kilometers of highways and roads have been built in the Zapata Swamp, through which the residents take out their charcoal and wood. The income of the population in this area has increased dramatically; there are people who earn 8, 10, 12 pesos a day or more, extracting wood. These are people who once lived in terrible conditions.

When the invasion took place there were two hundred teachers in the Zapata Swamp region participating in the literacy campaign. That gives an idea about the place these people chose.

This is very important, because it shows what the imperialist mentality is—the reverse of the revolutionary mentality. Imperialism examines geography; it analyzes the number of cannons, planes, tanks; it assesses positions. The revolutionary, on the other hand, examines the social composition of the population, what the population consists of. The imperialists don't give a damn what the population there thinks or feels, they could care less. The revolutionary thinks first of the population, and the population of the Zapata Swamp was entirely with us.

Why? Because it was a population that had been rescued from the worst misery, from the worst isolation. A child around here—in this area there are places called Santo Tomás, Vínculo, and Medioderos, which are little villages in the area, where before the main road was there—it has already reached Santo Tomás and will soon reach Vínculo—they had to use a road through Canaliso to take out what they produced, as well as everything else. And it took them three days to reach Batabanó. Children used to die there without a chance to reach the doctor, because from certain areas of the Zapata Swamp it took three days for anyone to reach civilization.

I remember a conversation I had with some residents of that area, around the zone of Santo Tomás. They told me: "Look, man can withstand more than a dog, because here there were dogs that died of starvation, while we didn't." [*Applause*] "There were dogs that starved to death while we didn't. Man can withstand more than a dog." That is the phrase of a resident of the Santo Tomás area.

The literacy campaign that was being carried out in those places was a fantastic thing. It was one of the pilot areas of the literacy campaign. All these towns—Jagüey Grande, Covadonga, Australia, all these towns around here—had no access to the sea, they were exclusively swampland. Now all these people have beaches; thousands of people visit Playa Girón and Playa Larga on Sundays, even though construction is not yet finished. There was a plan to officially open Playa Girón on May 20; and they were also working intensively on Laguna del Tesoro and Playa Larga

There are three hundred children of residents from the Zapata Swamp studying in Havana. They are studying ceramics, leather tanning, mechanics, carpentry; because a number of leather tanning, mechanical, ceramics, and carpentry shops are going to be established there. And we have three hundred boys and girls studying in Havana. Incidentally, the mother of two girls that were studying here was killed in the air attack by the mercenaries. There is a story about one of their little sisters, who had an obsession with a pair of white shoes. Right in the middle of the bombing, the little girl wanted to go and get her white shoes that were in the house. Finally she got the shoes, but they were all shot up, almost destroyed. And she lost her mother during the mercenaries' attack there.

But the fact was that there were two hundred teachers in the Zapata Swamp, and three hundred local children studying in Havana, in the wealthy Cubanacán area. And the standard of living of the population of the Zapata Swamp was very high: roads, doctors, jobs. It had become one of the most frequented places, one of the most visited.

Those were the conditions of the population in the place where the mercenaries landed. They disembarked at Playa Girón, where there is a town that has 180 new homes, and will have the capacity to house more than a thousand people. Because these are tourist centers, which will be organized so that the workers can go there, the poorest working families.

Playa Girón and the Zapata Swamp are places that we have filled with main roads. It is a town completely built by the revolution, with an airfield and everything else. This is where the mercenaries intended to establish their territory. There, of all places, is where imperialism was going to establish its occupied territory, at the place where the most has been done for the population in the least amount of time. Possibly there is no place in the world where more has been done for a population than in the Zapata Swamp over the last two years.

See how unaware they are. See how completely indifferent they are to how the population thinks. . . .

※

[Following a detailed account of the three-day battle, Castro described the victory over the U.S.-organized invaders by the people's militia and Rebel Army forces late in the afternoon of April 19. He continued:]

This does not mean that the danger is past. Quite the contrary. We believe that the danger now is great, above all, the danger of direct aggression by the United States. For example, in yesterday's wire dispatches, we read the following:

"MESA, Arizona—Conservative Republican leader, Senator [Barry] Goldwater, said he would recommend active military intervention in Cuba if all else failed.

"Goldwater, who held a 45-minute conference yesterday with President Kennedy, said that the United States cannot permit a Communist country to exist so close to its shores. The statement was made in this city before a group of Rotary Club leaders.

"'As of this morning'"—Goldwater continued—"'This country is in greater danger than it has ever been. Overnight we can become a second-rate world power. We can within a very few years come under a foreign philosophy.'

"Goldwater ended by saying that in regards to Cuba the United States should resort to an air and sea blockade. If this fails, then it should resort to the Organization of American States. If this also fails, then we would have to take action ourselves. The Senator stated: 'If this means a direct military intervention, and if all else should fail, I would support it.'"

See what concept of law this madman has. [Laughter] See what respect for the sovereignty of other peoples, what respect for international law. See how calmly they speak of direct military intervention. This shows the people the mentality of these gentlemen. They do not respect anything, they don't even know where they are. As if it were so simple, as if nothing more were required than landing the marines here, meeting no resistance. They just won't learn!

They don't think about trying to avoid becoming a second-rate world power through efforts in favor of peace, through efforts in favor of humanity. They don't think about not becoming a second-rate world power through their scientific achievements, through studying how they too can launch a man into space,[21] [*Laughter and applause*] and how they can send a rocket to Venus. They don't struggle in the field of science, in the field of peace, in favor of peace, to avoid a war, with all its calamities for humanity.

Because despite the short duration of the battle, just look at the number of lives it cost. Just look at the number of families that have to weep over their loved ones, because of a cowardly aggression, an unjustifiable aggression, an aggression paid for by thieves full of hatred, by the embezzlers, by the monopolies that want to starve our people to death, those who want to continue exploiting us.

Because of these gentlemen's vile motives—their millions of dollars, for instance—they make the people pay with an extremely high number of lives, they make the people pay with an extremely high number of sacrifices. They do all this to once again establish their privileges here, to once again establish the corruption that always existed in our country, to once again establish the repugnant past to which our people do not want to return—and to which they shall never return.

That's what war is. Why did they need to provoke this

---

21. On April 12, 1961, the Soviet Union launched the first manned space flight.

bloodshed in our country? Why did they have to come here, in a fruitless attempt? Not to mention getting themselves all worked up because they failed. Why do they threaten us with intervention? That's the odd part; these gentlemen have such a lack of conscience and are so irresponsible, so obsessed, that after they have made our people bleed, after they took a number of valuable lives, they still threaten to kill even more, to intervene even more.

That is why we must have an answer for them. And our answer is our determination to resist, our determination that if they dare launch an attack, that will be the end of imperialism, even though it may cost us our lives. Because to us, death, a glorious death, will always be a thousand times preferable to living in slavery, living in shame under the yoke of these gentlemen! [*Prolonged applause*]

Death does not frighten any man or woman of dignity. What does frighten a man or woman of dignity, what frightens the people, is the idea of the yoke, the idea of some day seeing themselves governed and oppressed by this group of gentlemen who have so little respect for the peoples, for the rights of the peoples, for the aspirations of the peoples, for the independence of the peoples, the sovereignty of the peoples, the peoples' hope for peace, the peoples' hope for progress.

That does cause fear—fear that those gentlemen could be dictating the law here, imposing their law of the scaffold and the sword, imposing their yoke upon the people. Those compañeros who fell in battle at Playa Larga, Playa Girón, San Blas, Yaguaramas, in all those places, died in a glorious manner, fighting successfully to inflict a defeat on imperialism. They deserve the most beautiful of monuments. They deserve a great monument built right there in the Zapata Swamp, in memory of the fallen, with the names of all those killed listed there. A monument telling the world that on this day in history, Yankee imperialism suffered its first great defeat in the Americas! [*Great applause*]

These arrows on the map show the troops' advance, how they fought their way through enemy fire, through enemy bombings. They fought their way through, paying with precious lives for each kilometer of land. All the units rivaled one another in courage. The army units and the militia battalions both displayed extraordinary courage, surprising the mercenaries, who had been led to believe the militiamen would not fight. The number of heroic feats carried out by the militia members in this battle are too numerous to count.

The antiaircraft batteries, the mortar batteries, the howitzers—all the units rivaled each other in courage. And some units that were not able to participate in the fighting were almost desperate when the battle ended. Such was their ardor, their desire to advance on the enemy, that some units that had rested for a day, or that still wanted to continue fighting the enemy, could be seen with disappointment on their faces, because the mercenaries had already surrendered and had not put up any more resistance.

Those are the things we observed.

We believe the people have passed an extraordinary test; they have defended their rights, they have defended their land, they have defended their honor. They have also earned, throughout the world, great admiration. They have achieved great prestige. They have inflicted a great defeat on imperialism. They have waged a battle in favor of peace, because it's indisputable that if the mercenaries had been successful in seizing a part of the national territory, in order to openly receive aid, to establish a base of operations, you can imagine how many lives it would have cost the revolution. You can imagine how much wealth it would have cost our country, how much it would have set back our progress.

So those 87 compañeros who died[22] have saved the lives of tens of thousands of Cubans, tens of thousands of women, tens of thousands of children, tens of thousands of combatants, because an enemy who had taken control of that piece of territory would have cost our people an untold number of casualties. It would have forced us into a long war, a war of attrition, of wastage of lives. It would have retarded our development. It would have retarded the work of the revolution.

Consider the fact that the literacy campaign has not stopped even during these days. We did not stop organizing this campaign even during these few days, that campaign continued forward. The organization of the Cattle Fair went ahead, and it will open today at Rancho Boyeros. The first brigadistas, who will leave shortly—today or tomorrow, I believe—met at Varadero. These are the first contingents of the Conrado Benítez Brigades, which will bring literacy to the mountains.[23] And that has great merit. The fact that the campaign has not stopped in the midst of tension and national disruption has extraordinary merit, and it demonstrates the faith, enthusiasm, and firmness of the revolution. It demonstrates how in the midst of blockades and economic and military aggressions, the people continue carrying out their work and moving it forward.

Those compañeros who died have saved tens of thousands of lives. They died precisely to prevent the formation of that beachhead, to destroy it immediately. The service rendered to the country by the soldiers, the pilots, is incalculable. Those pilots would leave one battle and come back to

---

22. In his testimony, Fernández gives the final casualty figures. See page 130.

23. Conrado Benítez was a nineteen-year-old literacy volunteer murdered by counterrevolutionary bandits in the Escambray mountains January 5, 1961.

reload in order to return again to confront the enemy. They would fight and come back again for ammunition to continue fighting, without a minute of rest. These pilots have created the Revolutionary Air Force, because they have set the precedent upon which the air force of the revolution will arise. The precedent of this air force of the revolution will be the extraordinary feats of the pilots, the tiny number of pilots of our small air force. I am sure that no air force has ever done what these pilots did. [*Applause*] That is why we believe April 17 should be established as the Day of the Revolutionary Air Force of Cuba. [*Applause*]

We all have the duty to generously assist the families of the compañeros who fell, so that they will not lack anything, because, I repeat, they saved tens of thousands of lives. Had the enemy established a beachhead there, had it established air bases, all our cities would have been threatened. They would have had to live under the terror of constant bombings and attacks; the fight would have been a long one. And this would have greatly complicated the international situation. It would have plunged our country into civil war, a war they were not able to launch and shall never launch.

This has served to unite the people. It has served to help the people see things as they truly are, in all their seriousness, in all their gravity, in all their importance. The people saw how the revolution demands these sacrifices, and that the revolution requires even greater sacrifices than depriving ourselves of a few material things.

Let those men who died, who gave their lives, serve as an example. Let them be an example for the whiners, for the weak, for those who constantly groan about every small inconvenience in a country that has begun to pay such a high price in sacrifices for its cause, for its revolution, for its independence, for its dignity. Sacrifices given in the struggle against a reactionary enemy, a powerful, aggressive, brutal enemy that not only causes us the loss of lives, but also threatens us with new aggressions.

Let me read the following:

"Senate Majority Leader Mike Mansfield stated that the Cuban crisis is too grave for the United States to stop and analyze who has been to blame for recent events.

"There is a time and a place for everything, he said, and in the interest of our country we must, of necessity, confront the present and plan for the future. The gravity of this moment demands a responsible unity with the President, who, under our constitution, bears a great load at all times.

"He added that at this particular moment a terrible and heavy responsibility rests on the President in reexamining and reevaluating our foreign policy. He has a right to and deserves full support.

"Apparently this support is what Kennedy has been looking for in his consultations with Congressional leaders and his scheduled meeting with ex-President Eisenhower."

Here's another one:

"WASHINGTON—Senator George Aiken, Republican of Vermont, stated that there is growing support in official circles for drastic action against Cuba.

"Aiken, who is a member of the Senate Foreign Relations Committee, said that recent events in Cuba reveal that the situation has been badly handled and erroneously judged.

"He added that Cuba constitutes a permanent threat to the Hemisphere"—as if *they* weren't the real threat to the hemisphere—"and warned that a decision of great importance will be taken before long."

Well, if the decision of great importance that will be taken before long is that they are going to invade Cuba, that frightens absolutely no one here. [*Applause*]

They should have no doubts that we will give them quite a reception here in our country.

The power of the empire cannot go beyond the dignity of a people, and their art of destruction can go no further than death. It will have to crash up against a people who are ready to face all the vicissitudes, all the risks, and all that may happen. But even more, we are going to confront these things with perfect calmness, confident that any attempt to destroy us will mean their own destruction, that any attempt to snuff out Cuban lives will mean the snuffing out of an incalculable number of their lives. And that any aggression against Cuba will be the beginning of the end of the Yankee empire. The day they attack Cuba will begin the countdown to the disappearance of the Yankee empire from the face of the earth! [Applause]

It is regrettable that the U.S. rulers are so erratic. It is regrettable they so often make mistakes, and that due to their propensity to make mistakes they commit errors such as these. Why did the U.S. government need to make such a fool of itself?

Ah! They calculated they were going to dominate the air, that they were going to take possession of that territory. They calculated. They calculated a lot. But they calculated badly, and they made a mistake. They could not destroy the planes because these were dispersed. And instead of destroying us they had our planes flying over their heads. The attack and the reaction of the people were immediate, the advance of our forces was like lightning.

Did they think we did not know how to operate the cannons? That we did not know how to operate the antiaircraft batteries? Their planes that were shot down proved the opposite. The concentrated fire of our antiaircraft guns proved the opposite, and proved we had been right when we said: If they come, they stay! [Applause]

What they believed was based on a miscalculation, and they made a mistake. But in the end, this error has been painful for us, it cost us lives. Yet it didn't go further. If instead they commit the error of invading our country, then the consequences of that error could be incalculable. In the first place, they are not going to be left in peace in Latin America. The struggle will be waged both here and there. Because if they invade our country, then, as a matter of course, all Cubans who sympathize with the revolution, and all Latin Americans who sympathize with the revolution, will carry the war there also—to the very heart of the empire! [*Applause*]

If they invade our country, the armies of Latin America will have to be entirely dedicated to protecting the ambassadors, the consuls, the Yankee diplomatic representatives. The armies of Latin America will not be sufficient to protect their presidents of corporations, their presidents of monopolies, their ambassadors and consuls. Because if they start a war against Cuba, the peoples of Latin America will also start a war against them everywhere. That should make them stop and think. . . .

History is on our side

Imperialism has to disappear just as feudalism did, just as the ancient societies passed, just as feudalism passed. In the same way that slavery passed, imperialism has to pass, the exploitation of man by man has to pass, the exploitation of peoples by other peoples has to pass. That is an inevitable historical reality. Are they going to fight history? Try to imagine the feudal lords battling history to prevent the disappearance of feudalism. Feudalism was a form of society that existed at one time, by virtue of which a lord had a number of rights over the individuals who lived on his land, a number of privileges. And that disappeared, the ancient societies disappeared, slavery disappeared. Why shouldn't colonialism, imperialism, and capitalism disappear? It has to disappear, at some time or another; in some countries it will disappear in one manner, in other countries in a different manner; some countries evolve, other countries do not evolve but march backwards. The more a social regime marches backwards, the sooner it is called upon to disappear.

Unfortunately for the world, at the moment we are now living in, it's obvious that the dangers of war have much more terrible consequences than they had in other times. If wars were terrible in 1914, and even more terrible at the end of the 1930s and beginning of the 1940s, then war at this moment would be incomparably more terrible.

Was Nazism saved? No. Was fascism saved? No. Then why should those following the methods of Nazism and fascism be saved, these men who make statements with the effrontery of a Goering, a Goebbels, a Himmler, a Hitler? With the same effrontery and the same tranquility with which a Hitler stated his willingness to invade a neighboring country, these gentlemen who rule the United States state their willingness to invade a small country. It's clear that the times in which the world is now living are different; the progressive forces of the world are very great, the forces in favor of peace in the world are very great. And who are the ones in favor of peace? Those who know that history is on their side, and that history, far from pointing out that their end is near, is pointing out to them the future; and then they do not get impatient with history. They do not fight history, but struggle alongside history and move forward with history.

Imperialism, which is out of fashion, which is outdated by history, tries to fight history and tries to accomplish through force, violence, destruction, and death, what it cannot accomplish through peace, that is: to preserve its system and preserve its privileges. It would be a true disgrace for the world if these gentlemen were incapable of thinking carefully, a true disgrace for the world, because they are going to cause the world many calamities. Notwithstanding the fact, of course, that the calamities they cause the world will be much more calamitous for them than for anyone else.

That is the question we have to analyze. That is the question we have to think about serenely. Now we have to free ourselves from all worry, to act with much serenity, to analyze things just as they are, and respond to the situation. That is what we are called upon to do.

Today, at this minute, Cuba is part of the world, and there can be no problem of Cuba that is not a world problem. [*Applause*]

We are going to keep all the revolutionary forces mobilized. We are going to continue with the organization of the May Day celebration. We are going to continue our revolutionary effort for the victory of the revolution and of the people. We are going to strengthen our spirit. We are going to prepare ourselves to make all the sacrifices that are necessary.

The people have tasted this hour of triumph. The joy of this victory over the mercenaries has been cause for great happiness, a just and deserved happiness by the people, a cause for confidence by the people. But remember that victories are achieved as this one was: as a result of sacrifice, as a result of 87 men who died to save tens of thousands of lives; of 87 men who died to preserve wealth; of 87 men who died—87 so far, and perhaps there may be more—to guarantee the future of the homeland. They sacrificed themselves for everyone else, they sacrificed themselves to guarantee the wealth, the independence, the dignity, the sovereignty of the nation, and to build a better homeland.

No one can be so selfish as to linger on petty questions in face of these examples. We should always remember that we owe today's happiness to those who died. And that future generations will owe tomorrow's happiness to those of us willing to sacrifice ourselves today. [*Ovation*]

GRANMA

Workers at Havana May Day celebration, 1961. Sign at left labels U.S. President Kennedy as "Ku Klux Klan, Arrogant, Negative, Noxious, Rich, Diabolic, etc." Sign at right says, "Happy and sovereign, defend your marvelous future."

If Mr. Kennedy does
not like socialism, well,
we do not like imperialism!

Fidel Castro
May 1, 1961

The annual parade in Havana in 1961 on May 1, International Workers' Day, celebrated the victory at Playa Girón and the public declaration of the revolution's socialist goals. Marching in the parade were troops who had participated in the fighting at the Bay of Pigs, at the front of which were the 339th militia battalion, which was the first to engage the invaders in battle; the battalion of the Revolutionary National Police; and three tank companies. Also parading were organized contingents of working people—from industrial workers and health care personnel, to workers who shined shoes for a living—as well as young brigadistas participating in Cuba's massive literacy drive and visitors to Cuba from around the world expressing their solidarity with the revolution.

Castro addressed the crowd at the conclusion of the parade. The following is the opening half of his remarks.

Speech to Havana May Day rally

Fidel Castro

Distinguished visitors from Latin America and the entire world [*Applause*]; combatants of the armed forces of the people [*Applause*]; workers [*Applause*]:

We have had fourteen and a half hours of parading. I think that only a people imbued with infinite enthusiasm is capable of enduring such tests. In any case, I will try to be as brief as possible. [*Shouts of "No!"*] We are very happy about the people's attitude. [*Applause*]

I believe that today we should outline a course to follow. We should think a little about what we have done up to today, determine what point in our history we find ourselves at, and look at what we have ahead. We have all had a chance to see the parade. Perhaps those of us on this platform can appreciate it better than you in the plaza, perhaps better even than those who have marched.

This May Day says a lot. It says a lot about what the revolution has been thus far, what it has achieved up to today. [*Applause*] Perhaps it tells our visitors more than it tells us. All Cubans have witnessed every step taken by the revolution, so perhaps we don't realize how much we have advanced as fully as visitors do, particularly those from Latin America, [Applause] where today they are still living in a world very similar to the one we lived in yesterday. It's as if they were transported from the past that we know so well and suddenly parachuted into this very moment of our revolution, with everything that is new in it, and the wonders it displays compared to the past. We do not intend tonight to stress the merits of what we've done. We merely want to look at where we are at and think about the revolution's genuine results up to now.

This May Day is different from those of the past. In the past, this date was the occasion for each sector of labor to set forth its demands, its aspirations for improvement, to those who were completely deaf to working-class interests, to those who could not even grant basic demands because they did not govern for the people, for the workers, for the peasants, for the country's poor. They governed solely for the privileged, solely for the dominant economic interests. Doing anything in the interests of the people—of the peasants and workers—would have meant harming the interests they really represented. For this reason they could not in general grant any just demand by the people. The May Day marches of those days expressed the complaints and protests of the workers.

How different today's parade has been from that! How different even from the first parades after the triumph of the revolution. Today's parade shows us how much we have advanced. [Applause] The workers no longer have to subject themselves to those ordeals. The workers no longer have to implore rulers deaf to their appeals. The workers no longer are subject to the rule of an exploiting class. The workers no longer have a government at the service of the interests that exploit their class. The workers now know that everything the revolution does, everything the government does or can do, has one and only one goal: helping their class, helping their people. [*Applause*]

Otherwise, there could be no explanation for this spontaneous show of support for the revolutionary government, this outpouring of identification that every man and woman has expressed today as they marched past the stage. [*Applause*]

Wherever we look we see fruits of the revolution. The first ones to parade today were the children of the Camilo Cienfuegos school complex. [*Applause*] We saw the Pioneers march by [*Applause*] with smiles of hope, confidence, and affection. We saw the Young Rebels march by.[1] [*Applause*] We saw the women of the Federation [of Cuban Women] go by. [*Applause*] We saw children march by from innumerable schools created by the revolution. [*Applause*] We saw the students studying artificial insemination here in the capital [*Applause*]—there are a thousand of them, from 600 sugarcane cooperatives. We saw young people, ordinary youth from working families, wearing the uniforms of the school where they're studying to become diplomatic representatives of our country in the future. [*Applause*]

We saw the pupils of the schools for children of peasants from the Zapata Swamp, the place the mercenaries chose for their attack on our country. We saw thousands and thousands of peasants march by, peasants who are also studying in the capital, coming from every corner of the island: from

1. The Camilo Cienfuegos school complex in the Sierra Maestra was built in 1960. The Union of Rebel Pioneers was an organization for Cuban children formed April 4, 1961; it has since changed its name to the José Martí Organization of Pioneers. On the initiative of the July 26 Movement leadership, the Association of Rebel Youth was born out of the Rebel Army in late 1959. In 1960 it fused with two other organizations of revolutionary-minded youth and in 1962 became the Union of Young Communists (UJC).

the mountains of Oriente or Las Villas, to the sugarcane cooperatives or people's farms. We saw the young women studying to be workers at child care centers. [*Applause*]

Every one of these groups of students have put on displays that are doubly praiseworthy, given the very brief time they had to prepare them. And not only did we see those who *came from* the countryside, but also those who are *going to* the countryside. Because the volunteer teachers marched by, as well as representatives of the 100,000 young people on their way to the country's interior to carry out the plan to completely eradicate illiteracy from our country in a single year.

Where does this strength come from? It comes from the people, and it goes toward the people. [*Applause*] These young people are truly children of the people. [*Applause*] When we saw them today with the words spelled out, "Long live our socialist revolution!" [*Prolonged applause*] I thought, how difficult all this would have been without a revolution. How difficult it would have been for any of these children from the mountains to have marched by here today. How difficult it would have been for any of these boys and girls from our countryside to have a chance to even know the capital, or to study in any of these schools, or to march by with the joy and pride shown here today, evoking admiration in us all, including our visitors, marching with the faith in the future shown here today. Because schools, university careers, art, culture, and honors were never meant for the children of working families, either in city or countryside. [*Applause*] They were never meant for the peasant from the remote mountainous areas. [*Applause*] They were never meant for the poor youth—black or white—from our countryside or cities. [*Applause*]

Art, culture, university careers, opportunities, honors, elegant clothes—these were all the privilege of a tiny minority, a minority portrayed today with that wit and humor shown by several contingents of workers in the parade imitating the rich, with their elegant costumes and all the things typical of well-heeled youth from wealthy families. [*Shouts of "Out with them!"*]

It is truly astounding to think that today more than 20,000 athletes and gymnasts paraded by, [*Applause*] keeping in mind that we are just beginning.

And we haven't even touched on the most marvelous thing we've had a chance to see today: which is an armed people and a united people. That is what has been on display this May Day. [*Prolonged applause*]

How would this have been possible without a revolution? How can one compare the present with the past? How can one not feel emotion on seeing endless lines of workers march by, followed by athletes and militiamen? At times all went by mixed together. After all, workers, athletes, militiamen, and soldiers are one and the same thing. [*Applause*]

All this explains why our people will emerge victorious whenever they are put to the test. We noted the many women in the ranks of the union contingents. [*Applause*] The explanation is simply that the men were in the artillery units, the mortar units, the antiaircraft units, and the militia battalions that followed behind the union contingents. And the women were the wives, sisters, mothers, or girlfriends of the militiamen who marched by later. [*Applause*]

And those boys from the secondary schools, the Pioneers who opened the parade or else marched by with the athletes— they too were the sons of those militiamen. [*Applause*]

In this way, one can appreciate the working people as a whole. Workers of every profession; manual workers and intellectual workers; the writer marching together with the artist, the actor, the radio announcer. The doctor marching together with the nurse, the health care worker. And marching together in massive numbers under the banner of the National Union of Education Workers were the teachers, the instructors, the employees of the Ministry of Education. [*Applause*]

Today we have had the opportunity, more so than ever before, to understand everything truly worthy in our country, everything that produces in our country. We have been able to understand better than ever that there are two classes of citizens—or rather there used to be two classes of citizens: those who worked, who produced, who created; and those who lived without working or producing. Those who simply lived as parasites.

In this young and combative nation, this enthusiastic and fiery nation, who was it that did not march today? Who could not march here today? The parasites. The ones marching today were the working people, those who work and those who produce with their hands or their brain—manual and intellectual workers. They are the producers of material goods or services for society, for the people.

I do not mean that workers who were unable to march because they had to work, or because they had to take care of their children, are parasites. Or those who were ill, or even those who just didn't want to march today. I'm speaking only of those who were not represented here because they *could not* be represented by those who work and those who produce. [*Applause*]

This truly is the people. The person who lives as a parasite, or wants to live as a parasite, does not really belong to the people. The only ones entitled to live without working are the disabled, the sick, the elderly, and the children. They are entitled to have us work for them and look out for them; they are entitled to benefit from the work of everyone else. All of us have the duty to work for the children, the elderly, the sick, and the disabled. [*Applause*] What no moral law will ever be able to justify is for the people to work for parasites. [*Applause*] The ones marching today were the working people who will never resign themselves to working for parasites ever again. [*Applause*]

In this manner our nation has come to understand what the revolution is. It has come to understand clearly what the revolution consists of, and how a country frees itself of foreign and domestic parasites. [*Applause*]

We remember that when the largest industries in the country were nationalized, the same way we nationalized U.S. factories[2]—some asked: "But isn't this factory Cuban?" They asked, "How can you nationalize a Cuban factory?" The reason is that such a factory was not Cuban; it was the property of a gentleman. It did not belong to the people; it did not belong to the nation. That's why it was correct to nationalize this factory. In other words, it should pass from the hands of this or that gentleman into the hands of the people, into the hands of the nation. [*Applause*]

It used to be the custom of certain gentlemen to talk a lot about the homeland. They had a very stunted idea of what the homeland is or should be. They were always talking about the homeland and the need to defend the homeland. But which homeland? The homeland of a few? The homeland of the privileged handful? The homeland of a gentleman with a thousand *caballerías* of land[3] and three houses, while others lived in miserable dirt-floor huts on a *guardarraya*?[4]

Which homeland did you have in mind, sir? A homeland where a few have all the opportunities and live off the labor of the rest? Or the homeland of a man who doesn't even have

---

2. In October 1960 the holdings of major Cuban capitalists had been nationalized, following the expropriation of major U.S. imperialist interests a few months earlier in August.

3. One caballería is approximately 33 acres, or 13.5 hectares.

4. Guardarrayas were strips of land located between canefields or on the edge of landed estates. During the many months of unemployment between sugar harvests many agricultural workers, if allowed, planted food crops in these areas in order to survive.

a job? The homeland of a family that lives in a slum? The homeland of the hungry and barefoot child who is begging in the street? Which homeland are you referring to?

What concept of homeland was this? A homeland that was the property of a few, to the exclusion of the rest of the country? Or the homeland of today, where we have won the right to control our destiny, where we have won the right to construct the future that will of necessity be better than today? A homeland that will never again be the property of a few and exist for the enjoyment of a few. The homeland will be, now and forever—as Martí said[5]—"with the participation of all, and for the good of all." Not the homeland of a few, for the good of a few. In the future the homeland will be a place where such injustices—where a few have everything and everyone else has nothing—will no longer exist.

Now we truly can speak of a homeland. Now we truly can have a genuine conception of homeland. Because when we say we are defending the homeland and willing to die for the homeland, it's not for the few, but for all Cubans! [*Applause and shouts of "Patria o muerte!"*]

That is why the privileged and exploiting classes could not have a true conception of homeland. For them, the homeland was a privilege by which they appropriated the labor of others. They wanted others to defend the homeland that belonged to them. That's why when a Yankee monopolist, [*Shouts of "Out with them!"*] a member of the U.S. ruling circles, talks about homeland, he's talking about the homeland of the monopolies, of large banking

---

5. José Martí, a noted poet, writer, speaker, and journalist, founded the Cuban Revolutionary Party in 1892 to fight against Spanish rule and oppose U.S. designs on Cuba. In 1895 the party helped initiate a war of independence against Spain, and Martí was killed in battle the same year. His revolutionary anti-imperialist program is part of the political foundation of the Cuban revolution, and he is considered Cuba's national hero.

capital, of the big businesses owned by a few.

When they talk about homeland, they are thinking about sending Black people from the U.S. South, or Puerto Ricans, or young people from working families in the United States to die, kill, or even murder in defense of those monopolies and those millions—all of which they call "homeland." [*Shouts of "To the wall!"*]

What moral right do they have to do this, other than the right imposed by a ruling and exploiting class? Black people in the U.S. South are denied all rights, made to sit at the back of the bus, and prohibited from entering many places. Deprived of all respect, they don't have millions and they don't have monopolies. What right does the ruling class have to draft a poor Black man to go die to defend their millions, their monopolies, their landed estates, their mines, and their factories? Puerto Ricans have had their right to a sovereign and independent country systematically denied, down to the smallest degree. What right does the ruling class have to draft Puerto Ricans—who have Latin American blood, Latin American traditions, and a Latin American origin—to go die on the battlefield to defend the policy of the great monopolies and the great financial and industrial magnates?

This idea they have of homeland and this fear about security that they often resort to—or often speak of as a pretext—is simply a matter of seeing their monopolies in danger, of seeing their economic interests in danger. Their conception of homeland, of morals, and of law is to mobilize millions of men who have nothing—often men with no rights, as is the case with Puerto Ricans and with Blacks in the U.S. South—and send them to fight and die on the battlefield. That is the conception of homeland held by the ruling classes, the privileged and exploiting classes.

That is why a nation only acquires a genuine idea of homeland when the interests of the privileged minority are eliminated, when a country's wealth becomes the patrimony of everyone, the opportunity of everyone, and the happiness of everyone. Any of these thousands of young people from poor families today have opportunities that they could not even have dreamed of yesterday. Working people know their sons or daughters can go to a school, can receive a scholarship, can go to the university, including to the best universities abroad—which in the past were reserved solely for rich families. Today any family, however poor, has the opportunity to send their child to the best school inside or outside the country, if that young person's talent merits it. Any family knows that thanks to the revolution, their children have the opportunities that previously only children from a handful of families had. And the opportunities multiply fantastically, until they encompass every single family.

Because a country that puts all its mental and physical energy toward a specific aim—whether it's defending the country, creating new wealth for the country, creating new opportunities for the country—can achieve this aim in a way that no ruling and exploiting minority can. Such a minority can never rally the people behind it, with all their fervor and enthusiasm. [Applause]

But the revolution can indeed rally the people, [Applause] with their infinite fervor and enthusiasm. The revolution can indeed take all the people's intelligence, energy, spirit of struggle, and creativity, and channel these onto the road of well-being and progress.

The people we see today are the same ones who yesterday had a skeptical attitude. Today's enthusiastic people who have been standing for fifteen or sixteen hours—men and women, young and old, equally—they are the same ones who yesterday, when it was a case of a public rally they were compelled or paid to attend, were not capable of being on their feet for even an hour.

Today's enthusiastic, heroic, and courageous people are the same ones who were indifferent yesterday. There is one simple reason: yesterday they were working for others; yesterday their sweat, energy, and blood were for others. Today their sweat, energy, and blood are for themselves. [*Applause*]

Think of the men who died in the recent battles. Would it have been worth a single drop of Cuban blood to defend the privileges of the past? Think of those Cubans who were killed—the young workers or children of workers who died less than two weeks ago to defend what we've seen here today. They died to defend those rights that the revolution has given the people. They died to defend today's enthusiasm, today's hope, and today's happiness. For that reason, earlier today, whenever we saw a happy or smiling face full of hope, we thought of each smile as a flower on the graves of the militiamen and soldiers who died. Each smile is a recognition and an expression of gratitude to those who gave their lives.

Had it not been for those lives cut down by selfishness, treachery, and the imperialist aggressor; had it not been for those men willing to die, there would not have been a May Day today. There would not have been a parade today by the Pioneers, the Young Rebels, the women, or the workers who unfurled those flags of the homeland. The athletes would not have marched by.

What would have happened to those young antiaircraft gunners, antitank gunners, or artillerymen? What would have happened to those gallant and disciplined battalions of workers—well armed, well trained, and now a bit more experienced—who marched today through this plaza?

What would have happened to the workers leaders? What would have happened to the workers and the militiamen? What would have happened to their wives, their children, their brothers and sisters, to their factories? What would have happened to them had imperialism been able to establish a beachhead on our territory?

What would have happened to them, their children and

wives, their homes, had the imperialist aggressor been able to take over a piece of our territory? And from there, send their Yankee planes, their Yankee bombs, their napalm bombs, their explosives and shrapnel, to wage a war of attrition against our nation?

This is on top of the economic aggression, the blockade of our exports, the cancellation of our quotas, the embargo of all exports of spare parts or raw materials to our country. Amid all these difficulties presented by imperialist economic aggression, we would simultaneously have had to confront almost daily bombing of our communications lines, our transport system, our production centers, and our cities.

Let's not even talk about what would have become of the people's hopes and aspirations had imperialism been able to defeat the revolution. Because there is no more terrible spectacle in the history of humanity than that of a defeated revolution.

There is the history of the uprising of the slaves in Rome to win their freedom, with thousands of slaves nailed to crosses all along the roads leading to Rome. This should give us an idea of what a defeated revolution is.

There is the history of the Paris Commune, with its frightening toll of workers murdered. This too should give us an idea of what a defeated revolution is.[6]

History teaches that a defeated revolution has to pay an extraordinary toll in blood to victorious reaction. The victorious ruling class demands payment for the anxiety it experienced, for all the interests that were affected, or that were threatened with being affected. But it not only demands payment for present debts; it also seeks to collect, in blood,

---

6. Following the defeat of a slave rebellion against the Roman Empire in 73–72 B.C. led by Spartacus, over 6,000 captured slaves were crucified. After the defeat of the Paris Commune in 1871, over 20,000 were killed, 7,000 deported, and thousands imprisoned.

payment for future debts. It tries to annihilate the revolution down to its very roots.

Of course, under certain circumstances it's impossible to
smash a revolution. I've spoken of revolutions that were defeated before conquering power. What has never happened
before in history is to defeat a revolutionary people that has
truly conquered power. [*Applause*]

I'm only trying to point out what the situation of this
country would have been had imperialism got what it wanted.
I'm trying to point out the kind of May Day our workers
would be having had imperialism got what it wanted!

For this reason, we were thinking about all we owe to
those who fell. This is why we were thinking that every
smile today is a tribute to those who made possible this
happy and hopeful day. [*Applause*]

The blood that was shed in the battle was the blood of
workers and peasants. It was the blood of sons of poor and
working families. It was not the blood of plantation owners, millionaires, thieves, criminals, or exploiters. The blood
that was shed was of those who yesterday were exploited
but today are free. [*Applause*] It was humble blood, honest
blood, working-class blood, creative blood. It was the blood
of patriots, not mercenaries. It was the blood of workers
who voluntarily and spontaneously enlisted in the army of
the homeland. [*Applause*] It was not the blood of conscripts
forced into service by some law. It was the blood of those
who spontaneously and generously offered to confront all
the risks of battle, to defend an ideal, a true ideal they felt
deeply. Not the false and hypocritical ideal that the Yankees
inculcated in their mercenaries, as if they were parrots repeating the word "ideal." [*Applause*]

Not an ideal of parrots; not an ideal to which you pay lip
service. But an ideal from the heart. Not an ideal of those
coming to recover their lost privileges, their lost lands, their
lost banks, their lost factories, their lost riches. Not an ideal

of those who came to recover the easy life, by those who never had a drop of sweat on their brow while always living off the sweat and blood of everyone else. [*Applause*] Not the ideal of the mercenary who sells his soul for the powerful empire's gold.

Rather, it is the ideal of the worker who does not want to continue being exploited. The ideal of the peasant who does not want to lose his land again. The ideal of the young person who does not want to lose his teacher. The ideal of the black person who does not want to be discriminated against anymore. The ideal of the woman who wants to live with rights and dignity. The ideal of working people, those who never lived off the sweat of others. The ideal of those who never considered life as a gift, but as work. The ideal of those who never stole anything from anyone, nor killed anyone in defense of illegitimate interests.

It is the ideal of a working person who defends the revolution because the revolution is everything for him. Because before he was nothing; he was lowly and downtrodden, subject to humiliation, discriminated against and mistreated. He was a man whom the ruling and exploiting class considered to be a nobody. Today he is a somebody, one amongst millions of his people. [*Applause*] And he defends the revolution because the revolution is his life, and because he identifies it with his life, his future, and his hopes.

Before sacrificing these hopes, he would rather lose his life a thousand times. Because he is not thinking selfishly about himself. He is thinking that while he may fall, it won't be in vain, because the cause for which he falls will bring happiness to millions of his brothers and sisters. [*Applause*]

Working-class blood, peasant blood, the blood of the poor was shed by the homeland in the battle against imperialism's mercenaries. What kind of blood and what kind of men did imperialism send here to establish a beachhead? A beachhead from which they could plunge our people into a war of attrition—systematically burning our canefields with incendiary bombs, as they have been doing without even a piece of the national territory from which to try to give some legitimacy for launching their planes. Launching a war of destruction against our factories and our people, as they have been doing when they didn't even have a base here, sending their planes from abroad, at the same time as they were tricking the world in the most cynical manner.

We have a right to say to the people, above all to our visitors, that at the same time three of our airports were simultaneously being bombed by U.S.-made planes, with Yankee bombs and bullets, U.S. news agencies were telling the world that our airports had been attacked by planes from our own air force, with pilots who had deserted that same day. . . .

Who were the people that fought against those workers and peasants? I'm going to tell you.

Of the first thousand mercenaries captured by the revolutionary forces—at the present moment, not counting the crew members of ships, there are close to 1,100 mercenary prisoners.[7] We analyzed the social composition of the first thousand, with the following results: approximately 800 are from wealthy families, whose property collectively comes to 27,566 caballerías of land taken over by the revolution; 9,666 houses, 70 factories, 10 sugar mills, 2 banks, 5 mines, and 2 newspapers. In addition, more than 200 of these 800 belonged to the most exclusive and aristocratic clubs in Havana. Of the remaining 200, 135 were former members of the Batista army, and the other 65 were lumpen or declassed individuals.

---

7. Facts on the four-day trial of 1,179 captured members of Brigade 2506 can be found in the April 7, 1962, entry in the chronology. A separate trial was held in June 1961 of fourteen former Batista henchmen who were notorious murderers and torturers. After being convicted, five were shot and nine were imprisoned. The last of these nine prisoners was released in 1986.

You will remember that during a discussion with the prisoners, I asked if any of them had cut sugarcane and no one came forward. Finally one raised his hand and said that he had once been a sugarcane cutter. If instead of this question, I had asked how many owned large landed estates, 77 would have raised their hands. So this is the social composition of the invaders: 27,556 caballerías of land, 9,666 buildings and houses, 70 factories, 10 sugar mills, 2 banks, 5 mines, and 2 newspapers.

We are sure that if we were to ask all those here how many owned sugar mills, or how many were bank owners, or how many owned large landed estates, there would not be one. Had we asked the combatants who were killed, members of the militias or soldiers of the Revolutionary National Police or Rebel Army; had we asked about the wealth of those who were killed or who fought, you can be sure there would not have been a single bank, a single mine, a single sugar mill, a single apartment building, a single factory, a single plantation, nor would there be a single member of any of the aristocratic clubs that used to exist in this city.

And some of those shameless individuals said they came here to fight for ideals, for free enterprise. Let some idiot come here today to say he was fighting for free enterprise. As if this people did not know more than enough about what free enterprise is. Free enterprise was the slums of Las Yaguas, Llega y Pon, Cueva del Humo, and dozens of other places that surrounded this city. Free enterprise was unemployment for 500,000 Cubans. Free enterprise was hundreds or thousands of families living in guardarrayas. Free enterprise was more than 100,000 peasant families working the land in order to pay a considerable part of their produce to absentee landlords who had never even seen a single seed being planted in those lands. Free enterprise was discrimination, arbitrary acts, outrages against workers and peasants, beatings by police, murders of workers' leaders, Mujalism,[8] contraband, gambling casinos, vice, exploitation, lack of education, illiteracy, and poverty.

How are they going to talk about free enterprise to a people that had almost half a million unemployed, a million and a half illiterates, half a million children without schools, a country where you had to stand in line to get into a hospital—in addition to finding some politician to help, in exchange for selling him your vote! How can they come talk about free enterprise to a people that knows what free enterprise is: aristocratic clubs for a few thousand families while there are beggars in the streets, while hungry children go swimming at El Morro, next to sewage, because they could not afford to go to a beach—because the beaches were off-limits and for the aristocrats; the beaches were for the fortunate beneficiaries of free enterprise.

They could not even dream of going to Varadero beach, because Varadero was for a few wealthy families. They could not even dream that the child of a poor person could go to a university, because the universities were only for the privileged of free enterprise. They could not dream that this child would go study languages in Europe, because the only ones who went to Europe were the privileged of free enterprise. They could not dream that the child of a construction worker or any low-paid worker could attend high school. A sugar worker could not dream that his child could graduate from high school, not to mention become a doctor or engineer. Because the child of a worker could only go to school if the worker lived in the capital and could af-

---

8. Eusebio Mujal was general secretary of the Confederation of Cuban Workers (CTC) under the Batista dictatorship. During these years the union officialdom, amid widespread corruption, attempted to police the labor movement for the bosses and Batista. Mujal fled Cuba on January 1, 1959.

ford to send him—even then the possibilities were few—
but 75 or 90 percent of the workers' children lived in areas
where there were no secondary schools and they lacked the
resources to pay for room and board in the city, so there
was no opportunity to go to school. That opportunity was
exclusively for the children of the beneficiaries of free enterprise. A cart driver or a sugarcane cutter could not even
dream that his daughter would march in this parade, or do
a tap dance and wear elegant clothing. A peasant could not
even dream that his son could go study agriculture in the
Soviet Union. Nor could working families dream that their
children would have the opportunity to study diplomatic
law, mechanics, or any other profession, because these opportunities, with only a few exceptions, were for the children of wealthy families.

Some little rich boy, who doesn't know what it means to
work, to sweat, or to suffer, and who came to murder peasants
and workers—how can he tell us that he shed the people's
blood in order to defend free enterprise? [*Prolonged applause*]
And not just the free enterprise owned by his daddy, but the
free enterprise of United Fruit Company, the free enterprise
of the Yankee electric power monopoly, the free enterprise
of the company that used to control the telephones, the free
enterprise of the companies that used to control the refineries.
These weren't even free enterprises; they were monopolies
that as such virtually eliminated competition.

When these gentlemen who came here, armed by imperialism, say they were defending free enterprise, what they
were really defending were the monopolies. Monopolies in
fact are against free enterprise, because they control the
entire industry, its prices and its resources. Its method consists precisely in ruining everyone else. They were not even
defending free enterprise, properly speaking. These very
ignorant or very stupid people were defending the Yankee
monopoly interests here and abroad. [*Applause*] How can

they tell the Cuban people that they came to defend the interests of free enterprise?

They also say they came to defend the 1940 constitution.[9] [*Laughter*] It's curious that they did nothing to defend the 1940 constitution when it was being torn to shreds by the Batista tyranny. They did nothing to defend the constitution when it was being destroyed in the March 10 barracks coup with the complicity of first, the U.S. embassy; second, the reactionary clergy [*Shouts of "Out with them!"*]; and third—or rather first, together with the others—the economically dominant classes, the monopolies, and the rich of our country, with the complicity of a judiciary corrupted down to the marrow of their bones, and of a whole series of corrupt politicians. It's truly cynical to see a little rich boy together with mayors, representatives, and politicians of all types from the Batista years saying they were coming to defend the 1940 constitution. Because it was precisely Batista who trampled on and destroyed that constitution, with the complicity of imperialism and the ruling classes. Also accompanying these little rich boys were hundreds of former members of the army of the Batista tyranny, and along with them a bunch of criminals and torturers, as well as a bunch of corrupt politicians—all saying they were coming to defend the 1940 constitution. [*Applause*]

In point of fact, inasmuch as there were any advanced or revolutionary aspects of the 1940 constitution, the only

9. The Cuban constitution of 1940 was a document that reflected the anti-imperialist sentiment that remained strong among the Cuban people in the years following the 1933 revolutionary upsurge that toppled the U.S.-supported dictatorship of Gerardo Machado. It included language advocating land reform and other democratic measures, but these provisions remained dead letters under the successive pro-imperialist regimes. The 1940 constitution was abrogated entirely when Fulgencio Batista seized power in a 1952 coup. Its restitution was a demand of the July 26 Movement in the fight against Batista.

government that has respected it, abided by it, and moved it forward is precisely the revolutionary government.

Because that constitution said, "The system of large landed estates is prohibited," and that "to bring about its disappearance"—the constitution spoke of "its disappearance"— "the law will establish the maximum amount of landed property that any agricultural or industrial enterprise can possess." Obviously that provision was never carried out. Why not? Because there needed to be a subsequent law brought into Congress. And who was in Congress? The politicians, the lawyers for the Yankee monopolies, the owners of the large landed estates, the millionaires, the rich. Only by way of exception was a tiny handful of workers leaders in that House and Senate, where they were condemned to remain in the minority, because all the newspapers, all the radio and television stations belonged to the same ruling economic sectors who owned and had a monopoly over the means of dissemination of ideas. Any attempt to do something on behalf of the peasants was drowned in lies.

Back then it was very difficult for the people to learn about the evictions of peasants, about the frightful misery the peasants lived in, about the extremely high infant mortality rate. Because tens of thousands of children of all ages died without a single doctor. The fact that tens of thousands of children died for lack of doctors and medicine was not a crime as far as the ruling class was concerned. It was not a crime as far as the beneficiaries of free enterprise were concerned. This did not pain them. This was not important for them. Society hardly even knew of these things!

The members of that Congress who had to decide on the supplementary provisions of the constitution were precisely the owners of large landed estates, the millionaires, and the lawyers for the Yankee monopolies. There was no Agrarian Reform Law then. Despite the fact that the law said, "The system of large landed estates is prohibited," a single Yankee company owned 17,000 caballerías of land. And despite the fact that another provision of the 1940 constitution said that "the law will determine the appropriate norms so that the land returns to Cuban hands," in nineteen years after the 1940 constitution was approved and went into effect, there was not a single law that took even a single caballería from a single Yankee monopoly that owned 17,000.

Another monopoly had 15,000 caballerías, another had 10,000, which is almost 140,000 hectares. There were companies here with more than 200,000 hectares, of the best land in Cuba. The constitution said that "the system of large landed estates is prohibited," that "the law shall establish the maximum amount of land," and that "the land shall revert to Cuban hands." But it was never carried out.

The constitution also stated that "the state shall exhaust all means at its disposal to give work to every worker, manual or intellectual." Does this refer to teachers? The revolution found over 10,000 teachers without a classroom, without work, and it immediately gave them jobs, because there were also half a million children who needed schools. Let me repeat: "The state shall exhaust all the means at its disposal to give work to every worker, manual or intellectual, in order to provide them a decent existence." This is what the revolution did. It exhausted all the means at its disposal for this. And if it didn't exhaust all the means at its disposal, it was prepared to exhaust all the necessary means to give them jobs. Yes, jobs, because that's what the constitution ordered. [Applause]

Those basic principles, which would have resolved the problem of hundreds of thousands of peasants, hundreds of thousands of unemployed, were set forth in the constitution but not complied with. . . .

Those who follow the instructions of the U.S. State Department, promoting the policy of isolating Cuba, those complying with imperialism's orders and breaking relations with a Latin American country under attack by imperialism, are miserable traitors to the interests and feelings of the Americas. [*Applause*]

These facts show us the rotten and corrupt politicking that prevails in many Latin American countries. It shows how the Cuban Revolution has turned those business-as-usual and corrupt forms upside down in order to establish completely new forms of life in our country.

To those who talk to us about the 1940 constitution, we say that the 1940 constitution is already too outdated and old for us. We are way beyond it, and have outgrown the 1940 constitution like an old jacket. That constitution was good for its time although it was never carried out. That constitution has been bypassed by this revolution, which, as we have said, is a socialist revolution. [*Applause*]

We must talk of a new constitution. Yes, a new constitution, but not a bourgeois constitution, not a constitution corresponding to the rule of an exploiting class over other classes. What we need is a constitution corresponding to a new social system, one without the exploitation of man by man. That new social system is called socialism, and this constitution will therefore be a socialist constitution. [*Applause*]

If Mr. Kennedy does not like socialism, well, we do not like imperialism! We do not like capitalism! [*Shouts*]

We have as much right to protest the existence of an imperialist and capitalist system ninety miles from our shore as he feels he has the right to protest over the existence of a socialist system ninety miles from his shore. [*Applause*]

Militia members ready artillery during Bay of Pigs invasion.

Appendix 1

CUBAN REVOLUTIONARY GROUND FORCES
IN THE BATTLE OF PLAYA GIRÓN

From Australia through Playa Larga to Playa Girón

Captain José Ramón Fernández

Infantry, tanks, artillery, antiaircraft units
Rebel Army, Revolutionary National Militias,
Revolutionary National Police

From Covadonga through San Blas to Playa Girón

Commander Filiberto Olivera Moya

Infantry, tanks, artillery, antiaircraft units
Rebel Army, Revolutionary National Militias

From Yaguaramas through San Blas to Playa Girón

Commander René de los Santos

Infantry, tanks, artillery
Rebel Army, Revolutionary National Militias

From Yaguaramas to Cocodrilo

Commander Raúl Menéndez Tomassevich

Infantry
Revolutionary National Militias

From Cienfuegos through Caleta Redonda to Caleta Buena

Captain Orlando Pupo Peña

Infantry
Revolutionary National Militias

Information provided by the Revolutionary Armed Forces of Cuba

José Ramón Fernández (center) inspects weapons captured from Brigade 2506.

Appendix 2

Military units

5 infantry batallions

1 heavy gun battalion

1 paratroop batallion

1 tank company

1 underwater demolition team

Weaponry and equipment

5 M-41 Sherman tanks, with 76 mm. guns.

10 armored cars equipped with .50 caliber machine guns

75 bazookas

60 mortars

21 recoilless 75 mm. and 57 mm. cannon

44 .50 caliber machine guns

39 light and heavy .30 caliber machine guns

8 flame throwers

22,000 hand grenades

108 Browning automatic rifles

470 M-3 submachine guns

635 Garand rifles and M-1 carbines

465 pistols and other light weapons

1 tanker truck for air fuel

1 mobile crane

1 bulldozer

2 large water trucks

numerous small trucks and tractors

This list has been compiled by the editors from various sources.

Naval craft

5   armed freighters (*Houston, Atlántico, Río Escondido, Caribe, Lake Charles*)

2   LCIs [Landing Craft, Infantry] (*Blagar, Barbara J*), from which the main CIA personnel escorting the brigade operated

3   LCU barges [Landing Craft, Utility] for transport of tanks, armored trucks, and other heavy equipment

4   LCVP barges [Landing Craft, Vehicle, Personnel] for troop transport

36   aluminum boats

Air power

16   B-26 bombers

8   C-54 troop transport planes

6   C-46 troop transport planes

2   PBY Catalina seaplanes

U.S. Navy escort*

1   aircraft carrier (USS *Essex*), with squadron of 40 fighter jets and 1 Marine battalion

1   amphibious helicopter carrier (USS *Boxer*)

5   destroyers (USS *Conway*, USS *Cony*, USS *Eaton*, USS *Murray*, USS *Wailer*)

2   submarines (USS *Cobbler*, USS *Threadfin*)

2   destroyer escorts (USS *Bache*, USS *Beale*)

1   LSD [Landing Ship, Dock] (USS *San Marcos*), which transported the mercenaries' LCVPs and LCUs from Nicaragua to the waters off Cuba

1   destroyer off the coast of Oriente province (USS *Northampton*)

The U.S. task force personnel consisted of some 6,000 servicemen.

---

* These are partial figures. Some accounts, including Edward Ferrer's *Operation Puma*, report that up to nine other U.S. warships were deployed as part of the Bay of Pigs support operation.

Chronology, glossary, further reading

Chronology

1952

March 10 – Coup d'état brings retired general Fulgencio Batista to power in Cuba. Batista cancels scheduled elections and, with Washington's support, consolidates brutal military dictatorship. Fidel Castro, a leader of anti-imperialist struggles in Cuba since his student days at the University of Havana in the latter 1940s, begins organizing a revolutionary movement to overthrow the Batista tyranny.

1953

July 26 – Some 160 revolutionaries led by Fidel Castro launch insurrectionary attacks on the Moncada army garrison in Santiago de Cuba and on the Carlos Manuel de Céspedes garrison in nearby Bayamo. The combatants fail to take their objectives, and more than 50 captured revolutionaries are murdered. Fidel Castro and 27 other fighters are subsequently captured, tried, and sentenced to up to 15 years in prison.

1955

May 15 – Following a nationwide amnesty campaign, Fidel Castro and the other imprisoned Moncadistas are released. Within several weeks the July 26 Revolutionary Movement is formed, taking as its program Castro's 1953 courtroom defense speech during his trial for the Moncada attack:

"History Will Absolve Me." In July Castro and other revolutionaries go to Mexico, where they prepare to launch a revolutionary war in the Sierra Maestra mountains of eastern Cuba.

1956

November–December – 82 members of the July 26 Movement, including Fidel Castro, Raúl Castro, Che Guevara, Camilo Cienfuegos, and Juan Almeida, depart Mexico aboard the yacht *Granma* and land in southeastern Cuba to initiate the revolutionary war against the U.S.-backed dictatorship. After surprise attack by Batista's forces in which 42 rebels are killed or captured, the newborn Rebel Army is consolidated by other expeditionaries and initial peasant recruits. It encompasses 24 combatants at the end of the year.

1957

January 17 – Rebel Army overruns army unit in La Plata, a coastal outpost in the Sierra Maestra.

May 28 – Rebel Army defeats Batista forces at well-fortified army garrison at El Uvero.

July 21 – Rebel Army organizes second column under command of Che Guevara.

August – General strike in Santiago de Cuba protests dictatorship's assassination of July 26 Movement leader Frank País.

1958

February 16–17 – Rebel victory at Pino del Agua marks decisive shift in military relation of forces, opening several months of expanded operations by Rebel Army.

April 9 – July 26 Movement calls general strike throughout Cuba. Announced without adequate preparation, the strike fails. Batista forces step up repression.

May–July – Batista launches "encircle and annihilate" offensive, sending 10,000 troops into the Sierra Maestra. Rebel Army, with 300 fighters and 200 usable rifles, concentrates forces around command post of Fidel Castro's Column no. 1, draws in government troops, and defeats them in course of several decisive battles. The regime's offensive is crushed in late July.

August–December – After breaking Batista army offensive, Rebel Army launches counterattack. Columns commanded by Che Guevara and Camilo Cienfuegos lead westward campaign from Sierra Maestra mountains to Las Villas province in central Cuba. Rebel Army fronts in eastern Cuba led by Fidel Castro, Raúl Castro, and Juan Almeida establish a liberated territory. By late December major cities and towns in eastern and central Cuba are cut off and surrounded by Rebel Army. The December 31 victory of Guevara's Las Villas column in taking Santa Clara, Cuba's third-largest city, seals the fate of Batista dictatorship.

1959

January 1 – In face of the advancing Rebel Army under the command of Fidel Castro and a popular insurrection led by the July 26 Movement, U.S.-backed dictator Fulgencio Batista flees to the Dominican Republic.

January 2–8 – Fidel Castro and main rebel columns march from Santiago de Cuba to Havana. Along the way and in the capital, hundreds of thousands turn out to greet the victorious army. Camilo Cienfuegos and Che Guevara assume command of the two main army bases in Havana, Camp Columbia and La Cabaña respectively.

February 13 – Sugarcane fields in San Carlos and in Jovellanos in central Cuba are set on fire by counterrevolutionary forces.

February 16 – Fidel Castro becomes prime minister at the request of the Council of Ministers, replacing José Miró Cardona.

February 27 – Revolutionary government approves law reducing electricity rates.

March–April – In acts of economic sabotage, 375 tons of sugarcane is burned in Jagüey Grande, and cane is set afire in Jovellanos as well. Two Cuban passenger planes are hijacked and forced to fly to Miami.

March 6 – Law reducing house and apartment rents by 30–50 percent is approved by revolutionary government.

March 10 – Revolutionary Air Force created.

March 22 – In response to initiative by workers in San Antonio de los Baños requesting military training to defend the revolution, Castro calls for creation of popular militias. Later that week, militias begin to be set up in cities and towns across Cuba. These include the establishment of workers militias in factories, as well as special militia units of peasants and of students.

– Racial discrimination in jobs and public facilities is outlawed and militias begin to enforce.

May – School in Matanzas province is burned down and Tinguaro sugar mill in that same province is attacked.

May 17 – Revolutionary government initiates an extensive agrarian reform, confiscating the large landed estates of foreign and Cuban owners, and distributing titles to some 110,000 tenant farmers, sharecroppers, and squatters.

June 5 – Cuban embassy in Dominican Republic is attacked and two Cuban diplomats assaulted. The attack results in the death of a Dominican child.

June 10 – The car of the Cuban ambassador to Haiti is machinegunned. The ambassador is unhurt but the driver and a Cuban sugar industry official are seriously wounded.

July 4 – Cuba's consul in Miami, Alonso Hidalgo, is beaten by former Batista henchmen and hospitalized.

July 14 – A Cuban DC-3 plane is hijacked and forced to land in Miami.

July 25 – A Cessna plane, on a flight originating in the United States, is shot down in Havana province. The plane is attempting to pick up Cubans wanted for crimes committed during the Batista dictatorship and help them flee the country.

August 13 – A plane bearing armed counterrevolutionaries organized by the dictatorship of Rafael Trujillo in the Dominican Republic is captured after landing at the airport of Trinidad in south-central Cuba. The plane is the same one used by Fulgencio Batista to flee Cuba seven months earlier. The counterrevolutionaries belong to the Anti-Communist Legion of the Caribbean, which includes individuals from various countries, among them a large number of Cubans, several of whom were officers in Batista's army. In the fighting two of them are killed and nine taken prisoner; two Cuban citizens are also killed and nine wounded.

September 21 – A Rebel Army soldier is killed in Pinar del Río during the capture of a group of counterrevolutionaries led by U.S. citizens Austin Young and Peter John Lambton. Weapons and other equipment are taken from them.

October – Planes taking off from the United States bomb two sugar mills in Camagüey province several times each. Another sugar mill in Pinar del Río province is bombed by a plane originating in the United States. Another plane taking off from U.S. territory is shot down by Cuban forces while attacking the town of Sagua la Grande.

October 2–10 – Two Cuban planes and a Cuban yacht are hijacked and taken to Florida.

October 16 – Creation of Ministry of the Revolutionary Armed Forces, headed by Raúl Castro. The new ministry puts under a single command the Rebel Army, Revolutionary Navy, Revolutionary Air Force, and Revolutionary National Police.

Late October – President Dwight D. Eisenhower approves a proposal by the State Department and CIA to organize armed Cuban counterrevolutionary groups. As part of this program, Cuban exiles based in the United States mount sea raids against Cuba.

October 21 – A B-25 plane strafes Havana, killing two people and wounding 50. The plane had taken off from the Pompano

Beach airport, 35 miles north of Miami.

– Huber Matos, military commander of Camagüey province, tries to spark a mutiny among Rebel Army officers there. A revolutionary mobilization in Camagüey puts down the attempt. Matos is arrested by Rebel Army commander Camilo Cienfuegos.

October 22 – A passenger train is machine-gunned in Las Villas.

October 26 – Announcement of creation of Revolutionary National Militias, consolidating local workers and peasants units formed earlier in the year.

October 28 – Plane carrying Camilo Cienfuegos is lost at sea. Cienfuegos is returning to Havana after suppressing mutiny led by Huber Matos.

November 10 – Water pumping station in the municipality of Matanzas is sabotaged.

December 2 – Railroad in Pedro Betancourt in Matanzas province is sabotaged.

December 11 – J.C. King, head of the CIA's Western Division, writes Richard Bissell, deputy director for plans (covert operations), and CIA Director Allen Dulles. King urges "violent action" against the Cuban government aimed at "the overthrow of Castro within one year." He recommends that "thorough consideration be given to the elimination of Fidel Castro."

1960

January – With Cuban sugar harvest in full swing, planes taking off from United States burn cane fields in Santa Cruz del Norte; in Las Villas province (5,000 tons plus several houses); in Sagua la Grande and again in Las Villas; in Camagüey (187,500 tons); in Oriente province, killing one person; and in Marianao (more than 525 tons).

– Task Force WH/4, Branch 4 of the Western Hemisphere Division of the CIA is established. Its job is to carry out Eisenhower's request for a clandestine program to overthrow the revolutionary government.

January 2 – Counterrevolutionaries burn down several houses at a peasant cooperative in Jovellanos.

January 10 – Gunmen open fire on Capt. Manuel Borjas, Rebel Army director of operations in Pinar del Río province, seriously wounding him.

January 21 – A plane drops four bombs—of 100 pounds each—on Havana. The pilot is U.S. citizen Bob Spining and the co-pilot is Eduardo Whitehouse, a former officer of the Batista regime.

January 27 – Members of the pro-Batista group "Rosa Blanca" (White Rose) attack a rally of 200 defenders of the revolution in New York's Central Park. Police join the attack. Several participants in the rally are hospitalized.

February – Planes taking off from the United States bomb several sugarcane fields in Camagüey, Matanzas, and Las Villas (75,000 tons).

February 1 – Counterrevolutionaries organized by CIA burn more than 1,250 tons of sugarcane in Matanzas.

February 18 – A Piper Comanche 250 blows up in mid-air during attempted bombing of sugar mill in Matanzas province. The pilot, U.S. citizen Robert Ellis Frost, is killed. The plane had taken off from the Tamiani airport in Florida, and documents found in the wreckage show Frost had carried out three previous bombing missions against Cuba.

March – The CIA begins training 300 Cuban exiles for armed action against the revolution. The training begins in the United States and the Panama Canal Zone; it moves to Guatemala in June.

– Planes taking off from the United States burn sugarcane fields in Oriente and Las Villas (a total of 6,500 tons); in Pinar del Río; in Matanzas (25,000 tons); and again in Las Villas and Matanzas.

March 4 – *La Coubre*, a French ship carrying Belgian small arms to Cuba, explodes in Havana harbor, killing eighty-one people. The weapons had been purchased with contributions by Cuban workers. At a mass rally the following day

Fidel Castro proclaims slogan of Cuban Revolution: *"Patria o muerte!"* [Our country or death].

March 17 – U.S. President Eisenhower approves "A Program of Covert Action against the Castro Regime." The CIA plan includes setting up a radio station to broadcast into Cuba, and calls for training paramilitary cadres for immediate deployment in Cuba. During White House meeting, Eisenhower says he knows of "no better plan" but that "our hand should not show in anything that is done."

March 21 – A Piper Comanche 250 is shot down over Cuba, and its crew members Howard Lewis Rundquist and William J. Shergales—both U.S. citizens—are arrested. The plane, which had taken off from Fort Lauderdale, Florida, had the mission of smuggling out criminals from the Batista regime who had been detained by the revolutionary government.

Mid-April – CIA director of covert actions, Richard Bissell, orders that an anti-Cuba radio station on Swan Island off the Caribbean coast of Honduras be in operation within a month.

April 23 – Cuba's foreign minister Raúl Roa states publicly, "I can guarantee categorically that Guatemalan territory is being used at this very time with the complicity of President Ydígoras and the assistance of United Fruit, as a bridgehead for an invasion of our country."

May 8 – Cuba and the Union of Soviet Socialist Republics establish diplomatic relations.

May 12 – Piper Apache plane piloted by U.S. citizen Matthew Edward Duke is shot down west of Havana, near Mariel. Duke had carried out 33 incursions into Cuban airspace.

May 17 – Radio Swan goes on the air, reaching Cuba and the entire Caribbean. Its programs are taped in Miami and broadcast from Swan Island. The station is ostensibly operated by the Gibraltar Steamship Corporation of New York City, a CIA front. In September the *New York Times* publishes a front-page story about the station and its ownership.

May 19 – CIA officials assemble team of counterrevolutionary Cuban exiles on Useppa Island off Florida for training. This is the initial nucleus of what eventually becomes Brigade 2506.

June 5–7 – Two Cuban boats are hijacked. One is forced to go to Miami, the other to Key West.

June 16 – A new rural school is burned down in Pinar del Río.

June 29–July 1 – Revolutionary government takes over Texaco, Esso, and Shell refineries following their refusal to refine petroleum purchased by Cuba from the Soviet Union.

Early July – Counterrevolutionary forces training on Florida's Ussepa Island are transferred to the 5,000-acre Helvetia plantation in the mountains of Guatemala, owned by the brother of that country's ambassador to the United States. The training camp becomes known as "Base Trax."

July 5 – A plane en route to Cuba from Spain is hijacked to Miami by two crew members. The rest of the crew and passengers are allowed to return to Cuba, as they demand.

July 6 – Eisenhower orders 95 percent reduction in quota of sugar Washington had earlier agreed to purchase from Cuba. Across the island, Cubans respond by proclaiming: *"Sin cuota pero sin bota"*—without the U.S. sugar quota but without the Yankee boot.

July 9 – Soviet Union announces it will purchase all Cuban sugar the U.S. refuses to buy.

July 23 – CIA director Allen Dulles meets with Democratic presidential candidate John F. Kennedy at the Kennedy family compound in Hyannis Port on Cape Cod. Among other things, Dulles informs Kennedy of the training operation and plans of Cuban counterrevolutionaries.

July 28 – Che Guevara addresses some 900 young people from across the Americas and the world at opening session of First Latin American Youth Congress in Havana. "If this revolution is Marxist," he tells them, ". . . it is because it discovered, by its own methods, the road pointed out by Marx."

August – To carry out assassination attempts on Fidel Castro, Richard Bissell approves hiring organized crime figures who had been linked to gambling casinos and brothels in Havana closed down by the revolution. Over the next several months, a series of unsuccessful plots are organized with help of mafia figures Johnny Rosselli and Sam Giancana. Fifteen years later, Giancana is murdered in his home shortly before he is scheduled to testify before 1975 hearings on White House assassination plots before the U.S. Senate Intelligence Committee. Rosselli, who appears before the Senate committee in June 1975, is murdered shortly afterwards; his decomposed remains are found in a drum in waters off North Miami Beach in August 1976.

– *Miami Herald* learns of CIA training of Cuban exiles near Homestead, Florida. After meeting with CIA director Allen Dulles, the editors suppress their reporter's story.

August 6 – In response to escalating U.S. economic aggression and sabotage, the revolutionary government in Cuba, following massively popular outpourings, expropriates major U.S. companies. By October virtually all major Cuban-owned industry is also nationalized, involving further mass mobilizations.

August 23 – The Federation of Cuban Women (FMC) is founded, with the aim of increasing the participation of women in city and countryside in building the militias, organizing the literacy campaign, promoting the establishment of child care facilities, and advancing the place of women in all aspects of social and political life.

August 25 – A plane taking off from the United States strafes the La Palma sugar mill in Pinar del Río, seriously wounding a Cuban citizen. The following day another sugarcane field is burned in Camagüey.

August 28 – At meeting of foreign ministers in San José, Costa Rica, the Organization of American States (OAS) adopts a U.S.-sponsored document aimed against Cuba asserting that all member states are "under obligation to submit to the discipline of the Inter-American system" to reject aid from the Soviet Union or China. The Cuban delegation submits a counterresolution to this so-called Declaration of San José and walks out of the meeting after its proposal is defeated.

September – Four Cubans are murdered in Las Villas province by counterrevolutionary bands. Another band robs a peasant cooperative.

September 2 – Rally of 1 million in Havana approves by acclamation the First Declaration of Havana condemning the Declaration of San José as an assault by U.S. imperialism on the "sovereignty and dignity" of the peoples of the Americas and on the "right of each nation to self-determination." It calls for "the right of the peasants to the land; the right of the workers to the fruit of their labor . . . and the right of nations to nationalize the imperialist monopolies."

September 4 – Electrical power service in Havana is hit by dynamite explosion.

September 26 – Fidel Castro addresses United Nations General Assembly. Among many U.S. attacks on Cuba Castro describes, he denounces the Swan Island radio station. In the course of his address, Castro announces that in 1961 Cuba will eliminate illiteracy.

September 28 – Formation of Committees for the Defense for the Revolution (CDRs) is announced in Cuba. These are to be popular organs of vigilance and mobilization against counterrevolutionary activity organized and financed by the U.S. government.

– First attempted CIA weapons drop to counterrevolutionaries inside Cuba. The air crews miss the drop zone by 7 miles. That same day the CIA undertakes its first supply mission by sea, which succeeds. Of some 68 air drops between then and March 1961, all but 7 fail to reach rightist bands.

October 4 – Some 25 counterrevolutionaries, among them 3 U.S. citizens, land near the Guantánamo Naval Base, armed with 100 weapons.

October 7 – Foreign minister Raúl Roa speaking before the UN, denounces U.S plans to invade Cuba and describes the exact location and other details of Guatemala bases run by the CIA.

October 13 – Revolutionary government nationalizes Cuban- and foreign-owned banks, as well as 382 large Cuban-owned industries.

October 14 – Urban reform law approved, nationalizing housing; Cubans are guaranteed right to their dwellings.

– Miami office of Cubana Airlines is attacked.

October 19 – The U.S. government, with bipartisan support, decrees a partial embargo against trade with Cuba.

October 24 – Remaining U.S. companies in Cuba are expropriated by the revolutionary government. The law nationalizing these properties assesses them at the value the companies themselves stated for taxation purposes under the previous pro-imperialist regimes, and it offers payment in 30-year bonds at 2 percent interest compounded annually. Payments are to be funded by setting aside 25 percent of the dollars received from sugar sales to the United States each year.

November 8 – John F. Kennedy elected president. Transition briefings begin.

December – Close to 600 counterrevolutionary Cubans begin seven-week training program in Guatemala. José Pérez San Román is appointed brigade commander by CIA.

– Over 40,000 members of the Revolutionary National Militia are mobilized to fight the counterrevolutionary bands in the Escambray mountains. Over the next two months, in what becomes known as the "cleanup" operation, they create a cordon, and, with the help of peasants in the area, eliminate or capture the members of most of the bands.

December 8 – The CIA calls for creation of an air strip at Puerto Cabezas, Nicaragua, for supply missions to counterrevolutionaries operating in Cuba.

December 31 – Arson attack by counterrevolutionaries destroys La Época department store in Havana.

1961

January 3 – Washington breaks diplomatic relations with Cuba.

– Eisenhower tells his advisers he would like to take military action against the Cuban government prior to the January 20 inauguration of the new administration. In discussing a possible pretext, according to a White House memorandum on the meeting, the president asks the advisers if they "could think of manufacturing something that would be generally acceptable." Secretary of State Christian Herter suggests staging an attack on the U.S.-controlled Guantánamo Naval Base and blaming it on the Cuban government.

– Anticipating increased danger of an assault during the transition in U.S. administrations, Cuba orders a general mobilization of the Revolutionary National Militias. Tens of thousands of workers and peasants are put on active duty. Mass meetings and demonstrations of workers take place throughout the country.

January 4 – CIA officials outline plan for invasion of Cuba by forces it is organizing. The plan states: "The initial mission of the invasion force will be to seize and defend a small area. . . . There will be no early attempt to break out of the lodgment for further offensive operations unless and until there is a general uprising against the Castro regime or overt military intervention by United States forces has taken place. . . . If matters do not eventuate as predicated above, the lodgment . . . can be used as the site for establishment of a provisional government which can be recognized by the United States. . . . The way will then be paved for United States military intervention aimed at pacification of Cuba."

– That same day, addressing the United Nations, Cuban foreign minister Raúl Roa states: "At this moment Cuba is imminently threatened with an invasion by the United States," a threat greatly increased by "the initiative taken by the United States in breaking off relations with Cuba." After detailing once again Washington's recruitment, training, and equipping of counterrevolutionary forces in Guatemala and the United States, Roa warns that once the invaders have "established their beachhead, the 'patriots' could form a provisional government and ask for assistance of the government of the United States in order to pacify the country."

January 5 – Volunteer teacher Conrado Benítez and peasant Eliodoro Rodríguez Linares are murdered by members of a counterrevolutionary band near Trinidad in the Escambray mountains.

January 6 – Che Guevara reports to Cuban people on economic agreements signed with Soviet Union and other countries.

January 7 – Cuban worker Manuel Prieto is arrested and beaten by U.S. soldiers from the Guantánamo Naval Base.

January 9 – Four Cuban fishermen are killed when their fishing boat, *El Pensativo*, is attacked from a speedboat.

January 17 – U.S. government imposes ban on travel by U.S. citizens to Cuba.

January 19 – On the eve of Kennedy's inauguration, Eisenhower tells the president-elect that preparations for the assault on Cuba are going well and that the new administration's job is to carry the operation through to completion.

January 20 – John F. Kennedy inaugurated president of the United States.

– A mass rally is held in Havana to greet militia members returning to their workplaces following the conclusion of the mobilization. Fidel Castro tells them, "If they attack us, they will not find our people sleeping, but awake and in the trenches."

January 25 – At meeting with Joint Chiefs of Staff, Kennedy approves increase in size of the invasion force, in view of Cuba's increasing strength and preparedness.

February 1–5 – Three bombs explode in Havana and one in Santa Clara. A tobacco warehouse is burned down.

February 8 – Kennedy authorizes creation of a junta of anti-Castro leaders to give political cover to the counterrevolutionary brigade.

February 28 – A girl's academy in Havana is bombed; nine students and teachers are wounded.

March 4 – A U.S. plane is shot down over Havana.

March 8 – A gas station is torched in Oriente province. Simultaneously 12 delivery trucks at the nationalized Coca Cola factory are vandalized and an explosive device is detonated at the nationalized electricity company.

March 13 – The Hermanos Díaz oil refinery in Santiago de Cuba, formerly owned by Texaco, is attacked by a sabotage team. A Cuban sentry is killed, another Cuban seriously injured, and fire damage done to the refinery. The saboteurs disembark from the U.S. ship *Barbara J*, used a month later as a base of CIA operations during the invasion at the Bay of Pigs.

March 16 – Allen Dulles and Richard Bissell present Kennedy with alternative plans for the Cuba invasion. Kennedy rejects plan to land near Trinidad south of the Escambray mountains and authorizes proposed invasion in the area of the Bay of Pigs.

– Cuba announces that 420 counterrevolutionary bandits in the Escambray have been captured or killed.

March 18 – The CIA's former Havana station chief assembles leaders of the various Cuban exile groups in a Miami motel and threatens to cut off their support unless they put aside factional rivalries and create a unified body. Three days later they form the Cuban Revolutionary Council, with José Miró Cardona as president.

March 31 – Kennedy abolishes remaining 5 percent of Cuba's sugar quota.

Early April – The CIA's mafia contacts organize a new assassination attempt on Castro, through poison pills. The CIA authorizes funds for the operation to be taken from the invasion budget.

– *U.S. News and World Report* informs White House it will withhold details from scheduled article on invasion plan. The *New Republic*, at Kennedy's request after reading galleys of article headlined "Our Men in Miami," agrees not to run it.

April 4 – The Revolutionary Armed Forces forms the Central Army, commanded by Juan Almeida. Its responsibilities encompass the central part of the island. Within the next two months, Eastern and Western armies are also formed.

April 7 – *New York Times* runs a story on counterrevolutionary training bases in Florida, saying plans for invasion of Cuba are in final stages. Following a direct intervention by Kennedy, the *Times* publisher reduces the front-page story from a four-column lead article to a one-column account.

April 12 – *New York Times* runs two-column front-page article headlined, "President Bars Using U.S. Force to Oust Castro."

April 13 – Counterrevolutionary agents set fire to the El Encanto department store in Havana. The fire kills one worker, Fe del Valle.

April 14 – Hijackers divert a Cubana Airlines plane to Jacksonville, Florida, and request asylum there.

April 15 – As prelude to planned invasion, eight planes attack airfields at Santiago de Cuba, San Antonio de los Baños, and Havana in an attempt to destroy Cuba's air force planes on the ground. The attacks kill seven and wound fifty-three. The strikes had been formally authorized by Kennedy the day before.

– After shooting up the tail wing of a plane at their air base in Puerto Cabezas, Nicaragua, a B-26 bomber is flown to Miami. Implementing a plan approved by Kennedy ten days earlier, the pilot says he is a disaffected Cuban air force pilot who was responsible for one of the bombing attacks on Cuba. This transparent lie is widely spread by U.S. media and presented at the United Nations by U.S. Ambassador Adlai Stevenson. In UN debate, Cuba's foreign minister Raúl Roa accuses Washington of responsibility for the crime, saying it is "undoubtedly the prologue to a large-scale invasion planned, organized, provisioned, armed, and financed by the government of the United States."

– Cuba orders mobilization of all combat units and places them on alert.

– Some 160 counterrevolutionaries trained in New Orleans hover off the eastern end of Cuba with the objective of making a diversionary landing near Imías in the Baracoa region, 30 miles northeast of Guantánamo. Fearing engagement with Cuban defense forces in the area, squad leader Nino Díaz aborts the landing.

April 16 – At a mass rally to honor the victims of the previous day's air attacks, Fidel Castro proclaims the socialist character of the Cuban Revolution and calls the people of Cuba to arms in its defense (see pp. 55–64). The revolution's central leaders are each sent to take responsibility for different areas of the country: Raúl Castro to Oriente province, Che Guevara to Pinar del Río, and Juan Almeida to Santa Clara to head the Central Army.

– Kennedy gives final approval for the Bay of Pigs invasion. The assault ships transporting the mercenary brigade, together with their U.S. Navy escort fleet, approach the landing site by separate routes.

– The first mercenaries disembark at Playa Girón at 11:45 p.m., accompanied by two CIA operatives, Grayston Lynch and William "Rip" Robertson. Militia members spot them and Lynch fires opening shots of the invasion. Almost simultaneously five militia members confront the invaders at nearby Playa Larga.

April 17–19 – See detailed account of the battle by Cuban Brigadier General José Ramón Fernández (pp. 121–135).

April 18 – At the United Nations, Adlai Stevenson denies responsibility for the invasion and rejects the detailed accusation presented by Raúl Roa the day before.

April 19 – The central leaders of Brigade 2506 having taken to the woods a few hours earlier, the last invaders surrender at Playa Girón at 5:30 p.m. Over the next days and weeks, Cuban forces round up and imprison 1,179 members of the brigade.

– José Miró Cardona, Antonio Maceo Mackle, Tony Varona, and Manuel Ray—the nominal president and other top officials of the Cuban Revolutionary Council—are released by White House representatives from confinement in a barracks at the blacked-out Opa-Locka airfield near Miami. Held behind doors and guarded by U.S. soldiers since the wee hours of April 17, these supposed political leaders of the invasion force had first learned of the landing in the barracks and listened over the radio to the communiqué written by the CIA and issued to the press in their name.

April 21 – Addressing accountability for Bay of Pigs defeat, Kennedy says at State Department press conference: "What matters is only one fact, I am the responsible officer of the government."

April 23 – In a televised address, Castro reports on the victory and its implications to the Cuban people (see pp. 169–221).

May 1 – Castro sums up the lessons of the battle in a speech to Havana's May Day celebration (see pp. 225–246).

May 28 – Counterrevolutionaries set fire to movie theater in Pinar del Río, injuring 26 children and 14 adults.

August – The Alliance for Progress is proclaimed at a meeting of the Organization of American States (OAS) in Punta del Este, Uruguay. The U.S.-sponsored program, established as a response to the Cuban Revolution and its example, aims to prop up compliant capitalist regimes and enrich U.S. bankers and investors. It allocates $20 billion in loans to Latin American governments over a ten-year period in exchange for their cooperation in opposing Cuba's revolutionary regime.

September 8 – Trial is held of fourteen of the captured mercenaries who, as henchmen of the Batista dictatorship, had committed acts of torture and murder. After being convicted and sentenced, five are executed. The remaining nine are sentenced to 30-year prison terms. The last of these is released in 1986.

November 4 – A new covert action program to overthrow the revolution, code-named Operation Mongoose, is developed during a White House meeting, involving more extensive engagement of U.S. armed forces than ever before. Later that month, Kennedy signs a memorandum formally placing his brother, Attorney General Robert F. Kennedy, directly in charge.

November 24 – Lyman Kirkpatrick's "Inspector General's Survey of the Cuban Operation" is distributed to six top CIA officials. The agency's deputy director, Gen. C.P. Cabell, orders a halt to any further distribution of the report.

November 26 – Young literacy campaigner Manuel Ascunce Domenech and peasant Pedro Lantigua Ortega are murdered by counterrevolutionaries near Trinidad.

1962

January 31 – The OAS, meeting in Punta del Este, Uruguay, votes to expel Cuba.

February 3 – Kennedy orders a total embargo on U.S. trade with Cuba.

February 4 – Rally of one million in Havana's Plaza of the Revolution denounces U.S. imperialist economic embargo and proclaims the Second Declaration of Havana, a call to support revolutionary struggles throughout the Americas.

March 16 – President Kennedy approves guidelines for Operation Mongoose, drafted by Gen. Maxwell Taylor, stating that "final success will require decisive U.S. military intervention." CIA covert operations director Richard Bissell later explains that, "Operation Mongoose was a more ambitious and more massive paramilitary activity than the Bay of Pigs had been," involving "significantly more personnel." The operation, Bissell says, "was closely monitored" by President Kennedy and "all actions received his explicit authorization."

April 7 – Following a four-day trial, 1,179 captured members of Brigade 2506 are convicted of treason and sentenced to 30-year prison terms. In May 1961 Fidel Castro had proposed that the Cuban government would free the mercenaries upon indemnification for some of the damages Washington had inflicted on the Cuban people. Ultimately, Washington agrees to pay $53 million in food, medicine, and medical equipment.

In December 1962, 1,113 prisoners are released and flown to Miami; another 60 wounded prisoners had been freed seven months earlier. Soon after they are released,

Attorney General Robert Kennedy organizes a clandestine operation, based in Costa Rica and Nicaragua, led by Manuel Artime, San Román, and other leaders of Brigade 2506. Its task is to mount commando raids on Cuban shore installations.

October 15 – CIA informs White House that U.S. military spy planes have photographed Soviet-supplied nuclear missiles in Cuba. The missiles have been shipped following a mutual defense agreement between Cuba and the Soviet Union in face of Washington's accelerated preparations to launch another invasion of Cuba that would include "decisive U.S. military intervention."

October 22 – Washington orders a naval blockade of Cuba and places U.S. armed forces on nuclear alert to demand removal from the island of Soviet-supplied nuclear missile defense. At White House meeting with congressional leaders earlier in the day, President Kennedy reports plan to assemble an invasion force of some 90,000 troops for combined air strikes and ground assault against Cuba. "We are going to move, with maximum speed, all of our forces to be in a position to invade Cuba within the 7-day period," Kennedy says. Defense Secretary Robert McNamara adds that, "The President ordered us to prepare an invasion of Cuba months ago, . . . I believe it was November of last year [1961]."

October 23 – In response to Washington's threatened aggression, millions of Cuban workers and farmers mobilize to defend the revolution. In a speech broadcast to the entire population, Fidel Castro says that the U.S. rulers "menace us with nuclear attack but they don't scare us. We will see if the U.S. congressmen, bankers, etc. possess the same serenity as we. We are serene in the knowledge that, if they attack us, the aggressor will be annihilated."

October 23–28 – Assessing revolutionary Cuba's mass military readiness, Pentagon planners respond to White House inquiry, informing Kennedy that an invasion would cost the U.S. military more than 18,000 casualties in the first ten days alone. Faced with this fact and the enormous political consequences it would entail, the Kennedy administration steps up efforts to find an alternative course to end the crisis.

– Following an exchange of communications between Washington and Moscow, Soviet premier Nikita Khrushchev, without consulting the Cuban government, announces his decision to remove the missiles.

November 25 – A statement signed by Cuban President Osvaldo Dorticós and Prime Minister Fidel Castro presents five points "essential to a genuine and final settlement of the crisis." First, "cessation of the economic blockade" against Cuba imposed by Washington. Second, an end to air drops and sea landings "of weapons and explosives [and] of infiltration by spies and saboteurs." Third, "cessation of the pirate raids carried out from bases in the U.S. and Puerto Rico." Fourth, "the cessation of all violations of our airspace and territorial waters by U.S. aircraft and warships." And fifth, "withdrawal from the Guantánamo naval base and the return of the Cuban territory occupied by the U.S."

The statement rejects Washington's demand that the Cuban government agree to "international inspection" of military installations on the island. "It was the U.S. government, by its repeated and overt attacks on our country, that made it necessary for the Cuban people to arm ourselves," Castro and Dorticós say. "It was President Kennedy himself who ordered an army of mercenaries to land at Playa Girón. . . . What would have become of our country and its revolution if our people had not offered stubborn and heroic resistance to the actions of that powerful and aggressive country?"

Glossary

Ahrens, Edward (d. 1990) – Miami district director of U.S. Immigration and Naturalization Service (INS), 1959–64.

Arbenz, Jacobo (1914–1971) – President of Guatemala 1951–54. During his regime a limited land reform was initiated that accompanied an upsurge in worker and peasant struggles. In 1954 a CIA-organized mercenary force invaded the country. Arbenz refused to arm the population and was forced out of office in June. A slaughter of "suspected communists" ensued.

Artime, Manuel (1932–1977) – As a student in 1958, Artime joined the rebel forces in the last days of the Batista dictatorship. He was appointed head of an agricultural development zone for the National Institute of Agrarian Reform (INRA) in 1959. Following the defeat of an abortive counterrevolutionary mutiny led by Huber Matos in October 1959, Artime left Cuba and organized the counterrevolutionary Movement of Revolutionary Recovery (MRR), which worked with the CIA to organize armed actions against the Cuban Revolution. A leader of Brigade 2506, Artime was chosen by the CIA to accompany the invasion force as the political representative of the new provisional government they intended to establish in Cuba. Taken prisoner at the Bay of Pigs, he was released December 1962. At the initiative of Robert Kennedy, he was put on a CIA retainer in 1963–64 to revive the MRR and, operating from bases in Costa Rica and Nicaragua, to mount commando raids on Cuban shore installations. He participated in a failed assassination attempt against Fidel Castro in 1965. In the 1970s Artime organized the Miami Watergate Defense Relief Fund, collecting $21,000 for the convicted Watergate burglars, a number of whom were U.S. or Cuban veterans of the Bay of Pigs operation.

Batista, Fulgencio (1901–1973) – Former army sergeant who helped lead a military coup by junior officers in September 1933, in the wake of a popular uprising that had overturned the dictatorship of Gerardo Machado a few weeks earlier. He rose to chief of staff and became government strongman in 1934, remaining in power until 1944. He left office but retained base of support within army officer corps, living in Florida 1944–48. Batista led a coup on March 10, 1952, establishing military dictatorship that collaborated closely with Washington. He fled to the Dominican Republic on January 1, 1959.

Bissell, Richard (1909–1994) – As CIA "deputy director for plans" 1959–62, he was in charge of covert operations for the agency and was the architect of the Bay of Pigs invasion. Prior to the U.S. defeat, Bissell, a liberal Democrat, was widely considered Kennedy's top choice to replace CIA director Allen Dulles. Following the Bay of Pigs defeat, Kennedy told Bissell he would have to resign his top-level post in the agency, and shortly afterwards offered Bissell a newly created position as the CIA's deputy director of science and technology. Bissell refused the consolation gesture and left the agency in February 1962.

Borges, Luis – Commander of the 111th Revolutionary National Militias battalion during the Bay of Pigs.

Bourzac, Gustavo (1934–) – Pilot in Cuba's Revolutionary Air Force during the Bay of Pigs invasion. A Rebel Army combatant in Cuba's revolutionary war, he held the rank of captain.

Burke, Arleigh (1901–1996) – Admiral in U.S. Navy. In 1955 he became chief of naval operations. As the member of the Joint Chiefs of Staff most directly engaged in organizing support for the Bay of Pigs invasion, he was in charge of the U.S. Navy fleet that accompanied Brigade 2506. He was transferred to the Retired List on August 1, 1961.

Carreras, Enrique (1922–) – Cuban division general, considered the father of Cuba's Revolutionary Air Force. A member of the Cuban air force since 1942, he participated in a movement within the military to oppose the Batista dictatorship. Arrested in 1957, he was imprisoned on the Isle of Pines until January 1, 1959. Joining the revolutionary armed forces, he helped train pilots for the new air force. He was senior pilot and at the Bay of Pigs shot down two aircraft and sank two enemy ships.

Castro, Fidel. See biography on pages 9–10.

Castro, Raúl (1931–) – Currently General of the Army, the second-ranking officer of the Revolutionary Armed Forces. A participant in student protests against the Batista dictatorship, he joined in the 1953 Moncada attack and was sentenced to thirteen years in prison. He was released in May 1955 following a national amnesty campaign. A member of the July 26 Movement, he was a founding member of the Rebel Army and part of the *Granma* expedition. In February 1958 he was promoted to commander and headed the Second Eastern Front. He was minister of the Revolutionary Armed Forces from 1959 until 2008. He was vice premier from 1959 until 1976, first vice president of the Council of State and Ministers from 1976 until 2008, and has been president of the Council of State and Ministers since 2008. Since 1965 he has been second secretary of the Communist Party of Cuba.

Cienfuegos, Osmany (1931–) – A member of the Socialist Youth, affiliated with the Popular Socialist Party, during Cuba's revolutionary war, he served as minister of public works 1959–63. He has been a member of the Communist Party Central Committee since 1965, and is currently a vice president of the Executive Committee of the Council of Ministers. He is the older brother of Camilo Cienfuegos, a leading Rebel Army commander during Cuba's revolutionary war.

Curbelo, Raúl – Head of the Revolutionary Air Force in 1961. During the Bay of Pigs, he was in charge of communications between the armed forces central command in Havana and the pilots at the front. He later served as minister of communications.

del Valle, Sergio (1927–2007) – Joined July 26 Movement as a student at the University of Havana; joined Rebel Army in 1957 as combatant and physician, becoming captain in Guevara's column; head of the air force in 1960; later chief of General Staff of armed forces; minister of the interior, 1968–79; member of Communist Party Central Committee 1965–97. Holds rank of division general in the Revolutionary Armed Forces.

Dorticós, Osvaldo (1919–1983) – A lawyer who was regional coordinator of July 26 Movement in Cienfuegos, he was expelled by Batista from Cuba in 1958. In July 1959 he became president of Cuba, holding that position until 1976. He was a member of the Communist Party Central Committee and Political Bureau at the time of his death.

Doster, George Reid (b. 1918) – Commanding general of the Alabama Air National Guard. He was recruited by the CIA to assemble U.S. and Cuban pilots for actions against Cuba, and he supervised their training and operations from Guatemala and Nicaragua. Eventually a force of eighty U.S. pilots was assembled; several flew combat missions at the Bay of Pigs and at least four were killed during the battle.

Dulles, Allen (1893–1969) – As director of the Central Intelligence Agency 1953–61, Dulles organized the operations to overthrow the government of Iran in 1953 and Guatemala in 1954. He was forced to resign from the CIA in 1961 following the Bay of Pigs fiasco.

Fernández, Alberto – A pilot on a crop fumigation plane at the triumph of the revolution, he became a member of the Revolutionary Air Force and participated in the battle at the Bay of Pigs. He subsequently worked for Cubana Airlines.

Fernández, José Ramón. See biography on pages 11–12.

Ferrer, Edward B. (1930–) – A commercial pilot for Cubana Airlines who organized an armed hijacking of a plane in July 1960 and flew it to Miami. He then became a pilot in the counterrevolutionary "Liberation Air Force" organized by Washington, based out of Guatemala and Nicaragua. He flew missions to supply terrorist bands in the Escambray. He participated in the Bay of Pigs invasion, providing air support to the mercenary troops.

González Suco, José Ramón (1937–) – A native of Cienfuegos, he participated as a militia member in the fight against the counterrevolutionary bands in the Escambray mountains. During the Bay of Pigs invasion he was a member of the 339th Battalion. As a shortwave operator, he was named head of the observation point.

Goodpaster, Andrew J. (1915–2005) – Staff secretary and assistant for national security activities to President Dwight D. Eisenhower, 1954–61. Assistant to the Chairman of the Joint Chiefs of Staff, 1961–67. In 1967–68 he was commander of NATO, and in 1968–69 served as deputy commander of U.S. forces in Vietnam.

Guevara, Ernesto Che (1928–1967) – Argentine-born leader of the Cuban Revolution. A founding member of the Rebel Army, he was the first combatant to be promoted to the rank of commander during Cuba's revolutionary war. In late 1958 he commanded the column that captured Santa Clara, Cuba's third-largest city. Following the 1959 triumph, in addition to his military tasks, Guevara held a number of positions and responsibilities in the revolutionary government including head of the National Bank and minister of industry; he was often a spokesman for the revolutionary leadership internationally. In April 1965 he led the Cuban contingent that aided anti-imperialist forces in the Congo. In late 1966 he led a vanguard detachment of internationalist volunteers to Bolivia. Wounded and captured by the Bolivian army in a CIA-organized operation on October 8, 1967, he was murdered the following day.

Hawkins, Jack – A colonel in the U.S. Marines with experience in amphibious landings at Iwo Jima during World War II and Inchon during the Korean War. He was assigned to the CIA by the Pentagon to be chief of the paramilitary staff for what became the Bay of Pigs invasion. He was the top U.S. officer directly involved in the operation.

Kirkpatrick, Lyman (1916–1995) – Inspector general of Central Intelligence Agency 1953–61, and in that capacity author of report on failure of the Bay of Pigs operation. Executive director of CIA 1962–65.

Lemnitzer, Lyman (1899–1988) – U.S. Army general; chairman of the Joint Chiefs of Staff, October 1960 to September 1962.

Lobo, Julio (1898–1983) – Wealthy sugar baron prior to the revolution, Lobo owned fourteen sugar mills in Cuba. His lands were nationalized by the first agrarian reform in 1959. His sugar mills were nationalized in October 1960 and Lobo left Cuba. He later lived in Spain.

Lugo, Ismael de – Pseudonym of Fermín Asla Polo, a Spanish Capuchin priest who accompanied Brigade 2506, with authorization of the hierarchy of the Capuchin Order. He fought as part of Gen. Francisco Franco's Falangist forces in the 1936–39 Spanish civil war.

Lynch, Grayston – Retired U.S. Army captain who joined the CIA in 1960. Accompanied Brigade 2506 during the Bay of Pigs invasion. Coming ashore with a team of frogmen the night of the landing, Lynch fired the first shot in the battle. The senior CIA operative on the scene, he handled radio contact with the mercenaries during the battle from aboard the *Blagar* off the Cuban coast. Between April 1961 and 1967, Lynch directed 2,126 clandestine CIA actions against Cuba out of Miami, personally participating in 113 of them. Retired from the CIA in 1971.

Maciques, Abraham – In charge of economic development in the Zapata Swamp region. Served as guide for revolutionary troops during battle at Bay of Pigs.

Martínez Sánchez, Augusto (1923–) – Rebel Army commander; he later served as minister of labor and social security. A retired brigadier general of the Revolutionary Armed Forces.

Miret, Pedro (1927–) – Participant in 1953 Moncada attack; leader of July 26 Movement; Rebel Army commander during revolutionary war; member of Communist Party Central Committee since 1965; currently a vice president of Council of State and Council of Ministers.

Miró Cardona, José (1902–1974) – A prominent figure in the bourgeois opposition to Batista in the 1950s, Miró Cardona was Cuba's prime minister from January 5 to February 13, 1959, when he was replaced by Fidel Castro. Subsequently ambassador to Spain, he resigned in July and left Cuba in November. In October 1960 he became secretary general for public relations of the counterrevolutionary Democratic Revolutionary Front (FRD). In March 1961 Miró Cardona became president of the newly formed Cuban Revolutionary Council, set up at the initiative of the CIA to become a "provisional government" following the Bay of Pigs invasion.

Mustelier, Mariano – Militia leader who first spotted the invaders at Playa Girón shortly after midnight on April 17, 1961.

Oliva, Erneido (1932–) – Commissioned as lieutenant in the Batista army in 1958, Oliva worked as an artillery instructor. In early 1959 the Rebel Army decided to keep him on as an instructor, which they did until August, when the new army was purged of former soldiers of the dictatorship. He left Cuba shortly thereafter. Oliva was second in command of Brigade 2506. Captured at the Bay of Pigs, he was released in December 1962 and became involved in a White House-organized counterrevolutionary unit led by Manuel Artime based in Costa Rica and Nicaragua that staged commando raids on Cuban shore installations. Subsequently he was commissioned in the U.S. Army, appointed to represent Cuban-American personnel. He later became a major general in the U.S. Army Reserves, and retired in 1993 as deputy commanding general of the Washington, D.C., National Guard.

Pérez San Román, José (d. 1989) – Former captain in the Cuban army before the revolution, Pérez San Román had been associated with anti-Batista conspirators within the armed forces. In 1959 he worked briefly for the National Institute of Agrarian Reform (INRA) but left Cuba and was recruited by the CIA. Appointed by the CIA as military commander of Brigade 2506. Taken prisoner at the Bay of Pigs, he was released in December 1962. Subsequently, as unofficial adviser to Robert Kennedy, Pérez San Román commanded a unit based in Costa Rica and Nicaragua that organized commando raids on Cuban shore installations. He later joined the U.S. Army and became a captain.

Roa García, Raúl (1907–1982) – Prominent left-wing student leader in Cuba in the 1920s and 1930s; later dean of social sciences at the University of Havana. Member of July 26 Movement's

Civic Resistance Movement during Cuba's revolutionary war. In January 1959 Roa was named Cuba's ambassador to the Organization of American States. In June of that year, he became Cuba's foreign minister. In that capacity, he addressed the United Nations regularly, including during the debate over the Bay of Pigs invasion and the U.S. preparations for it. He remained foreign minister until 1976. Roa was a member of the Central Committee of the Communist Party and was vice president of National Assembly at time of his death.

Rodiles, Samuel (1932–) – Joined July 26 Movement in 1955 in Guántanamo. During the revolutionary war, Rodiles first participated in the urban underground. In early 1958 he joined the Rebel Army's Second Eastern Front, as a lieutenant in Column no. 6. By December 1958 he had been promoted to commander. As second in command of the Revolutionary National Police (PNR), he was sent to the Bay of Pigs as second in command of a battalion of PNR fighters that saw some of the heaviest combat of the invasion. Arriving on April 18, he took part in the capture of Playa Larga and the advance on Playa Girón. Between 1977 and 1989 Rodiles volunteered for three internationalist missions in Angola, where he served as second in command of the Cuban volunteer contingent of the Revolutionary Armed Forces. He is a division general of the FAR.

Ruiz-Williams, Enrique (Harry) – General manager of Cuba's largest copper mine before the revolution, he left Cuba after the mine was nationalized in August 1960. Second in command of Brigade 2506's heavy gun battalion, he was wounded in the fighting and captured. He was released in April 1962, together with the other mercenaries who had been wounded. Subsequently Ruiz-Williams helped organize further armed actions against the revolution, working directly under Attorney General Robert Kennedy.

Silva Tablada, Alfonso (1914–1961) – A pilot in the Cuban air force prior to the revolution, he joined the July 26 Movement. A member of the Rebel Army during Cuba's revolutionary war, he was the sole pilot in the Rebel Army's Air Force in 1958, carrying out combat missions in the rebels' Second Eastern Front. A captain in the Revolutionary Air Force, he was killed during the Bay of Pigs invasion when his B-26 was shot down over one of the mercenaries' ships on April 17, 1961.

Stevenson, Adlai (1900–1965) – U.S. liberal capitalist politician. Governor of Illinois 1948–53. Democratic Party candidate for president, 1952 and 1956. U.S. ambassador to United Nations 1961–65.

Ulloa, Carlos (d. 1961) – A member of the Nicaraguan air force, Ulloa was arrested in 1957 for activities against the Somoza dictatorship. In 1958 he escaped from prison and, from Costa Rica, helped ferry supplies to anti-Somoza forces in Nicaragua. In August 1959 he went to Cuba and was introduced to Camilo Cienfuegos, who recruited him to Cuba's Revolutionary Air Force as a pilot. He was killed during the Bay of Pigs invasion when his plane was shot down on April 17.

Further reading

Báez, Luis, ed., *Secretos de generales* [Secrets of generals] (Havana: Editorial Si-Mar S.A., 1997). Interviews with forty-one generals of the Revolutionary Armed Forces in which they tell of their experiences during Cuba's revolutionary war, the battle at Playa Girón, internationalist missions, and other efforts to defend and strengthen the Cuban Revolution.

Barnes, Jack, "U.S. Imperialism Has Lost the Cold War" in New International no. 11 (1998). Discusses the impact on the class struggle internationally of revolutionary Cuba's ongoing example that it's possible to stand up to U.S. imperialism and win. This issue of *New International* also contains "Socialism: A Viable Option" by Cuban Communist Party Political Bureau member José Ramón Balaguer.

Bissell, Richard, *Reflections of a Cold Warrior: From Yalta to the Bay of Pigs* (New Haven: Yale University Press, 1996). Memoirs, written thirty years after the Bay of Pigs, by the top CIA official responsible for the operation.

Carreras, Enrique, *Por el dominio del aire: Memorias de un piloto de combate (1943–1988)* [Controlling the air: memoirs of a combat pilot 1943–1988] (Havana: Editora Política, 1995). An account by the Revolutionary Air Force pilot who sank two Brigade 2506 ships and downed two of its B-26 bombers. Includes Raúl Castro's April 15, 1961, call to arms in Santiago de Cuba.

Castro, Fidel, *El pensamiento de Fidel Castro* [The thought of Fidel Castro] (Havana: Editora Política, 1983), 2 vols. Contains substantial excerpts from numerous speeches by Castro between 1959 and 1961.

Castro, Fidel, and Guevara, Ernesto Che, *To Speak the Truth: Why Washington's Cold War against Cuba Doesn't End* (New

York: Pathfinder, 1992). Includes Castro's September 1960 speech before the United Nations General Assembly in which he detailed Washington's economic, political, and military assaults against Cuba in preparation for what would become the Bay of Pigs invasion.

Diez Acosta, Tomás, *La crisis de los misiles, 1962: Algunas reflexiones cubanas* [The 1962 missile crisis: some Cuban reflections] (Havana: Ediciones Verde Olivo, 1997). Details Washington's covert efforts against Cuba in the period between the Bay of Pigs invasion and the October 1962 "missile crisis."

Escalante Font, Fabián, *Cuba: la guerra secreta de la CIA* [Cuba: the CIA's secret war] (Havana: Editorial Capitán San Luis, 1993). The story of covert CIA operations against Cuba, told by the former head of Cuba's State Security.

Ferrer, Edward B., *Operation Puma: The Air Battle of the Bay of Pigs* (1975). The account of a pilot for Brigade 2506.

Guevara, Ernesto Che, *Che Guevara Talks to Young People* (New York: Pathfinder, 2000). Includes Guevara's October 20, 1962, talk, "What a Young Communist Should Be," pointing to the example set for communist youth by the combatants who fought selflessly at Playa Girón to defend Cuba's socialist revolution.

Hansen, Joseph, *Dynamics of the Cuban Revolution* (New York: Pathfinder, 1979). This collection of articles by a leader of the communist movement in the United States includes the April 19, 1961, front-page statement on the Bay of Pigs from the *Militant* newsweekly headlined, "Stop the Crime against Cuba!"

History of an Aggression: The Trial of the Playa Girón Mercenaries, (Havana: Ediciones Venceremos, 1962). Includes excerpts from the testimonies of captured mercenaries, detailing the U.S. government role in organizing every aspect of Brigade 2506 and its invasion of Cuba.

Johnson, Haynes (with Manuel Artime, José Pérez San Román, Erneido Oliva, and Enrique Ruiz-Williams), *The Bay of Pigs: The Leaders' Story of Brigade 2506* (New York: W.W. Norton and Company Inc., 1964).

Kirkpatrick, Lyman B., "The Inspector General's Survey of the Cuban Operation, October 1961," together with a reply by Richard Bissell, the top CIA official who directed the operation. Published in Kornbluh, Peter, *Bay of Pigs Declassified: The Secret CIA Report on the Invasion of Cuba* (New York: The New Press, 1998).

Malcolm X, *Malcolm X Speaks* (New York: Pathfinder, 1965). Includes December 1964 speech at meeting of Organization of Afro-American Unity in Harlem to which Malcolm X read a message from Ernesto Che Guevara.

Pino Machado, Quintín, *La batalla de Girón: Razones de una victoria* [The battle of Girón: reasons behind a victory] (Havana: Editorial de Ciencias Sociales, 1985). A detailed account of the background to the invasion as well as combat operations.

Rodríguez, Juan Carlos, *La batalla inevitable: La más colosal operación de la CIA contra Fidel Castro* [The inevitable battle: the CIA's biggest operation against Fidel Castro] (Havana: Editorial Capitán San Luis, 1996). An account of the April 1961 invasion and preparations for it, produced by the Cuban State Security Historical Research Center. The 2009 English edition is titled *The Inevitable Battle: From the Bay of Pigs to Playa Girón.*

Sentencia del Tribunal Provincial Popular de Ciudad de La Habana *en el proceso por la demanda del pueblo de Cuba contra el gobierno de Estados Unidos por los daños económicos ocasionados a Cuba* [Sentence of the People's Provincial Court of the City of Havana in the lawsuit by the people of Cuba against the U.S. government for economic damages caused to Cuba] (Havana: Editora Política, 2000). The testimony of José Ramón Fernández in this book was presented as part of these 1999 proceedings.

Torreira, Ramón, and Buajasón, José, *Operación Peter Pan: Un caso de guerra psicológica contra Cuba* [Operation Peter Pan: an example of psychological warfare against Cuba] (Havana: Editora Política, 2000). A study of Washington's 1959–62 campaign to spread the slander that Cuba's revolutionary government intended to take children away from their parents. Operation Peter Pan resulted in some 14,000 Cuban children being sent to the United States, many of whom were separated from their families for years.

Waters, Mary-Alice, ed., *Making History* (New York: Pathfinder, 1999). Interviews with Cuban generals Néstor López Cuba, Enrique Carreras, José Ramón Fernández, and Harry Villegas—among them three leaders of the Cuban forces at the Bay of Pigs that defeated the invaders within seventy-two hours. With a preface by Juan Almeida Bosque.

Wyden, Peter, *Bay of Pigs: The Untold Story* (New York: Simon and Schuster, 1979).

Index

Agrarian reform, 16, 79, 94, 183, 258
Ahrens, Edward, 58–59, 277
Aiken, George, 217
Air force. *See* Brigade 2506 air force; Revolutionary Air Force
Air strikes (April 15), 70, 201–6; casualties from, 52, 53, 55, 57, 61–62, 72, 270; destruction of Cuban aircraft, 203, 204; failure of, 63, 202–4, 218; as indication of imminent invasion, 201, 206; Kennedy approval, 52, 59, 99, 270; mercenary planes shot down, 53, 62, 204; objective of, 52, 63, 203, 270; statement to Cuban people on, 53–54; U.S. cover story, 57–61, 99–100, 239, 270; U.S. tactical error in, 206
Alabama Air National Guard, 104, 280
Alliance for Progress, 272
Almeida, Juan, 68, 269, 271
Arbenz, Jacobo, 170–71, 176, 277
Arrests of counterrevolutionaries, 72–73, 77, 141
Artime, Manuel: book by, 95, 104, 106, 108–9; as Brigade 2506 leader, 95, 274, 277–78
Ascunce, Manuel, 273
Assassination attempts on Fidel Castro, 91, 107, 263–64, 269, 277
Associated Press, 15–16, 18, 58–60
Association of Combatants of the Cuban Revolution (ACRC), 88
Association of Rebel Youth, 70, 72, 227

Atlántico, 106
Attorney General's List of Communist or Subversive Organizations, 26, 30
Austerity policies: directed against capitalists, 178–80; in Latin America, 180
Australia Sugar Mill, 119–21, 122–24, 207–8

Bacallao, Valentín, 111
Baracoa, aborted diversionary landing at, 100, 105, 198, 270–71
Barbara J, 99, 269
Barnes, Jack, 14, 19, 25–26, 35, 37–38
Base Trax (Helvetia), Guatemala, 109, 263
Batalla inevitable, La: La más colosal operación de la CIA contra Fidel Castro (Rodríguez), 96, 289
Batista, Fulgencio, 9, 11, 16, 93, 177–78, 243, 255, 256–57, 278
Bay of Pigs Declassified: The Secret CIA Report on the Invasion of Cuba (Kornbluh, ed.), 96, 289
Bay of Pigs invasion: aim of Kennedy administration, 93, 102, 140, 198–99, 236, 267; causes of U.S. defeat, 40, 91, 93–94, 218; CIA diversionary maneuvers, 100, 125–26, 198, 270–71; consequences of a U.S. victory, 79–80, 213–15, 216, 235–37; Cuba's anticipation of, 20, 112–13, 169; as culmination of stage of U.S. assaults, 55–56, 90; first great U.S. defeat in the Americas, 17,

See also Revolutionary Armed
Forces
Miret, Pedro, 133, 282
Miró Cardona, José, 18, 99, 257, 269,
271, 282–83
Molasses, 186
Molina, Francisco, 23–24
Moncada attack, 9, 255
Monopolies, 175–76, 182, 242. *See
also* Capitalism
Montero, Noelio, 111
Montero, Ricardo, 111
Morales Cruz, 110
Movement of Revolutionary Recov-
ery (MRR), 277
Mujal, Eusebio, 241
Murray, USS, 106, 136
Mustelier, Mariano, 113, 283

Napalm, 134, 139, 236
National Association of Small Farm-
ers (ANAP), 88
Nationalization of industry, 16, 35, 79,
231, 264, 265–66; U.S. response
to, 176–77
Navarro, Manuel, 104
Navy. *See* Revolutionary Navy
Nazi Germany, 200, 203, 220
New York Times, 56, 262, 270
Nicaragua: anti-Somoza activity in,
285; mercenary bases in, 98–99,
101, 105–6, 108, 199, 266; as U.S.
ally, 172–73
Nixon, Richard, 26, 96

October Crisis. *See* Cuban "missile
crisis" (1962)
Oil, U.S. economic aggression around,
181–82, 263
Oliva, Erneido, 95, 104, 106, 108–
9, 283
Olivera Moya, Filiberto, 249
Operation 40, 110
Operation Marte, 100, 105

Operation Mongoose, 37, 272, 273
Operation Peter Pan, 91–92, 289
*Operation Puma: The Air Battle of
the Bay of Pigs* (Ferrer), 95, 100,
103–4, 106, 135, 252, 288
Organization of American States
(OAS), 171, 184–85, 197, 211,
272–73; Declaration of San José,
172, 184, 264
Oriente province, 68, 271

País, Frank, 256
Pálpite, 120–21, 124–25, 127
Panama, 98, 102, 105, 261
Paris Commune, 236
Pazos, Felipe, 181
Peace, through defeat of imperialism,
70, 193, 214
Pearl Harbor, 203
Peasants: agrarian reform and, 16, 79,
94, 183, 258; before revolution, 179,
209, 231, 240, 244; and defense of
revolution, 62–64, 177, 237
*People of Cuba v. the U.S. Govern-
ment*, 88, 289
Pérez San Román, José: as commander
of Brigade 2506, 102, 266, 274,
283; books by, 93, 95, 100, 102–3,
104, 106, 108–9
Pérez San Román, Roberto, 112
Pinar del Río: Che Guevara in, 68,
69–71, 271; CIA plan for, 98
Pioneers, 88, 227
Playa Girón, 83, 209; Cuban capture
of beachhead, 132–34, 135–36;
mercenary landing at, 113, 114,
206–7, 271. *See also* Bay of Pigs
invasion
Playa Larga, 111–12, 209; Cuban
advance on, 121; Cuban capture
of, 129; failed attacks on, 122–23,
124, 126; mercenary defenses at,
121; mercenary landing, 101–2,
113–14, 206–7, 271

Class Struggle in the United States

Is Socialist Revolution in the U.S. Possible?

A Necessary Debate

MARY-ALICE WATERS

In two talks, presented as part of a wide-ranging debate at the Venezuela International Book Fairs in 2007 and 2008, Waters explains why a socialist revolution in the United States is possible. Why revolutionary struggles by working people are inevitable, forced upon us by the crisis-driven assaults of the propertied classes. As solidarity grows among a fighting vanguard of working people, the outlines of coming class battles can already be seen. $7. Also in Spanish, French, and Swedish.

Cuba and the Coming American Revolution

JACK BARNES

The Cuban Revolution of 1959 had a worldwide political impact, including on working people and youth in the imperialist heartland. As the mass, proletarian-based struggle for Black rights was already advancing in the US, the social transformation fought for and won by the Cuban toilers set an example that socialist revolution is not only necessary—it can be made and defended.

This second edition, with a new foreword by Mary-Alice Waters, should be read alongside *Is Socialist Revolution in the U.S. Possible?* $10. Also in Spanish and French.

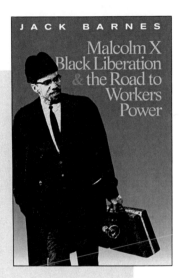

The Cuban Revolution and

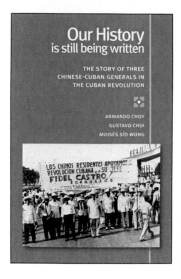

Our History Is Still Being Written
THE STORY OF THREE CHINESE-CUBAN GENERALS IN THE CUBAN REVOLUTION

In Cuba, the greatest measure against racial discrimination "was the revolution itself," says Gen. Moisés Sío Wong, "the triumph of a socialist revolution." Armando Choy, Gustavo Chui, and Sío Wong talk about the historic place of Chinese immigration to Cuba, as well as more than five decades of revolutionary action and internationalism, from Cuba to Angola and Venezuela today. Through their stories we see how millions of ordinary men and women changed the course of history, becoming different human beings in the process. $20. Also in Spanish and Chinese.

From the Escambray to the Congo
IN THE WHIRLWIND OF THE CUBAN REVOLUTION
Víctor Dreke

The author describes how easy it became after the Cuban Revolution to take down a rope segregating blacks from whites in the town square, yet how enormous was the battle to transform social relations underlying all the "ropes" inherited from capitalism and Yankee domination. Dreke, second in command of the internationalist column in the Congo led by Che Guevara in 1965, recounts the creative joy with which working people have defended their revolutionary course—from Cuba's Escambray mountains to Africa and beyond. $17. Also in Spanish.

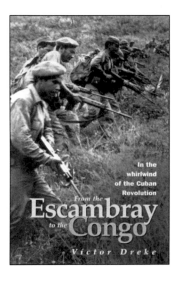

Renewal or Death
Fidel Castro

"To really establish total equality takes more than declaring it in law," Fidel Castro told delegates to the 1986 congress of the Cuban Communist Party, pointing to the revolution's enormous conquests in the fight against anti-black racism. "We can't leave it to chance to correct historical injustices," he said. "We have to straighten out what history has twisted." In *New International* no. 6. $16

World Politics

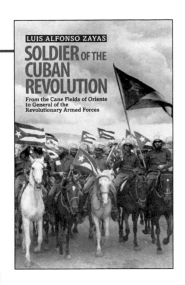

Soldier of the Cuban Revolution
FROM THE CANE FIELDS OF ORIENTE TO GENERAL
OF THE REVOLUTIONARY ARMED FORCES
Luis Alfonso Zayas
The author recounts his experiences over five
decades in the revolution. From a teenage
combatant in the clandestine struggle and
1956–58 war that brought down the US-
backed dictatorship, to serving three times as
a leader of the Cuban volunteer forces that
helped Angola defeat an invasion by the army
of white-supremacist South Africa, Zayas tells
how ordinary men and women in Cuba changed
the course of history and, in the process,
transformed themselves as well. $18. Also in Spanish.

Che Guevara Talks to Young People
The Argentine-born revolutionary leader challenges youth
of Cuba and the world to study, to work, to become
disciplined. To join the front lines of struggles, small
and large. To politicize themselves and the work of their
organizations. To become a different kind of human being
as they strive with working people of all lands to transform
the world. Eight talks from 1959 to 1964. $15. Also in
Spanish.

The Inevitable Battle
FROM THE BAY OF PIGS TO PLAYA GIRÓN
Juan Carlos Rodríguez

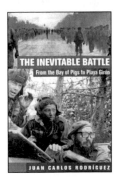

The US-led invasion of Cuba in April 1961 was defeated
in 66 hours by militia battalions composed of worker and
peasant volunteers, along with soldiers from the Cuban
armed forces. Cuban historian Juan Carlos Rodríguez
explains that the human material available to Washington
could not match the courage and determination of a people
fighting to defend what they had gained through the
continent's first socialist revolution. $20. Also in Spanish.

www.pathfinderpress.com

From the dictatorship of capital...

The Communist Manifesto

Karl Marx, Frederick Engels

Why is all recorded history "the history of class struggles"? Why is the capitalist state "but a committee for managing the common affairs of the whole bourgeoisie"? How does the fight for "the proletariat organized as the ruling class" open the only way forward for humanity? The answers to these questions, addressed in the founding document of the modern working-class movement in 1848, remain as vital today as they were at the time. $5. Also in Spanish, French, and Arabic.

The Civil War in France

Karl Marx

In 1871 insurgent working people in Paris rose up and established the first workers government in history, one crushed in blood 72 days later by troops of the French bourgeoisie. In his 20th anniversary introduction to Marx's contemporary account of the Paris Commune, Engels wrote that middle-class misleaders in the workers movement have "been filled with wholesome terror at the words: Dictatorship of the Proletariat. Well and good, gentlemen, do you want to know what this dictatorship looks like? Look at the Paris Commune." $5

State and Revolution

V.I. Lenin

"The relation of the socialist proletarian revolution to the state is acquiring not only practical political importance," wrote V.I. Lenin in the preface to this booklet, finished just months before the October 1917 Russian Revolution. It also addresses the "most urgent problem of the day: explaining to the masses what they will have to do to free themselves from capitalist tyranny." In *Essential Works of Lenin*. $12.95

...to the dictatorship of the proletariat

Their Trotsky and Ours
Jack Barnes

To lead the working class in a successful revolution, a mass proletarian party is needed whose cadres, well beforehand, have absorbed a world communist program, are proletarian in life and work, derive deep satisfaction from doing politics, and have forged a leadership with an acute sense of what to do next. This book is about building such a party. $16. Also in Spanish and French.

The History of the Russian Revolution
Leon Trotsky

A classic account of the social and political dynamics of the first socialist revolution, told by one of its central leaders. Trotsky describes how, under Lenin's guidance, the Bolshevik Party led the working class, peasantry, and oppressed nationalities to overturn the monarchist regime of the landlords and capitalists and bring to power a workers and peasants republic that set an example for toilers the world over. Unabridged, 3 vols. in one. $38. Also in Russian.

The Transitional Program for Socialist Revolution
Leon Trotsky

In this 1938 founding document drafted for the Socialist Workers Party in the US and the world movement it is part of, Bolshevik leader Leon Trotsky explains an interconnected program of slogans and demands that "lead to one and the same political conclusion: the workers need to break with all traditional parties of the bourgeoisie in order, jointly with the farmers, to establish their own power." $20

www.pathfinderpress.com

New International
A MAGAZINE OF MARXIST POLITICS AND THEORY

NEW INTERNATIONAL NO. 12

CAPITALISM'S LONG HOT WINTER HAS BEGUN

Jack Barnes

and "*Their Transformation and Ours*," Resolution of the Socialist Workers Party

Today's sharpening interimperialist conflicts are fueled both by the opening stages of what will be decades of economic, financial, and social convulsions and class battles, and by the most far-reaching shift in Washington's military policy and organization since the US buildup toward World War II. Class-struggle-minded working people must face this historic turning point for imperialism, and draw satisfaction from being "in their face" as we chart a revolutionary course to confront it. $16

NEW INTERNATIONAL NO. 13

OUR POLITICS START WITH THE WORLD

Jack Barnes

The huge economic and cultural inequalities between imperialist and semicolonial countries, and among classes within almost every country, are produced, reproduced, and accentuated by the workings of capitalism. For vanguard workers to build parties able to lead a successful revolutionary struggle for power in our own countries, says Jack Barnes in the lead article, our activity must be guided by a strategy to close this gap.

Also in No. 13: "Farming, Science, and the Working Classes" *by Steve Clark.* $14

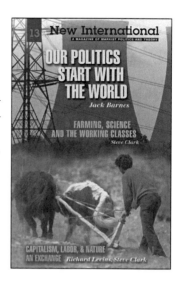

THESE ISSUES ARE ALSO AVAILABLE IN SPANISH, FRENCH, AND SWEDISH AT
WWW.PATHFINDERPRESS.COM

Building a PROLETARIAN PARTY

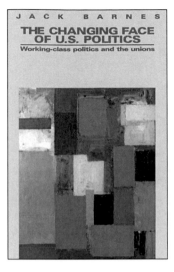

The Changing Face of U.S. Politics
Working-Class Politics and the Trade Unions
JACK BARNES

Building the kind of party working people need to prepare for coming class battles through which they will revolutionize themselves, their unions, and all society. A handbook for those seeking the road toward effective action to overturn the exploitative system of capitalism and join in reconstructing the world on new, socialist foundations. $24. Also in Spanish, French, and Swedish.

Revolutionary Continuity
Marxist Leadership in the U.S.
FARRELL DOBBS

How successive generations took part in struggles of the US labor movement, seeking to build a leadership that could advance the class interests of workers and small farmers and link up with fellow toilers around the world. Two volumes:
The Early Years, 1848–1917, $20; *Birth of the Communist Movement 1918–1922*, $19.

The History of American Trotskyism, 1928–38
Report of a Participant
JAMES P. CANNON

"Trotskyism is not a new movement, a new doctrine," Cannon says, "but the restoration, the revival of genuine Marxism as it was expounded and practiced in the Russian revolution and in the early days of the Communist International." In twelve talks given in 1942, Cannon recounts a decisive period in efforts to build a proletarian party in the United States. $22. Also in Spanish and French.

EXPAND *Your Revolutionary Library*

The Working Class and the Transformation of Learning
The Fraud of Education Reform under Capitalism
JACK BARNES

"Until society is reorganized so that education is a human activity from the time we are very young until the time we die, there will be no education worthy of working, creating humanity." $3. Also in Spanish, French, Swedish, Icelandic, Farsi, and Greek.

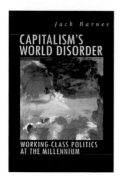

Capitalism's World Disorder
Working-Class Politics at the Millennium
JACK BARNES

Social devastation and financial panic, coarsening of politics, cop brutality, imperialist aggression—all are products not of something gone wrong with capitalism but of its lawful workings. Yet the future can be changed by the united struggle of workers and farmers conscious of their capacity to wage revolutionary battles for state power and transform the world. $25. Also in Spanish and French.

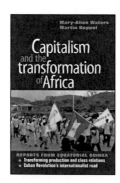

Capitalism and the Transformation of Africa
Reports from Equatorial Guinea
MARY-ALICE WATERS, MARTÍN KOPPEL

The transformation of production and class relations in a Central African country, as it is drawn deeper into the world market and both a capitalist class and modern proletariat are born. As Cuban volunteer medical brigades collaborate to transform social conditions there, the example of Cuba's socialist revolution comes alive. Woven together, the outlines of a future to be fought for today can be seen—a future in which Africa's toilers have more weight in world politics than ever before. $10. Also in Spanish.

www.pathfinderpress.com

Lenin's Final Fight
Speeches and Writings, 1922–23
V.I. LENIN

In 1922 and 1923, V.I. Lenin, central leader of the world's first socialist revolution, waged what was to be his last political battle. At stake was whether that revolution would remain on the proletarian course that had brought workers and peasants to power in October 1917—and laid the foundations for a truly worldwide revolutionary movement of toilers organizing to emulate the Bolsheviks' example. *Lenin's Final Fight* brings together the reports, articles, and letters through which Lenin waged this political battle. $20. Also in Spanish.

Thomas Sankara Speaks
The Burkina Faso Revolution, 1983–87

Led by Sankara, the revolutionary government of Burkina Faso in West Africa set an electrifying example. Peasants, workers, women, and youth mobilized to carry out literacy and immunization drives; to sink wells, plant trees, build dams, erect housing; to combat women's oppression and transform exploitative relations on the land; to free themselves from the imperialist yoke and solidarize with others engaged in that fight internationally. $24. Also in French.

The Jewish Question
A Marxist Interpretation
ABRAM LEON

Traces the historical rationalizations of anti-Semitism to the fact that, in the centuries preceding the domination of industrial capitalism, Jews emerged as a "people-class" of merchants, moneylenders, and traders. Leon explains why the propertied rulers incite renewed Jew-hatred in the epoch of capitalism's decline. $22

www.pathfinderpress.com

PATHFINDER AROUND THE WORLD

Visit our website for a complete list of titles and to place orders

www.pathfinderpress.com

PATHFINDER DISTRIBUTORS

UNITED STATES
(and Caribbean, Latin America, and East Asia)

Pathfinder Books, 306 W. 37th St., 10th Floor,
New York, NY 10018

CANADA

Pathfinder Books, 7107 St. Denis, Suite 204,
Montreal, QC H2S 2S5

UNITED KINGDOM
(and Europe, Africa, Middle East, and South Asia)

Pathfinder Books, First Floor, 120 Bethnal Green Road
(entrance in Brick Lane), London E2 6DG

AUSTRALIA
(and Southeast Asia and the Pacific)

Pathfinder, Level 1, 3/281-287 Beamish St., Campsie, NSW 2194
Postal address: P.O. Box 164, Campsie, NSW 2194

NEW ZEALAND

Pathfinder, 4/125 Grafton Road, Grafton, Auckland
Postal address: P.O. Box 3025, Auckland 1140

Join the Pathfinder Readers Club
to get 15% discounts on all Pathfinder titles
and bigger discounts on special offers.
Sign up at www.pathfinderpress.com
or through the distributors above.